D1253062

Michael Jackson:

For The Record

Chris Cadman & Craig Halstead

Visit us online at www.authorsonline.co.uk

An Authors OnLine Book

Cover design © Jamie Martin
Cover photograph © Emerson Sam/Corbis Sygma
Back cover montage © Yoann Galiotto

ISBN 0-7552-0267-8
ISBN 978-0-755202-67-6

Authors OnLine Ltd
19 The Cinques
Gamlingay, Sandy
Bedfordshire SG19 3NU
England

This book is also available in e-book format, details of which are available at www.authorsonline.co.uk

About the authors:

Chris and Craig's writing partnership began in 1990, when they compiled 'The Complete Michael Jackson Solo Discography 1972-90' for Adrian Grant's official fan magazine, *Off the Wall*. Chris also did much of the research for the first edition of Adrian's best selling book, *Michael Jackson – The Visual Documentary*.

Chris launched his own fanzine *Jackson* in 1995, with Craig as contributor, proof reader and eventual co-editor (*Jackson* is no longer published). Chris and Craig's first two books, *Michael Jackson – The Early Years* and *Michael Jackson – The Solo Years*, were published in 2002 and 2003, respectively. *Jacksons Number Ones* followed later in 2003, and their first non-Jackson book, *ABBA Gold Hits*, was published in 2004.

Chris was born in July 1961 in West Bromwich, England. A Karate Black Belt First Dan by the age of 15 years, he joined the family business on leaving school, a business he still helps to run today, supplying and servicing saws for companies across the West Midlands, where he still lives. He is married to the love of his life, wife Lynne, and has two daughters, Samantha and Stephanie.

Craig was born in June 1959 in Rochdale, England. He studied Applied Chemistry and Biochemistry at Huddersfield, gaining a B.Sc. (honours), but since November 1986 he has worked as a Community Worker at a small, multi-cultural Community Centre. He also writes fiction and is the author of one, as yet unpublished, novel. He lives in the North West with his young son.

9/09

for Shirley Cartman

ACKNOWLEDGEMENTS

Christina Chaffin: what can we say, that we haven't already said before, countless times? Thank you doesn't seem adequate, for all you have done for us, in supporting our Jackson projects so enthusiastically. Keep up the hard work with your web-sites and the mjjvault forum – *Go get 'em, Scoop!*

Jamie Martin & Tanja Kovac: special thanks for your encouragement, interest and support. Jamie, the cover you kindly designed for us is absolutely stunning – we love it, and so does everyone who has seen it!

Yoann Galiotto: special thanks for the montage – just what we were looking for, so we're delighted we could use it.

Christopher Kimberley: so glad you liked our ABBA book, thanks for your input into this one and our web-sites, and for your ongoing support.

Damiano Ciodi (mjfanclub.net): thanks for sharing some of your vast record collection with us, and for responding to our many queries – your support is much appreciated.

Paul Akinbanjo: thank you to you and your team at The Internet Michael Jackson Fan Club (mjnewsonline.com), for being so supportive of our previous Jackson books. We were shocked and saddened to learn of your resignation from the fan club, and wish you every success with your future ventures – you will be hugely missed.

Kathleen Horning & Justin: a special thanks for bringing to our attention new information on mjjvault. Kathleen, your j5-collector website is sadly missed.

Jayne Ross & the team at mjworld.net: many thanks for your support.

Martin Logan & the team at mjtkop.com: many thanks for your support.

Richard Fitt: it's amazing to think this is our fifth book together, many thanks to you and your team for helping to make one of our dreams come true.

We would also like to thank these people for all their tireless efforts, in supporting us and our research, many of them via the numerous Jackson forums there are on-line nowadays: Philippe (mjcollectorland), Nikki Harris, Ludovic Guyot (Foulcamp), Maximillian Muhammad (Mistermaxxx), Katie Doty (Gumbo 54), James (Bottle of Smoke), Franeck, L.K. Forney, Corey,

Jay Leggett (MJ_Brainace), Mark (thespecialone – good luck with your new life & baby daughter, Mia!), Manu, Deborah Dannelly, Paul Voth & Alex (Korgnex).

Chris would like to pay tribute to his wonderful parents, Ron and Brenda. Love to his brother Dean, sister-in-law Louise and nephews Oliver and Jake, sister-in-law Sue and family, and all other family members. To his best friend, Allan, his wife Pearl and father Ray. Last but not least, the three most important girls in my life, my wife Lynne and our daughters, Samantha and Stephanie.

Craig would like to say hello and love you lots to his son, Aaron, and pay tribute to his late father, Gordon – miss you much. Lots of love to mum Jean and Alf, Zoe and Garry, Kathy and Neil, and John. Not forgetting other family, friends and colleagues too numerous to mention – thanks for everything.

Finally, here are some of the web-sites we have found to be supportive, helpful and/or useful in the course of our research:

mjjvault.hosted-forum.com
sitekreator.com/Mijac/teenagesymphony.html
sitekreator.com/Jacksons/main_page.html
www.mjworld.net
www.mjnewsonline.com
www.mjfanclub.net
www.jacksonvillage.org
www.mjstrangersite.com
www.mjcollectors.com
www.mjdatabank.com
jetzi-mjvideos.com
www.jackson5abc.com
www.mjcollectorland.com
bubblesland.free.fr
www.mjjforum.com
mjbackstage.be
www.michaelmania.com
www.mj-ireland.com
www.mjtkop.com
www.cmjfc.ca
www.mjfrance.com

www.mattheweaston.co.uk
www.mjstreet.net
www.steady-laughing.com
www.michaeljacksoncatalog.com
www.mjj2005.com

All web-site addresses were correct, and the sites active, at the time of going to press – this, of course, can change at any time. We, as authors, have no involvement in any of these sites and the addresses are provided for information only: we cannot be held responsible for the content or accuracy of any of the sites.

By the same authors:

ABBA Gold Hits

Jacksons Number Ones

Michael Jackson – The Early Years

Michael Jackson – The Solo Years

www.cadman-halstead-musicbooks.com

www.mjjcharts.com

INTRODUCTION

Michael Jackson first entered a recording studio in November 1967, just three months after his ninth birthday. Two years later he and his older brothers scored their first hit, *I Want You Back* – and, despite setbacks that would have ended the career of a lesser man, Michael's legion of fans remain as loyal today as they have ever been.

The aim of this book is to document the many songs Michael has been involved with over the years – as singer, as writer, as producer, or simply as the inspiration or subject. The songs are listed numerically and alphabetically, and each listing includes the artist, release date and connection to Michael, together with other interesting information.

We have used a number of sources in compiling this book. The starting point, naturally, was the officially released singles and albums by Michael and his brothers, not forgetting the numerous collaborations he has been involved with over the years.

Many unreleased songs Michael has written or co-written have been registered – most commonly by his music company Mijac Music – with one or more professional bodies, including:

- The United States Copyright Office.
- The Songwriters Hall of Fame.
- The American performing rights organisation, BMI.
- The American Society of Composers, Authors & Publishers.
- The Canadian Musical Reproduction Rights Agency Ltd.
- EMI Music Publishing

Michael has name-checked numerous songs he has written or co-written in copyright court cases – most notably, in Mexico in 1993. All these titles are detailed, as are the poems – but not the reflections – featured in Michael's 1992 book of poems and reflections, *Dancing The Dream*. We have also included and detailed:

- Official remixes.
- Notable demo versions.
- Cover versions & other hit versions.
- Notable adaptations and tracks, especially hits, which have sampled a Jackson or Jackson-related song.

We recognise we have not included every demo version or every cover version or every song to sample one of Michael's recordings – to do so would be impossible.

Every song Michael has ever been involved with recording surely exists – or once existed – in at least one, and probably numerous, demo versions. The vast majority of these will never be heard and it would serve no purpose to simply mention 'demo version exists', for every title listed. Therefore, we have only detailed demos that have been officially or unofficially released, or where interesting facts about the demo are known.

Numerous unofficial remixes also exist – again, for the most part, we have made no attempt to detail these.

We are indebted to a number of contacts, who shall remain nameless, who have confirmed the existence of numerous unreleased songs – for example, one contact has in his possession some rare, unreleased Motown demo tracks, and a list of unreleased cover versions recorded by the Jackson 5.

It was inevitable, in compiling a book like this from scratch, we would come across songs Michael is rumoured to have written, or recorded, or been involved with, but which we didn't feel comfortable including in the main body of the book, due to a lack of hard evidence they actually exist.

At the same time, we didn't simply want to ignore such songs or omit them completely – hence, following the main body of the book, we have compiled a 'Rumour Has It' section. This features a list of titles that might exist and might be Michael-related, but equally might not.

We don't doubt some people will feel certain songs in the main body of the book should be in the rumour section, or not be in the book at all, or visa-versa. It's equally certain we have left out songs other people would have included and, while we have striven for 100% accuracy, we wouldn't be human if we didn't make the occasional error.

This book has taken us nearly three years to research and write, and it's no exaggeration to say we could have spent another two or three years working on it – it's that kind of project. But we had to draw the line somewhere, if the book was ever to see the light of day.

We hope you enjoy reading our book as much as we have enjoyed researching and writing it.

Chris Cadman & Craig Halstead

MICHAEL JACKSON: FOR THE RECORD

1-2-3

Early, rejected title for the Jackson 5's second hit single, *ABC*.

Chorus included the alternate lyrics, '1-2-3, easy as A-B-C, or simple as do-re-me. 1-2-3, A-B-C, baby you and me.' Bootleg recording known to exist – no official release.

2 BAD

Written by Michael with Bruce Swedien, Ivan Moore and Dallas Austin.

Featured on the album HIS*TORY PAST, PRESENT AND FUTURE BOOK 1* (hereinafter shortened to HIS*TORY*), released in June 1995, and in Michael's mini-movie, *Ghosts* – it was the only song in the mega-rare first version of the short film, with *Ghosts* and *Is It Scary* added later. The original version also had different effects, colours and sounds, other incidental music, plus a different transformation of the Mayor.

Official Versions:
Album Version.
Refugee Camp Mix.

Refugee Camp Mix featured on the 1997 album, *BLOOD ON THE DANCE FLOOR*.

2-4-6-8

Song the Jackson 5 recorded for their second album, *ABC*, issued in May 1970 in the States and August 1970 in the UK.

Featured in the 'Drafted' episode of the Jackson 5 cartoon series in 1971.

Snippet featured in the opening montage of clips from Michael's film, *Moonwalker*.

7 ROOMS OF GLOOM

Four Tops hit the Jackson 5 recorded a version of – remains unreleased.

The Four Tops took the song to no.10 on the R&B singles chart and no.14 on the Hot 100 in the States, and to no.12 in the UK, in 1967.

9 *FRAGMENTEN UIT NIEUWE ELPEE BAD*

Flexi disc issued free on the cover of the Dutch magazine *Top 10* in 1987, featured excerpts from all the tracks on the album *BAD* (except the CD-only bonus track, *Leave Me Alone*).

Later issued in Holland as a 7" vinyl promotional single with picture sleeve.

16 CANDLES

Song the Jackson 5 recorded for their album, *MAYBE TOMORROW*, issued in April 1971 in the States and October 1971 in the UK.

Featured in the 'Mistaken Identity' episode of the Jackson 5 cartoon series in 1971.

B-side of *How Funky Is Your Chicken* in Holland and Sweden.

Originally recorded by the Crests, for their album, *THE CRESTS SING ALL BIGGIES* – they took the song to no.2 on the Hot 100 and no.4 on the R&B singles chart in the States in 1959.

2000 WATTS

Written by Michael with Teddy Riley, Tyrese Gibson and J. Henson, and recorded by Michael for his album, *INVINCIBLE*, issued in October 2001.

Originally scheduled to appear on a Tyrese album in 2001, but Michael fell in love with the track and recorded it himself. Tyrese, although he decided against recording the song as well, nevertheless titled his album *2000 WATTS*.

2300 JACKSON STREET

Written by Jermaine, Jackie, Tito and Randy Jackson with Gene Griffin and Aaron Hall.

Title track of a Jacksons album recorded by Jermaine, Jackie, Tito and Randy (but not Michael and Marlon), issued in June 1989.

Featured backing vocals by 'The Jackson Family and Children', including Michael, Janet, Rebbie and Tito's sons, 3T.

Charted at no.9 on the R&B singles chart, but failed to make the Hot 100, in the States – peaked at no.76 in the UK.

Promo short film, directed by Greg Gold, featured members of the Jackson family, including Michael.

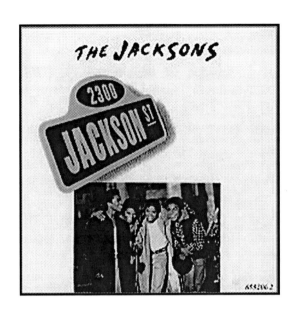

A BABY SMILES

Song Michael considered for his album, *DANGEROUS*, and cited he had written in his Mexican court disposition in November 1993 – remains unreleased.

Lyrics featured as a poem, titled 'When Babies Smile', in Michael's book of poems and reflections, *Dancing The Dream*.

Titled *Baby Smiles*, one of five songs hand-written by Michael circa 1979 – lyrics included in a personal notebook, with young actor Mark Lester on the cover, which formed part of a 10,000+ piece collection of Jackson memorabilia purchased by Universal Express and some of its entertainment partners, in November 2006.

A BRAND NEW DAY

Song featured in Michael's first movie, *The Wiz*, an all-black remake of *The Wizard Of Oz* with Diana Ross in the starring role, as Dorothy. Michael played the part of the scarecrow, and among his co-stars were: Lena Horne (Glinda, the good witch), Richard Pryor (the Wiz), Ted Ross (the cowardly lion) and Nipsey Russell (the tin man).

Movie premiered in 1978, and was accompanied by a double soundtrack album that achieved no.17 on the R&B albums chart in the USA, and no.40 on the pop albums chart.

Credited to 'The Wiz Stars', released as a single in several continental European countries (but not the UK or USA), going all the way to no.1 in Holland and Belgium – where it kept Michael's *Don't Stop 'Til You Get Enough* out of the top slot.

A CHANGE IS GONNA COME

Pre-Motown recording by the Jackson 5 first heard in 1993, when it featured on a Japanese release, *BIG BOY*; later the same year, included on *THE JACKSON FIVE FEATURING MICHAEL JACKSON*, issued on the Stardust label in the UK/Europe.

Two versions released, an over-dubbed extended remix and the track as it was originally recorded, way back in 1965-7.

Written and originally recorded by Sam Cooke, for his album *AIN'T THAT GOOD NEWS*, as a response to Bob Dylan's *Blowin' In The*

Wind. Sam's version achieved no.9 on the R&B singles chart in the States in early 1965. It peaked at no.31 on the Hot 100 but failed to chart in the UK.

A FOOL FOR YOU

One of 19 rare and previously unreleased tracks on the Jackson 5's *SOULSATION!* 4CD box set, released in 1995.

Penned by Ray Charles, the Jackson 5 originally recorded the song on 12th February 1970, with producer Bobby Taylor.

Ray's original version featured on the 1958 album, *RAY CHARLES AT NEWPORT*.

A PLACE IN THE SUN

Stevie Wonder song the Jackson 5 recorded a version of – remains unreleased.

Stevie took the song to no.3 on the R&B singles chart and no.9 on the Hot 100 in the States, and to no.20 in the UK, in 1966. Stevie's version featured on his album, *DOWN TO EARTH*.

A PRETTY FACE IS

Song written by Stevie Wonder circa 1974 (some sources say as far back as 1968), possibly intended for the Jackson 5 or as a duet by Stevie with Michael.

Stevie confirmed the song's existence in an interview in Japan in 1988, and he stated he envisioned the song as a duet with Michael. Michael and Stevie are reported to have recorded the song for Stevie's 1988 album, *CHARACTERS*, but it remains unreleased.

Other unreleased songs Stevie worked on around the time he wrote *A Pretty Face Is*, which may or may not have been written for Michael and his brothers, include: *No News Is Good News, Bumble-Bee Of Love, Sky Blue Afternoon, The Future, If Your Mama Could See You Now* and *Would I Live For You, Would I Die For You*.

Also known by the title, *A Pretty Face*.

ABC

Title track of the Jackson 5's second album, issued in May 1970 in the States and August 1970 in the UK.

Originally titled '1-2-3' and 'ABCD' – demo versions known to exist.

Premiered on the *American Bandstand* TV show in the States, on which Michael also revealed he was a big Beatles fan.

Appeared on a promotional film sent to concert promoters in 1970, to let them know who the Jackson 5 were – performance filmed at the group's first Motown concert in Philadelphia.

Released as a single in February 1970 in the USA and May 1970 in the UK. Achieved no.1 in the States on both the Hot 100 (for two weeks), where it toppled *Let It Be* by the Beatles, and the R&B chart (for four weeks). Charted at no.8 in the UK.

Outsold the Jackson 5's debut hit, *I Want You Back*, and was the no.8 best selling single of 1970 in the States.

Motown celebrated the success of *ABC* by pressing gold (yellow) vinyl copies, with an accompanying press release that stated: 'Because of all the million selling records we've had in the past, none soared beyond the million mark faster than *ABC* by the Jackson 5. It did it in less than 12 days!'

Grammy Award nomination: Best Contemporary Vocal Performance by a Duo, Group or Chorus (the Carpenters took the award, for *(They Long To Be) Close To You*).

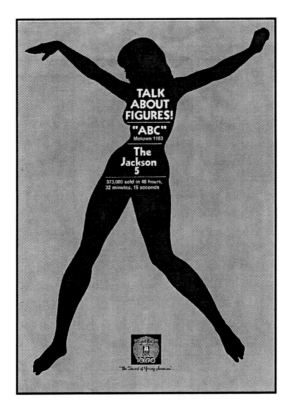

Featured in 'It All Started With', an episode of the Jackson 5 cartoon series, in 1971.

Following its success, co-writer Freddie Perren confessed the music of *ABC* is the chorus of *I Want You Back*. 'All we did was take that music and keep playing it, adding a couple of steps to it,' he admitted. 'We cut the track for *ABC* before *I Want You Back* was really a big hit!'

Cited by Michael, in the early 1970s, as one of his three favourite songs he had recorded for Motown, along with *I'll Be There* and *Never Can Say Goodbye*. Also named by Michael named as one of his three personal Motown favourites in his autobiography, *Moonwalk*, published in April 1988.

Previously unreleased live medley of *I Want You Back* and *ABC*, recorded at the Jackson 5's Los Angeles concert on 26th August 1972, featured on the TV soundtrack album, *THE JACKSONS: AMERICAN DREAM*, issued in October 1992 in the States and July 1993 in the UK.

Performed by the Jackson 5 on the *Carol Burnett Show* in 1974.

Salaam Remi's Krunk-A-Delic Party Mix, on the album *MOTOWN REMIXED* in 2005, featured alternate vocals.

Other remixes:
Love Stream Mix – from the album, *SOUL SOURCE – JACKSON 5 REMIXES*, released in Japan in 2000.
Kubota, Takeshi Remix – from the same album as above.
Readymade Super 524 Mix – from the album, *SOUL SOURCE – JACKSON 5 REMIXES 2*, released in Japan in 2001.

Justa Roots Rock Mix – from the same album as above; also included on the Jackson 5 album, *SOUL LEGENDS*.
DJ Friction Remix.

Sampled by:
Vanilla Ice on *Dancin'*, from his 1990 album, *TO THE EXTREME*.
Naughty By Nature on *O.P.P. (Other People's Property)* – charted at no.5 on the R&B singles chart and no.6 on the Hot 100 in the States, and no.35 in the UK, in 1991.

ABC – I'LL BE THERE – THE LOVE YOU SAVE

Medley of hits the Jackson 5 performed on their own TV special in the States in 1972.

ABC – THE LOVE YOU SAVE

Medley performed by the Jacksons during the *Michael Jackson: 30th Anniversary Celebration, The Solo Years* concerts, staged at New York's Madison Square Garden on 7th and 10th September 2001.

ABCD

Early, rejected title for the Jackson 5's second hit single, *ABC*.

AFTER THE STORM (THE SUN WILL SHINE)

Unreleased track from the Jackson 5's Motown era – written by Willie Hutch.

AIN'T NO MOUNTAIN HIGH ENOUGH

Classic song the Jackson 5 recorded two versions of, one mid-tempo with a spoken intro (as per the Diana Ross recording), and the other up-tempo – both remain unreleased.

Hit versions:
Marvin Gaye & Tammi Terrell – no.3 on the R&B singles chart and no.19 on the Hot 100 in the States in 1967.
Diana Ross – no.1 on the Hot 100 and R&B singles chart in the States, and no.6 in the UK, in 1970.

Boys Town Gang (medley) – no.46 in the UK in 1981,
Jocelyn Brown – no.35 in the UK in 1998.
Whitehouse – no.60 in the UK in 1998.

Marvin & Tammi's original version featured on their album, *UNITED*.

AIN'T NO SUNSHINE

Track on Michael's debut solo album, *GOT TO BE THERE*, released in January 1972 in the States and May 1972 in the UK.

Issued as Michael's third solo single in the UK in July 1970 (*I Wanna Be Where You Are* having been chosen as the third release in the States), peaking at no.8.

Alternate version remixed by Dean Burt included on the 1987 album, *THE ORIGINAL SOUL OF MICHAEL JACKSON*. SSY Remix featured on the album, *SOUL SOURCE – JACKSON 5 REMIXES 2*, released in Japan in 2001.

Original version by writer Bill Withers featured on his 1971 album, *JUST AS I AM*.

Title track of a budget compilation of Michael's Motown output, released in 1982 by the Pickwick label in the UK.

Other hit versions:
Bill Withers – no.3 on the Hot 100 and no.6 on the R&B singles chart in the States in 1971.
Sivuca – no.56 in the UK in 1984.
Sydney Youngblood – no.51 on the R&B singles chart in 1991.
Kid Frost – no.95 on the Hot 100 in the USA in 1995.
Ladysmith Black Mambazo featuring Des'Ree – no.42 in the UK in 1999.

AIN'T NOTHING LIKE THE REAL THING

Opening track on the Jackson 5's album, *LOOKIN' THROUGH THE WINDOWS*, issued in May 1972 in the States and October 1972 in the UK.

Released as the B-side of *Skywriter*, a single released in the UK (but not USA) in 1973, peaked at no.25.

Performed by the Jackson 5 on *The Flip Wilson Show* in the States in 1972.

Original version, by Marvin Gaye & Tammi Terrell, featured on their 1968 duets album, *YOU'RE ALL I NEED*. Single topped the R&B charts in the States for three weeks in 1968; also charted at no.8 on Billboard's Hot 100 and no.34 in the UK.

AIN'T THAT PECULIAR

One of several cover versions the Jackson 5 often performed in the early, pre-Motown days – co-written by Smokey Robinson.

Recorded by Jermaine for his debut solo album, *JERMAINE*, released in 1972.

Live recording with Jermaine singing lead featured on the album, *LIVE!*, credited to Michael Jackson with the Jackson 5, released in the UK (but not USA) in 1988. Album originally released in Japan, titled simply *IN JAPAN!* Recorded at the Osaka Koseinenkin Hall, Japan, on 30th April 1973.

Included on the limited edition CD, *IN JAPAN!*, released by Hip-Select in 2004 – only 5,000 copies pressed.

Marvin Gaye's original version – from the album *MOODS OF MARVIN GAYE* – hit no.1 for a single week on the R&B singles chart in the USA in 1965. It also achieved no.8 on the Hot 100 but wasn't a hit in the UK.

AIN'T TOO PROUD TO BEG

Temptations hit the Jackson 5 recorded a version of – remains unreleased.

One of several songs the Jackson 5 performed at their Motown audition – filmed by Johnny Bristol, but this part of the audition has never been publicly released.

Hit versions:

Temptations – no.1 on the R&B singles chart and no.13 on the Hot 100 in the States, and no.21 in the UK, in 1966.

Rolling Stones – no.17 on the Hot 100 in 1974.

Rick Astley – no.89 on the Hot 100 in 1989.

The Temptations' original appeared on their album, *GETTING READY*.

AL CAPONE

Song Michael cited he had written in his court disposition in November 1993 – failed to make his album, *BAD*. Demo version believed to exist, but remains unreleased.

ALL I DO

Track on Stevie Wonder's 1982 Grammy winning album, *HOTTER THAN JULY*, featuring Michael on backing vocals.

B-side of Stevie's single, *That Girl*.

ALL I DO IS THINK OF YOU

Track on the Jackson 5's album, *MOVING VIOLATION*, released in May 1975 in the States and July 1975 in the UK.

B-side of the last Jackson 5 single, *Forever Came Today*, issued while they were still a Motown act. Charted in its own right on the R&B singles chart in the States, peaking at no.50, after it became known the group were leaving Motown for CBS/Epic.

Performed by the Jackson 5 on *Soul Train* in the States in 1975, and live from Las Vegas, on the *Mike Douglas In Hollywood* TV show.

Cover version by Pasadena quintet, Troop (standing for 'Total Respect Of Other People'), hit no.1 on the R&B singles chart in the States in 1990.

Version by teen group B5 released in 2005.

Sampled by the Roots, on the track *Can't Stop This*, from their 2006 album, *GAMES THEORY*.

ALL IN YOUR NAME

Song about peace Barry Gibb of the Bees Gees confirmed, in October 2005, he worked on with Michael in the summer of 2002.

Originally believed to be titled *Prayer For Peace* – slated to appear on an album Michael was working on in 2003.

Demo version by Barry and Michael known to exist – remains unreleased.

ALL NIGHT DANCIN'

Song written by Michael and brother Randy, featured on the Jacksons' album, *DESTINY*, released in December 1978.

B-side of the single *Shake Your Body (Down To The Ground)* in the UK (but not USA).

Performed by the Jacksons during their Destiny Tour – featured in a concert screened on BBC2 in the UK.

ALL THE THINGS YOU ARE

Track on Michael's third solo album, *MUSIC & ME*, released in April 1973 in the States and July 1973 in the UK.

B-side of *Too Young*, issued as a single in Italy in 1973.

Included on the tribute album *MOTOWN CELEBRATES SINATRA*, released in 1998, which also featured a shot of Michael dressed as Frank Sinatra on the sleeve (taken from the 1971 TV special, *Diana!*). Same photo used on the sleeve of Michael's Swedish single, *Rockin' Robin*.

ALRIGHT NOW

Song written by Michael with John Barnes.

Recorded by Ralph Tresvant, for his 1990 album, *RALPH TRESVANT*.

ALRIGHT WITH ME

Track on the Jacksons' album, *2300 JACKSON STREET*, released in June 1989.

B-side of the Jacksons single, *Nothin (Compares 2 U)*.

Michael wasn't one of the Jacksons who recorded this song.

AM I BLUE

Song the Jacksons performed on their TV series in 1976, with their special guest star, Sonny Bono (of Sonny & Cher), as part of a medley with *More Than You Know*, *For Once In My Life* and *Try A Little Tenderness*.

ANGEL

Song written by Babyface, who described it as 'simply fantastic', and recorded around 1998 by Michael for a greatest hits compilation that didn't happen – remains unreleased.

ANOTHER DAY

Song Lenny Kravitz confirmed in an interview in *Blender* magazine he had been working on with Michael – failed to make the final track listing of Michael's album, *INVINCIBLE*.

'Working with Michael Jackson was probably the best recording experience of my life,' said Kravitz. 'He was totally cool, absolutely professional and a beautiful, beautiful guy – and let's not forget, Michael is a musical genius.'

Remains unreleased.

ANOTHER PART OF ME

Song written and recorded by Michael.

Originally featured in the short film *Captain EO*, a 17 minute 3D space fantasy shot for Disney, and premiered at the Epcot Center in Orlando, Florida, on 12th September 1986. Costing $30 million, *Captain EO* was billed as 'a celebration of triumph over evil', and was directed by Francis Ford Coppola and produced by George Lucas. The final screening was at Disneyland, Paris, on 16th August 1998.

Included on Michael's album, *BAD*, released in September 1987, ahead of another of Michael's compositions, *Streetwalker* (which was finally issued in 2001, as one of the bonus tracks on the special edition of the same album).

Sixth single lifted from *BAD*, hitting no.1 (for one week) on the R&B singles chart in the States. As the fifth R&B chart topper from *BAD* (*Dirty Diana* stalled at no.5), it equalled a record held by Janet Jackson, for the most no.1 singles from one album (in her case, from *CONTROL*).

The first five singles from *BAD* topped the Hot 100 (another record), but *Another Part Of Me* only made no.11, and peaked at no.15 in the UK.

Official Versions:

Album Version.	Extended Dance Mix.
A Cappella.	Instrumental.
Radio Edit.	Dub Version.
7" Version.	

Promoted with a 'live' video, filmed at Michael's Wembley Stadium concert, on 15th July 1988 – directed by Patrick T. Kelly. Premiered on 30th July 1988, during the 90 minute TV special, *Michael Jackson: Around The World*. HRH Princess Diana, Elizabeth Taylor, Sophia Loren and Tina Turner all attended the concert.

Part of a lawsuit heard in Mexico in 1993, when Robert Smith (*aka* Robert Austin), Reynard Jones and Clifford Rubin claimed it infringed the song, *Send Your Love* – the judgement was in Michael's favour.

Featured in the film, *Rush Hour* (1998).

ANTHOLGY MIX

17 minute medley of Michael's solo hits, featured on one of seven 12" singles from the rare promo box-set *Twelves*, released in the UK in 2003, to promote Michael's greatest hits compilation, *NUMBER ONES*. Placed together, the seven exclusive picture sleeves formed a large *Off The Wall* era picture of Michael.

Hits featured: *You Rock My World, Black Or White, Rock With You, Bad, Billie Jean, Don't Stop 'Til You Get Enough, Thriller, Off The Wall, Smooth Criminal, Wanna Be Startin' Somethin', P.Y.T. (Pretty Young Thing)* and *Beat It*.

ANYONE NAMED JACKSON IS A FRIEND OF MINE

Song performed by the Jackson 5 on *The Carol Burnett Show* in the States, on 21st January 1974.

ARE YOU LISTENING?

Poem written by Michael – included in his book of poems and reflections, *Dancing The Dream*, published in 1992.

ART OF MADNESS

Track on the Jacksons' album, *2300 JACKSON STREET*, released in June 1989. Issued as a single in several continental European countries, but not in the UK or USA.

Michael wasn't one of the Jacksons who recorded this song.

ASHES TO ASHES

Incidental piece of music Michael composed with Nicholas Pike, for his *Ghosts* short film, premiered in October 1996.

ASK THE LONELY

Song originally recorded by the Jackson 5 in 1970, but that remained unreleased until 1983, when a remixed version appeared on the

Motown compilation, *MOTOWN SUPERSTARS SING MOTOWN SUPERSTARS*.

Album also included a version of Michael's *I Wanna Be Where You Are*, performed by Thelma Houston. Liner notes incorrectly stated 'originally released by the Jackson 5'.

Original version included as one of 19 'Rare & Unreleased' tracks of the fourth CD of the Michael/Jackson 5 box-set, *SOULSATION!*, issued in June 1995 in the States and July 1995 in the UK – demo version also known to exist.

Song originally recorded by the Four Tops, for their eponymous 1964 album. They took the song to no.9 on the R&B singles chart, and no.24 on the Hot 100, in the States in 1965.

ATTITUDE

Song Michael co-wrote with Kathy Wakefield and Michel Pierre Colombier, and registered with EMI Music Publishing – remains unreleased.

AVE MARIA

Song the Jackson 5 recorded for their *CHRISTMAS ALBUM* circa 1970, but which failed to make the final track listing – remains unreleased.

For many years, Motown asserted no out-takes from the *CHRISTMAS ALBUM* sessions existed – however, an ex-employee has recently named 15 songs Michael and his brothers did record but which weren't used, of which this is one.

Hit versions:
Shirley Bassey – no.31 in the UK in 1962.
Lesley Garrett & Amanda Thompson – no.16 in the UK in 1993.
Andrea Bocelli – no.65 in the UK in 1999.

BABY BE MINE

Written by Rod Temperton, and recorded by Michael for his solo album, *THRILLER*, released in December 1982.

B-side of *Human Nature* in the States (not issued in the UK), and of *I Just Can't Stop Loving You* in both the USA and UK.

BABY I NEED YOUR LOVIN'

Four Tops hit the Jackson 5 recorded a version of – remains unreleased.

Hit versions:
Four Tops – no.11 on both the Hot 100 and R&B singles chart in the States in 1964.
Fourmost – no.24 in the UK in 1964.
Johnny Rivers – no.3 on the Hot 100 in 1967.
O.C. Smith – no.30 on the R&B singles chart and no.52 on the Hot 100 in 1970.
Eric Carmen – no.62 on the Hot 100 in 1979.

Song heard in the TV mini-series, *The Jacksons: An American Dream*, but not performed by the Jackson 5.

BABY IT'S LOVE

One of two songs allegedly penned for, and maybe recorded by, the Jackson 5 and Diana Ross in 1970, but unconfirmed by Motown.

BABY, YOU DON'T HAVE TO GO

Pre-Motown recording by the Jackson 5 first heard in 1993, when it featured on a Japanese release, *BIG BOY*; later the same year, included on *THE JACKSON FIVE FEATURING MICHAEL JACKSON*, issued on the Stardust label in the UK/Europe.

Extended four minute version made available in 2005, on the Jackson 5's download compilation, *SOUL MASTERS*.

BACK IN MY ARMS AGAIN

Supremes hit the Jackson 5 recorded a version of – remains unreleased.

Hit versions:
Supremes – no.1 on the Hot 100 and R&B singles chart in the States, and no.40 in the UK, in 1965.
Genya Ravan – no.92 on the Hot 100 in 1978.

BACK TO THE PAST MEDLEY

One of two promo medleys, released on 12" and CD as *The Medleys*, in Brazil in 1994:

Featured: *Rock With You, Burn This Disco Out, Off The Wall, Don't Stop 'Til You Get Enough, Shake Your Body (Down To The Ground), Blame It On The Boogie, Thriller* and *Billie Jean*.

BAD

Written and recorded by Michael, for his solo album of the same name, released in September 1987.

Originally intended as a duet with one of Michael's main rivals in the 1980s, Prince. 'Prince was excited to have been asked,' said Susan Rogers, 'but he said to me, "I just don't do that stuff", and I think he felt Michael was going to make himself look better.' Michael's idea was to have the two of them square off in the short film, taking turns to sing and dance, in order to determine who was the 'baddest'. Prince turned Michael down, but submitted *Wouldn't You Love To Love Me*, a song he had originally demoed in 1976, for *BAD*. Michael passed, so Prince gave the song to Taja Sevelle, for her self-titled 1987 album (released on Prince's Paisley Park Records).

Second single lifted from *BAD*, hit no.1 on the Hot 100 for two weeks and the R&B singles chart for three weeks, in the States. Charted at no.3 in the UK, where a limited edition red vinyl 12" single was issued.

American Music Award: Favourite Soul/R&B Single, Male.

Soul Train Awards: Best Single of the Year, Male.

Clip of Michael's performance from one of his Bad World Tour concerts at Wembley, UK, in 1988 screened at the MTV Video Music Awards. Different performance screened as part of a Bad concert shown on Nippon TV in Japan.

Official Versions:
Album Version.	Extended Dance Mix (incl. False Fade).
A Cappella.	7" Single Mix.
Dance Remix Radio Edit.	Dub Version.

Extended Dance Mix (incl. False Fade) featured additional vocals.

Short promo film directed by Martin Scorsese, recruited at producer Quincy Jones's suggestion, loosely based on the true story of Edmund Perry, a young black man shot dead when he returned home to Harlem, New York, from a private college. Around 17 minutes long, with a lengthy opening shot in black/white, in which Michael took on a 'serious' acting role for the first time – gang members included a young, and at the time unknown, Wesley Snipes. The musical, technicolor segment of the short film was filmed at a subway station in Brooklyn.

Short film premiered on 31st August 1987, on the TV special, *Michael Jackson: The Magic Returns*.

Bad: Pepsi Commercial – with new lyrics written by Michael in 1986 – registered with the United States Copyright Office in March 1987. Series of commercials began with The Magic Begins and The Dressing Room, followed by five shorts that ran as part of one story: The Magic Begins, The Chase, The Chopper, The Museum and The Finale.

In late 1988, Sammy Davis, Jr. performed a comedy version of *Bad* during one of his concerts. Before his performance, he said of Michael: 'I've seen him grow from a small boy to this huge star, and it's frightening to see where else he'll take it to.' Michael and choreographer Michael Peters helped out Sammy, on some break dancing steps for the film, *Cry Of The City*.

Featured as a sample in *I Got The Money*, from the stage musical *Sisterella*, which Michael supported financially.

Sampled in 2000 by rapper Trina on *Da Baddest Bitch*.

Sixth of Michael's 20 *'Visionary – The Video Singles'* reissues, with the music on one side of a Dual Disc and the accompanying short film on the other side. Issued in March 2006 in the UK – charted at no.16.

BAD GIRL

Song Michael cited he had written in his court disposition in November 1993 – remains unreleased.

BADDER

Entertaining re-make of Michael's *Bad* short film, as featured in his 'movie like no other', *Moonwalker*, premiered in 1989. Nine year old Brandon Adams played Michael, lip-synching to Michael's original recording. Michael's nephew, Jermaine Jackson, Jr., was among the *Badder* dancers.

BAREFOOTIN'

Song the Jackson 5 performed regularly in the early days, initially in and around their home town, Gary, Indiana. Whilst singing, young Michael often used to kick off his shoes, and dance around the stage.

The Jackson 5 won Gary's city wide Talent Search with *Barefootin'* in 1965, and earned their first press write-up in the *Gary Post-Tribune*.

A hit for Robert Parker in the States in 1966, making no.2 on the R&B singles chart and no.7 on the Hot 100.

BASSOUILLE

Song written by Michael with Bruce Swedien in 1994, but failed to make Michael's HIS*TORY* album, and remains unreleased.

BE A LION

Song featured in Michael's first movie, *The Wiz*, and on the accompanying double soundtrack album. Lead vocals by Diana Ross, who played Dorothy in the film, with Michael and his co-stars singing a few lines each.

BE A PEPPER II

Two short radio jingles (30 seconds and 60 seconds) recorded by the Jacksons, including Michael, for Dr Pepper's 'Be A Pepper II 1979 Campaign' in the States.

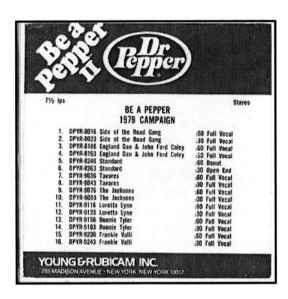

BE ME 4 A DAY

Song written by Michael with Grey Calix Days (who also worked with Michael's nephews, 3T), and registered with the BMI – remains unreleased.

Known by several alternative titles: *Be Me For A Day*, *Just For One Day Be Michael*, *Just For A Day*, *Me 4 A Day* and *Be Michael*.

BE MY GIRL

Song mentioned in the January 1973 issue of *Rock & Soul* magazine, as having been performed in concert by the Jackson 5 in mid-to-late 1972 – cited as the group's latest single, with Jermaine on lead.

Recorded by the Jackson 5 for Motown – remains unreleased.

Known among fans, mistakenly, by the title *Paper Doll*.

BE NOT ALWAYS

Song written and produced by Michael, with additional lyrics by brother Marlon.

Although effectively a solo cut by Michael, featured on the Jacksons' album *VICTORY*, released in July 1984.

Titled *Always, Be Not Always*, one of five songs hand-written by Michael circa 1979 – lyrics included in a personal notebook, with young actor Mark Lester on the cover, that formed part of a 10,000+ piece collection of Jackson memorabilia purchased by Universal Express and some of its entertainment partners, in November 2006.

BE WHAT YOU ARE

One of five songs the Jackson 5 performed as a medley at the Grammy Awards on 2nd March 1974, to introduce the nominees for Best Rhythm & Blues Vocal Performance by a Group, Duo or Chorus.

A hit in 1973 for the Staple Singers, achieving no.18 on the R&B singles chart and no.66 on the Hot 100, in the States.

BEAT IT

Track written and co-produced, with Quincy Jones, by Michael.

Featured a soaring guitar solo – inspired by the song *Eruption* – by Eddie Van Halen, who was invited to guest on the track by Quincy Jones. Van Halen initially believed he was receiving crank calls, before establishing proper communication with Jones – and recorded his contribution completely free of any charge, so keen was he to be involved.

'I did it as a favour,' said Van Halen. 'I was a complete fool, according to the rest of the band, our manager and everyone else. I was not used. I knew what I was doing – I don't do something unless I want to do it.'

'Quincy Jones and Michael took a skeleton version of *Beat It* up to Eddie's place, as they wanted him to solo over the verse section,' explained Steve Lukather, who also worked on the song. 'Initially, we rocked it out as Eddie had played a good solo – but Quincy thought it was too tough. So I had to reduce the distorted guitar sound and that is what was released.'

One of the last four songs Michael completed for *THRILLER*; the other three were *Human Nature, The Lady In My Life* and *P.Y.T. (Pretty Young Thing)*.

Third single from Michael's solo album, *THRILLER*, following *The Girl Is Mine* and *Billie Jean*. In the States, Frank Dileo (Vice President of Epic Records, and later Michael's manager) convinced everyone *Beat It* should be released whilst *Billie Jean* was still heading towards no.1, and predicted both singles would be in the Top 10 at the same time.

On the Hot 100, *Billie Jean* was replaced at no.1 by Dexy Midnight Runners' *Come On Eileen*, which spent a solitary week at the top, before Michael reclaimed the no.1 slot with *Beat It*. Both singles occupied Top 5 positions at the same time, a feat only matched by the Bee Gees, Olivia Newton-John, Linda Ronstadt and Donna Summer in the 1970s.

Beat It topped the Hot 100 for three weeks and R&B singles chart for one week, and peaked at no.3 in the UK.

RIAA Platinum Record Award (USA million seller).

Promo video, directed by Bob Giraldi, financed to the tune of $140,000 by Michael himself after CBS got cold feet. Inspired by *West Side Story*. Cast included 18 professional dancers and four break dancers, choreographed by Michael Peters, and real life members of two rival Los Angeles street gangs.

Billboard Video Awards: Best Overall Video Clip, Best Performance by a Male Artist, Best Use of Video to Enhance a Song, Best Use of Video to Enhance an Artist's Image, Best Choreography.

American Music Awards: Favourite Pop/Rock Video, Favourite Soul Video.

Grammy Awards: Record of the Year, Best Rock Vocal Performance, Male.

Billboard Video Awards: Best Overall Video, Best Dance/Disco 12" (joint with *Billie Jean*).

Rolling Stone: No.1 Video in both the Critics Poll and Reader's Poll.

Black Gold Awards: Best Video Performance.

Inducted into the Music Video Producer's Hall of Fame.

Official Versions:
Album Version.
Edit.
Moby's Sub Mix.

Featured in the National Highway Safety Commission's anti-drunk driving campaign in the States, with the slogan, 'Drinking and Driving can Kill a Friendship', and included on the accompanying NHSC promo album. Michael collected a special award from President Ronald Reagan at the White House, for his support of the campaign.

Eddie Van Halen joined Michael and his brothers on stage, to perform *Beat It* with them during the Jacksons' Victory Tour, on 4th July 1984.

Live performance by Michael, at his Dangerous Tour concert in Bucharest, Romania, on 1st October 1992, featured on the DVD released as part of his box-set, *THE ULTIMATE COLLECTION*, issued in November 2004.

Different concert performances screened by Nippon TV in Japan (from the Bad World Tour), and in Germany and New Zealand (both from the *History* World Tour).

Performed by Michael and Slash during the *Michael Jackson: 30th Anniversary Celebration, The Solo Years* concerts, staged at New York's Madison Square Garden on 7th and 10th September 2001.

Performed by the Chipmunks in a 1983 episode of *Alvin & The Chipmunks*, where the Chipmunks and Chipettes faced-off against bullies at an ice skating rink.

Featured in several films, including: *Back To The Future II* (1989), *Zoolander* (2001) and *Undercover Brother* (2002).

Performed by Metallica at the 2003 MTV Video Music Awards.

Latin influenced cover version by Señor Coconut released as a single in the UK in 2004.

Ranked no.4 'World's Favourite Song' by UK voters in Sony Ericsson's global poll in 2005, behind Michael's *Billie Jean*, *Thriller* and Queen's *Bohemian Rhapsody*.

Fifth of Michael's 20 *'Visionary – The Video Singles'* reissues, with the music on one side of a Dual Disc and the accompanying short film on the other side. Issued in March 2006 in the UK – charted at no.15.

BEAUTIFUL GIRL

Written by Michael, and recorded by him, between 1998 and 2004.

Demo version featured on Michael's box-set, *THE ULTIMATE COLLECTION*, issued in November 2004.

BEHIND THE MASK

Song written by Chris Mosdell and Ryuichi Sakamoto, with additional lyrics by Michael.

Original instrumental version, with choral backing, recorded by the Yellow Magic Orchestra, for their 1979 album, *SOLID STATE SURVIVOR*. Quincy Jones heard Yellow Magic Orchestra's version during the *Thriller* sessions, and brought it to Michael's attention.

'I didn't know who Michael Jackson was – I wasn't into that whole soul disco stuff,' confessed Chris Mosdell. 'When Michael Jackson recorded it, he also added an extra melody line and a few extra lyrics, so they wanted to split the royalties – which is quite impossible. You can't take a Beatles song and add a melody line, a few more lyrics, and ask for fifty percent.'

Legal battles meant Michael's version didn't make his *THRILLER* album and remains unreleased.

Michael's keyboardist, Greg Phillinganes, did record a version for his album, *PULSE*, issued in 1985. Released as a single, it achieved no.77 on the R&B singles chart in the States, but failed to make the Hot 100 and wasn't a hit in the UK.

Phillinganes first met Michael and his brothers during the sessions for the Jacksons' *DESTINY* album in 1978, and went on to serve as musical director for Michael's Bad World Tour.

Phillinganes, who also played with his band, brought the song to Eric Clapton's attention. Clapton's cover version, on which Phillinganes played keyboards and sang backing vocals, hit no.15 in the UK in 1987. This version, curiously, failed to credit Michael as one of the song's co-writers – but Chris Mosdell has confirmed Michael does takes 50% of the song-writing royalties.

BEI MIR BIST DU SCHON

Old standard the Jackson 5 sang as part of a 'Salute to the Vocal Groups' medley with *Opus One*, *Yakety Yak*, *Stop! In The Name Of Love*, an untitled Jackson 5 ditty and *Dancing Machine*, on *The Carol Burnett Show* in the States in January 1975 – clip included on the Vol.31 DVD of the show.

Originally written in Yiddish – translates as 'To me, you are beautiful'. English lyrics by Sammy Cahn and Saul Chaplin, and first recorded in English by the Andrew Sisters in 1937. Recorded by numerous other artists, including Cab Calloway and Benny Goodman.

BELONG 2

Song written by Michael with Teddy Riley in 1999, for Michael's *INVINCIBLE* album, but failed to make the final cut and remains unreleased.

BEN

Title track of Michael's second solo album, released in August 1972 in the States and December 1972 in the UK.

Initially intended for Michael's teen rival Donny Osmond, until lyricist Don Black suggested Michael might make a better job of it.

Title song for a tame horror movie, the sequel to *Willard*, in which youngster, David Garrison (played by Lee Montgomery), has a rat as his best friend. In the film, Montgomery sings the song whilst sat at a piano. Michael's version of *Ben* played at the end of the movie, when the rat reappears, after Garrison believes it has been killed. 14 year old Michael wasn't old enough to go see the film when it was first released.

Gave Michael his first no.1 on the Hot 100 in the States, where it also achieved no.5 on the R&B singles chart. In the UK it peaked at no.7.

Sold 1.7 million copies in the States.

Michael promoted *Ben* with several TV appearances in the States, including *American Bandstand, The Sonny & Cher Comedy Hour, Soul Train* and the Jackson 5's own TV special in November 1972 – also performed by Michael on *The Jacksons* TV series in 1976.

Golden Globe Award and Academy Award nomination for Song of the Year – Michael performed the song at the latter, but the song failed to pick up an Oscar. Also honoured with an ASCAP Award.

Red vinyl 7" single released in Japan with 'rats' sleeve. Rare one-sided 7" promo, on the Cinerama label, featured an excerpt of *Ben*, accompanied in the background by the sound of screaming rats.

Live version featured on the Michael/Jackson 5's *LIVE!* album, issued in September 1988 in the UK (no USA release). All songs on the album were recorded at a concert on 30th April 1973, at the Osaka

Koseinenkin Hall in Japan. Also included on the limited edition CD, *IN JAPAN!*, released by Hip-Select in 2004 – only 5,000 copies pressed.

Second live version, recorded at a concert at Madison Square Garden in September 1981, featured on the Jacksons album, *LIVE*, issued in November 1981.

Live performance by the Jacksons, at a concert in Mexico in 1976, included on the home video, *The Jacksons In Concert*, released in 1981 in the UK (no USA release). Michael also performed the song during the Jacksons' Destiny Tour, screened on BBC2 in the UK.

Short version featured in the 'Stark Raving Dad' episode of *The Simpsons*, in which Michael guested – however, contractual obligations meant a sound-a-like performed *Ben* and *Billie Jean*.

Remixed version titled HF Remix #2 featured on the album, *SOUL SOURCE – JACKSON 5 REMIXES 2*, released in Japan in 2001.

Used as the theme song for the Japanese soap, *Aikurshi*, in 2005 – reissued in Japan in May 2005 as a 3-track CD single, featuring the original recording and two new mixes (*HF Remix* and *Orchestral*). Charted at no.48, a four place improvement on the song's original placing in 1972.

Cover version recorded by Marti Webb in 1985, in aid of the Ben Hardwick Appeal, peaked at no.5 in the UK. Ben Hardwick was a terminally ill little boy whose story touched hearts across the country when it was told on the popular TV show, *That's Life!* Michael's version of *Ben* was played at Ben's funeral.

Also in the UK, talent show *Opportunity Knocks* winner Toni Warne recorded a version of *Ben*, which charted at no.50 in 1987.

Covered by Crispin Glover, to coincide with a re-make of *Willard*, the prequel to the film, *Ben*.

Irish boyband, Boyzone covered *Ben* for their 1996 album, *A DIFFERENT BEAT*.

Performed by Billy Gilman during the *Michael Jackson: 30th Anniversary Celebration, The Solo Years* concerts, staged at New York's Madison Square Garden on 7th and 10th September 2001.

BIG BOY

Written by Gordon Keith, released as the Jackson 5's first ever single by Steel-Town Records in January 1968 (USA only).

Demo recorded circa November 1967. Initially hand-sold by Michael and his brothers, at the many gigs they played. Picked up for national distribution by Atco, a subsidiary of Atlantic Records, who pressed 10,000 copies. Sold well locally, but failed to register on any of Billboard's charts.

Re-issued as a limited edition CD single in the States, on the Inverted record label, in June 1995.

An ex-engineer, who engineered on all the sessions, has confirmed the Jackson 5 recorded eight songs for Steel-Town, only six of which have been released, including:

- *Big Boy.*
- *You've Changed.*
- *We Don't Have To Be Over 21 (To Fall In Love).*
- *Jam Session* (the version on the B-side of *Big Boy*).

Two of the six released songs are unconfirmed, but are probably:

- *Some Girls Want Me For Their Lover* (*aka Michael The Lover*).
- *I Found A Love.*

The two unreleased Steel-Town recordings are confirmed as:

- *Take My Heart.*
- *Jackson Man.*

All the other 'lost Steel-Town recordings', it's speculated, were actually taped by Shirley Cartman, possibly in her own living room. According to Cartman, only one copy of the tape ever existed. Many years after the recordings were made (by which time she had moved to Atlanta), a friend recommended she have the recordings transferred to professional archival tape, to preserve them for historical purposes. This she did, using a local Atlanta company – then, just a year or so later, the first of many compilations of 'lost' recordings surfaced, released by S.D.E.G., a small Atlanta record label.

When she learned of the commercial release of her recordings, Cartman was understandably angry – more so, because some songs she had written especially for the Jackson 5 (including *Lonely Heart*), were credited to Gordon Keith (founder and owner of Steel-Town).

BILLIE JEAN

Track written and co-produced, with Quincy Jones, by Michael.

Originally titled 'Not My Lover' (to avoid any confusion with the tennis player, Billie Jean King), and inspired by an obsessive young women who accused Michael and his brothers of fathering their sons. Michael's mother, Katherine, expressed surprise at the song's lyrics, especially where Michael vehemently proclaimed, 'the kid is *not* my son!'

Producer Quincy Jones wasn't too impressed with the demo of *Billie Jean* – he didn't much care for the bass. Original demo version included on the special edition of *THRILLER*, issued in 2001. Second demo version, over six minutes with alternate vocals and ad-libs, is known to exist – remains unreleased.

Mixed by Bruce Swedien, who usually did just one mix of a song – but he did 91 of *Billie Jean*, before the second mix was eventually chosen.

'Quincy said, okay, this song has to have the most incredible drum sound that anybody has ever done, but it also has to have one element that's different, and that's sonic personality,' said Swedien, admitting he lost a lot of sleep over what exactly Quincy meant. 'What I ended up doing was building a drum platform and designing some special little things, like a bass drum cover and a flat piece of wood that goes between the snare and the hi-hat... the bottom line is that there aren't many pieces of music where you can hear the first three or four notes of the drums, and immediately tell what the piece of music is. But I think that is the case with *Billie Jean* – and that I attribute to sonic personality.'

Second single from Michael's 1982 solo album, *THRILLER*, following his light-weight duet with Paul McCartney, *The Girl Is Mine*.

Conquered the R&B singles chart in just three weeks – the fastest rising no.1 since 1970, when the Jackson 5 scored a hat-trick of equally quick chart toppers with *ABC*, *The Love You Save* and *I'll Be There*. Hit the top just one week after *The Girl Is Mine* was toppled by the Gap Band's *Outstanding*, and stayed at no.1 for an impressive nine weeks.

Also no.1 on the Hot 100 in the States for seven weeks, and no.1 in the UK for a single week. *Billie Jean* and *THRILLER* topped the singles charts and the albums charts on both sides of the Atlantic in the same week – a feat very few acts have ever achieved.

Short film directed by Steve Barron – premiered on MTV on 2nd March 1983, becoming the first music video screened that told a story, and resulted in Michael becoming the first black artist to be added to the MTV playlist.

No.3 best selling single of 1983 in the States, and no.9 best selling single of the same year in the UK.

RIAA Platinum Record Award (USA million seller).

American Music Award: Favourite Pop/Rock Single.

Grammy Awards: Best New R&B Song, Best R&B Vocal Performance, Male.

Cashbox Awards: Top Pop Single, Top Black Single.

Billboard Video Awards: Best Overall Video, Best Dance/Disco 12" (joint with *Beat It*).

NARM Awards: Best Selling Single.

Black Gold Awards: Best Single of the Year.

Canadian Black Music Awards: Top International Single.

Inducted into the Music Video Producers Hall of Fame in 1992.

Official Versions:
Album Version.	Original Demo Recording.
12" Extended Remix.	Pepsi Version.
Four On The Floor Radio Mix.	Instrumental Version.

Performed by Michael – to massive critical and popular acclaim – at *Motown 25: Yesterday, Today, Forever*, staged in the Pasadena Civic Auditorium on 25th March 1983. He 'moonwalked' in public for the first time, and went on to earn an Emmy nomination, for Best Individual Performance on a Variety or Music Program.

Victory Tour 'Live' Promo, directed by Patrick T. Kelly, used to promote the Jacksons tour of the same name – full version shown on *Night Flight Profile* in the States, and on *The Tube* in the UK.

Live performance by Michael, at his Dangerous Tour concert in Bucharest, Romania, on 1st October 1992, featured on the DVD released as part of his box-set, *THE ULTIMATE COLLECTION*, issued in November 2004.

Live performances also aired as part of concerts screened in Japan, Germany and New Zealand.

Cited by Michael as his favourite song to perform live: 'but only when I don't have to do it the same way,' he said. 'The audience wants a certain thing – I have to do the moonwalk in that spot. I'd like to do a different version.'

Coupled with Steely Dan's *Do It Again* in 1983, titled *Do It Again/Billie Jean*. Italian group Club House's version charted at no.11 in the UK and no.75 on the Hot 100 in the States. Slingshot – studio musicians from Detroit – took their version to no.25 on the R&B singles chart in the States.

Sampled by numerous artists, including:
LL Cool J's *Who's Afraid Of The Big Bad Wolf*, which he contributed to the 1991 Disney tribute album, *SIMPLY MAD ABOUT THE MOUSE*.
BLACKstreet's *Billie Jean Remix* of *No Diggity* in 1996 – hit no.1 for four weeks in the States on both the Hot 100 and R&B singles chart, and peaked at no.9 in the UK.
Bar-Kays (a parody) on *Dirty Dancers* – featured of the group's 1996 album, *THE BEST OF – VOLUME 2*.

Chanté Moore on *I Started Crying*, a track included on her 1999 album, *THIS MOMENT IS MINE*.

Pras on *Avenues*, from his 2001 album, *GHETTO SUPERSTAR*.

Babyface on the *Jammin' G-Clef Billie Jean Remix* of *There She Goes*, in 2001.

Featured in the film, *Charlie's Angels* (2000), and in the video game, *Grand Auto Theft: Vice City*.

Ranked no.16 'Best Song' on the UK's Channel 4 TV/HMV's 'Music of the Millennium Poll' in early 2000, in which over 600,000 votes were cast.

Ranked no.7 on MTV Europe's 'All-Time Top Ten R&B Songs' millennium poll.

Ranked no.35 on MTV USA/TV Guide's '100 Greatest Videos Ever Made' millennium poll.

Performed by Michael and Slash during the *Michael Jackson: 30th Anniversary Celebration, The Solo Years* concerts, staged at New York's Madison Square Garden on 7th and 10th September 2001. Also performed by Destiny's Child, as a medley with their own hit, *Bootylicious*.

Ranked no.3 'World's Favourite Song' on Sony Ericsson's global poll in 2005, in which over 700,000 people in more than 60 countries voted. UK voters placed *Billie Jean* at no.1, ahead of *Thriller*, with a further five of the Top 10 being solo recordings by Michael.

Fourth of Michael's 20 *'Visionary – The Video Singles'* reissues, with the music on one side of a Dual Disc and the accompanying short film on the other side. Issued in March 2006 in the UK – charted at no.11, and spent over 40 weeks on the Top 200, making it the most successful reissue by some distance.

Cover versions include:

The Bates – no.67 in the UK in 1996.

Linx – as *Billie Jean Got Soul*, in 1997.

Ian Brown (flip-side of *Dolphins Were Monkeys*) – no.5 in the UK in 2000.

Sound Bluntz – no.32 in the UK in 2002.

Chris Cornell (former Soundgarden frontman) – performed live during an acoustic set in Stockholm, Sweden, in September 2006.

Ian Brown commented: 'I love Jackson… I want to do a Jackson EP, with *Thriller*, *Beat It*, *Billie Jean* and *Rockin' Robin* or *ABC* on it. Hopefully I'll get it done.'

BLACK OR WHITE

Written by Michael, with rap lyrics by Bill Bottrell.

Opening guitar first recorded at Michael's Encino home. 'That piece of music, the beginning part that Slash plays on, was recorded at Michael's house,' confirmed Bottrell. 'Michael asked me to dig it out of the vault in August of 1989. He had in mind to use it as the intro to *Black Or White* – it took a long time before we got Slash on it.'

'For me, the best thing about *Black Or White*,' said Bottrell, 'was that his (Michael's) scratch vocal remained untouched throughout the next year (of work on *DANGEROUS*), and ended up being used on the finished song.'

Lead single from Michael's album *DANGEROUS*, single and album both released in November 1991.

Fastest no.1 on Billboard's Hot 100 in the States since 1969, when *Get Back* by the Beatles also conquered the chart in just three weeks. No.1 for seven weeks, but stalled at no.3 on the R&B singles chart.

RIAA Platinum Record Award (USA million seller).

No.8 best selling single of 1991 in the States.

First single by an American to enter the UK singles chart at no.1 since Elvis Presley's *It's Now Or Never* in 1960. Spent two weeks in pole position.

Also no.1 in Australia, Austria, Belgium, Cuba, Denmark, Finland, France, Israel, Italy, Mexico, Norway, Spain, Sweden, Switzerland and Zimbabwe.

Series of remixes by Richard Clivilles and David Cole of the C&C Music Factory. Issued in January 1992, charted in their own right in the UK, achieving no.14.

Official Versions:

Album Version.	Instrumental.
Clivilles & Cole House/Club Mix.	Radio Edit.
Clivilles & Cole House/Dub Mix.	Tribal Beats.
Clivilles & Cole Radio Mix.	Underground Club Mix.
House with Guitar Radio Mix.	

Grammy nomination: Best Pop Vocal Performance, Male.

Promo 11 minute short film, directed by John Landis, premiered on 14th November 1991. Estimated global audience in 27 countries of 500+ million – the highest ever for a music video. Co-starred: Macauley Culkin (*Home Alone*), George 'Norm' Wendt (*Cheers*), cartoon characters Bart and Homer Simpson, brother Jackie's daughter Brandi, and a cameo appearance from director Landis.

Final, non-musical segment of promo – in which Michael interpreted the black panther's wild and animalistic behavior – was highly controversial, with complaints flooding in from many shocked viewers. Michael issued a press statement that read:

> *It upsets me to think* Black Or White *could influence any child or adult to destructive behavior, either sexual or violent.*

I've always tried to be a good role model and, therefore, have made these changes to avoid any possibility of adversely affecting any individual's behavior. I deeply regret any pain or hurt that the final segment of Black Or White *has caused children, their parents or other viewers.*

Final segment edited out of most future screenings, but made available on the home video *Dangerous – The Short Films*, issued in 1993, with swastikas and Klu Klux Klan graffiti added to give focus to Michael's uncharacteristically violent outbursts.

International Monitor Awards: Music Video with the Best Special Effects.

NAACP Image Awards: Outstanding Music Video.

Michael performed *Black Or White* for the first time at MTV's 10th Anniversary Special in November 1991. Joined on stage by Slash, former Guns 'N Roses guitarist, who also played guitar on the recorded track. Slash also joined Michael on stage in Tokyo, Japan, at his Dangerous World Tour concerts on 30th and 31st December 1992.

Live segment, from Michael's Dangerous World Tour, screened at the Billboard Awards in December 1992.

Live performance by Michael, at his Dangerous Tour concert in Bucharest, Romania, on 1st October 1992, featured on the DVD released as part of his box-set, *THE ULTIMATE COLLECTION*, issued in November 2004.

Live performances from Michael's *His*tory World Tour shown as part of televised concerts in Germany and New Zealand.

Also in 1992, song used in Michael's Japanese advert for *Kirara Basso*.

Performed by Michael and Slash during the *Michael Jackson: 30th Anniversary Celebration, The Solo Years* concerts, staged at New York's Madison Square Garden on 7th and 10th September 2001.

Remixed version included on the first acetate version of the special, expanded edition of *DANGEROUS* – bonus disc later shelved.

Eleventh of Michael's 20 *'Visionary – The Video Singles'* reissues, with the music on one side of a Dual Disc and the accompanying short film on the other side. Issued in April 2006 in the UK – charted at no.18.

BLAME IT ON THE BOOGIE

Written by Mick Jackson – no relation – with Stevie Wonder in mind.

First brought to the attention of the Jacksons, after one of their representatives heard it, at the Midem Music Festival in 1978.

Lead single, and the only track the brothers didn't write themselves, from the Jacksons' album *DESTINY*, issued in December 1978.

Charted in the States at no.3 on the R&B singles chart and a lowly no.54 on the Hot 100, and peaked at no.8 in the UK. Special 7 Minute Extended Disco Remix featured slight alternate vocals.

Accompanied by the Jacksons' first promo video, featuring Michael and his brothers in an entertaining, toe-tapping feature with – for the time – advanced special effects. Peter Conn directed the promo.

Official Versions:
Album Version.
Special 7 Minute Extended Disco Remix.

Mick Jackson's original version rush-released, once it became known the Jacksons' cover was being issued as a single. Two versions by similarly named artists understandably led to confusion among record buyers, especially in the UK, where Mick's version charted at no.15.

Mick Jackson has confirmed he loves the Jacksons version of his song, and Jay Kay's 2003 cover as well. Michael and Mick Jackson have met several times. 'The first time was in a lift in the Montcalm Hotel in London, and we just said hi,' Mick recalls. 'Later, at the *Top Of The Pops* TV show in London, he asked me to sell him my jump suit I was wearing for the show and I declined... MJ was performing *Destiny* with his brothers.'

Performed by the Jacksons, when they guested on *The ABBA Special*, filmed in Switzerland in 1979, and on Germany's *Musik Laden* the same year. Also featured in a Destiny Tour concert screened on BBC2 in the UK.

Other hit versions:
Big Fun – no.4 in the UK in 1989.
Clock – no.16 in the UK in 1998.

Cover version by Nouvelle Star – from the French version of *American Idol*– hit no.1 in France in 2005.

BLESS HIS SOUL

Written and produced by Michael with brothers Jackie, Marlon, Randy & Tito, also featured on the Jacksons' album *DESTINY*.

B-side of Michael's solo single *Girlfriend* in the UK, and of the Jacksons' single *Lovely One* in the States, both released in 1980.

BLOOD ON THE DANCE FLOOR

Written by Michael with Teddy Riley, who came up with the evocative title.

Title track of Michael's solo album, sub-titled 'His*tory In The Mix*', issued in May 1997. Album opened with five previously unreleased songs, followed by eight remixed songs from Michael's HIS*TORY* album.

Originally recorded for Michael's *DANGEROUS* album in 1991, but failed to make the final track listing. Teddy Riley, reportedly, was angry Michael didn't call him to 'vacuum clean this old master' – that is, to give the song a more current sound, before its inclusion on *BLOOD ON THE DANCE FLOOR*.

Album dedicated to Elton John, as a thank you from Michael for putting him up and supporting him, following his troubles in late 1993.

Promo short film, directed by Michael and Vincent Paterson, premiered in the UK on *Top Of The Pops* on 28th March 1997 – several weeks ahead of its release as a single. Ploy generated enough interest to shift 85,000 copies in its first week, good enough to take the no.1 spot from R. Kelly's *I Believe I Can Fly*. Michael's seventh UK chart topper as a soloist, but tumbled from no.1 to no.8 in its second week on the chart.

Disappointed in the States, peaking at no.19 on the R&B singles chart and no.42 on the Hot 100.

Official Versions:

Album Version.	Refugee Camp Edit.
A Cappella.	Refugee Camp Mix.
Fire Island Dub.	T & G Pool Of Blood Dub.
Fire Island Radio Edit.	TM's O-Positive Dub.
Fire Island Vocal Mix.	TM's Switchblade Edit.
Refugee Camp Dub.	TM's Switchblade Mix.

The Refugee Camp Mix, rather than the original mix, featured on Michael's home video, His*tory On Film Volume II*.

Michael, interviewed in 1998 about the remixes on *BLOOD ON THE DANCE FLOOR*, confirmed he didn't really like remixes, as he didn't appreciate other producers altering his work – his record company, however, asserted 'kids love remixes.'

Live performance, from Michael's *His*tory World Tour, screened as part of a concert by Sat 1 TV in Germany.

Twentieth and last of Michael's 20 *'Visionary – The Video Singles'* reissues, with the music on one side of a Dual Disc and the accompanying short film on the other side. Issued in June 2006 in the UK – charted at no.19.

BLOWIN' IN THE WIND

Bob Dylan song the Jackson 5 recorded a version of – remains unreleased.

Hit versions:
Peter, Paul & Mary – no.2 on the Hot 100 in the States, and no.13 in the UK, in 1963.
Stevie Wonder – no.1 on the R&B singles chart and no.9 on the Hot 100 in the States, and no.36 in the UK, in 1966.

BLUE JEAN (SAFE SEX)

Track by Jeru The Damaja that refers to Michael and *Billie Jean*, from the 2000 album, *HEROZ4HIRE*.

BLUES AWAY

Written by Michael about a man coming out of depression, and featured on the Jacksons' eponymous debut album, released in November 1976.

B-side of *Show You The Way To Go* – the first time one of Michael's own songs was issued on a single.

Performed solo by Michael on *The Jacksons* TV series in 1976.

BODY

Written by, and essentially a solo recording by, Marlon Jackson, featured on the Jacksons' album *VICTORY*, issued in July 1984.

Third single lifted from *VICTORY*, but failed to match the success of the first two, *State Of Shock* and *Torture*.

Charted at no.39 on the R&B singles chart, and no.47 on the Hot 100, in the States. In the UK, failed to make the Top 75, but spent a solitary week at no.94 on 'The Next 25' section of the chart.

Official Versions:
Album Version.
Extended 12" Remix.
Extended 12" Instrumental.

7" Mix.
7" Instrumental.

Although credited by all six Jackson brothers, Michael and Jermaine declined to appear in the promo video.

BODY LANGUAGE (DO THE LOVE DANCE)

Song featured on the Jackson 5's album *MOVING VIOLATION*, issued in May 1975 in the States and July 1975 in the UK.

49

Scheduled to be released as the follow-up to *Forever Came Today/All I Do Is Think Of You* in the States on 18th September 1975. Promo single issued, but full release cancelled, when it became known Michael and his brothers (Jermaine apart) were leaving Motown for CBS/Epic.

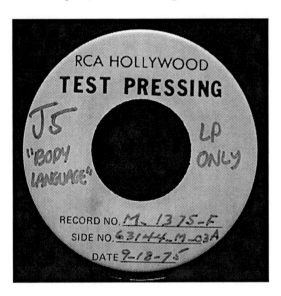

Performed by the Jackson 5, with Vicki Lawrence, on *The Carol Burnett Show* in January 1976, and on their own TV series the following year.

Live performance by the Jacksons, at a concert in Mexico in 1976, included on the home video, *The Jacksons In Concert*, released in 1981 in the UK (no USA release).

Remix – Fat's Camp Lovedance Mix – released in 2005 on Universal Music's DJ WhistleBump label.

BOOGIE MAN, THE

Song featured on the Jackson 5's album *SKYWRITER*, issued in March 1973 in the States and July 1973 in the UK.

Scheduled for release as a single in the States in March 1974, but withdrawn. Promo copies with a picture sleeve were issued – today, a great rarity.

Released as a single in the UK in April 1974. Failed to make the Top 50, but registered at no.58 on the 'breakers' section of the chart.

BOOTYLICIOUS

Destiny's Child hit Michael's sang to the female trio at their first meeting. Achieved no.1 on the Hot 100 and no.2 on the R&B singles chart in the States, and no.2 in the UK, in 2001.

BOOTYLICIOUS – BILLIE JEAN

Medley performed by Destiny's Child during the *Michael Jackson: 30th Anniversary Celebration, The Solo Years* concerts, staged at New York's Madison Square Garden on 7th and 10th September 2001. Destiny's Child paid homage to Michael with fedora hats and white gloves during their performance.

BORN TO LOVE YOU

Song featured on the Jackson 5's debut album, *DIANA ROSS PRESENTS THE JACKSON 5*, released in December 1969 in the States and March 1970 in the UK.

Originally recorded by the Temptations, for their 1965 album, *THE TEMPTIN' TEMPTATIONS*.

BOTTLE OF SMOKE

Song written by, and possibly recorded by, Michael circa 1989.

Considered for Michael's *DANGEROUS* album, but failed to make the final track listing, and remains unreleased.

BOYS AND GIRLS, WE ARE THE JACKSON FIVE

Originally released in 1989, titled 'Monologue', on the pre-Motown compilation *THE BEGINNING YEARS 1965-1967*.

First titled *Boys And Girls, We Are The Jackson Five* on a Japanese release, *BIG BOY*; later the same year, included on *THE JACKSON*

FIVE FEATURING MICHAEL JACKSON, issued on the Stardust label in the UK/Europe.

BOZO INTRODUCTORY SONG

Medley of the biggest Bozo songs of the past, performed to introduce the Bozo Awards on the *Sonny & Cher Show*, in 1976 – the entire cast, including the Jacksons and Sonny & Cher, sang the medley. The Jacksons also performed *Enjoy Yourself.*

BRACE YOURSELF

Promotional clip, accompanied by Orff's *Carmina Burana*, which featured excerpts from Michael's concerts, music videos, album and magazine covers, etc. – sub-titled 'A Kaleidoscope of Michael Jackson'. Originally, the term was used by Michael to introduce his *Black Or White* short film.

Clip, directed and edited by Bob Jenkins, included on Michael's home videos, *Video Greatest Hits* – History and History *On Film Volume II.*

BRAND NEW THING

Song written by Michael with brothers Jackie, Jermaine, Marlon and Tito, and performed by the Jackson 5 in concert in the 1970s, to introduce young Randy on to the stage – never recorded.

Registered with the United States Copyright Office in April 1972.

Performed by the Jackson 5 on the American TV show, *Hellzapoppin*, in 1972.

BREAK OF DAWN

Written by Michael with Dr. Freeze.

Featured on Michael's solo album *INVINCIBLE*, released in October 2001.

Following the success of *You Rock My World* and *Butterflies*, cited by many critics as the track most likely to give Michael a sizeable hit in the States, but never released to radio or as a commercial single.

Demo, reputedly of Michael working on the song, surfaced on the internet in 2005 – authenticity unconfirmed.

BREAKING FREE

Short poem written by Michael – included in his book of poems and reflections, *Dancing The Dream*, published in 1992.

BREEZY

Song that appeared on the Jackson 5's album *MOVING VIOLATION*, issued in July 1975.

BRIDGE OVER TROUBLED WATER

Cover version recorded, with Jermaine singing lead, by the Jackson 5 for *THIRD ALBUM*, released in September 1970 in the States and February 1971 in the UK.

Originally recorded by Simon & Garfunkel in early 1970, for an album of the same title – their version hit no.1 on both sides of the Atlantic, and in many other countries as well.

BUFFALO BILL

Written by Michael, and first mentioned just prior to the release of the Jacksons' album *VICTORY* in 1984, by Michael's manager at the time, Frank Dileo. Also considered by Michael for his solo album, *BAD*, but failed to make the final track listing.

Inspired by James 'Wild Bill' Hickok (*aka* Buffalo Bill) and the way he died: shot in the back by Jack McCall during a poker game in Deadwood, Dakota Territory, in August 1876.

Name-checked on the unofficial *Michael Jackson: Unauthorised* home video, released in 1992 in the UK.

Cited by Michael in his court disposition in November 1993, and mentioned by him on *THE MICHAEL JACKSON INTERVIEW* CD, released by Baktabak in the same year – remains unreleased.

BUMPER SNIPPET

Unreleased snippets that surfaced on the internet, from a recording session where Michael is awaiting the go ahead, and sings a few lines including, 'Girl, I wanna groove!'

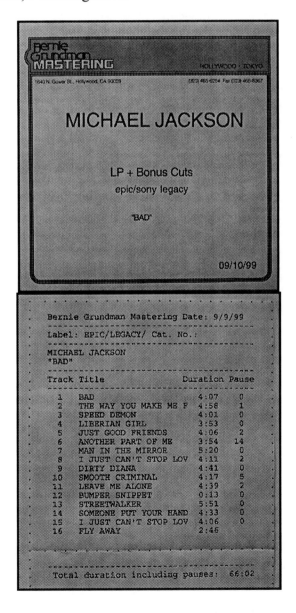

Included on the first acetate version of the special, expanded edition of *BAD*, but later withdrawn – no official release.

Another version features a child screaming into the microphone. This version was one of the Bonus Cuts included on the first acetate version of the special, expanded edition of *DANGEROUS*:

1. *Bumper Snippet (Kid).*
2. *Monkey Business.*
3. *Work That Body.*
4. *If You Don't Love Me.*
5. *Serious Effect.*
6. *Happy Birthday, Lisa.*
7. *She Got It.*
8. *Black Or White (Remix).*
9. *Dangerous (Alt. Version).*
10. *Who Is It (Remix).*

Bonus Cuts CD cancelled – no official release.

BURN THIS DISCO OUT

One of three song's Heatwave's Rod Temperton wrote for Michael, around the same time as *Rock With You*, for his first solo album for CBS/Epic, *OFF THE WALL*, released in August 1979.

Initially, Temperton was invited to deliver just one song, and was surprised when all three of his songs made the final selection. Michael recorded vocals for all three songs in one weekend, having already mastered the lyrics – professionalism that impressed Temperton.

B-side of Michael's single *Beat It* in the UK (but not USA).

BUTTERCUP

Song written circa 1974-75 by Stevie Wonder, at a time he said he was working on songs for a Jackson 5 album (that never happened). Article in the Spring 1975 issue of *Rock & Soul Songs* mentioned the collaboration, and cited *Buttercup* as a future single.

Recorded by Carl Anderson for his 1982 album, *ABSENCE WITHOUT LOVE* – released as a single three years later. Included on *THE WONDER OF STEVIE*, a two disc tribute to Stevie, featuring other artists singing his songs. Anderson died of leukaemia in February 2004 – Stevie played at his funeral service.

BUTTERFLIES

Song Michael recorded and co-produced with Andre Harris, for his solo album *INVINCIBLE*, issued in October 2001. Backing vocals by Marsha Ambrosius, who co-wrote the song with Harris. Ambrosius and Natalie Stewart, of the UK duo Floetry, were invited by Michael to visit the studio while he was recording the track.

'It was incredible because he asked,' said Ambrosius, 'he continually asked, "Marsh, what's the next harmony? Girls, does this sound right? What do you think? Is this what you were looking for?" He was so open.'

Released to American radio stations in October 2001, and became the second of Michael's singles to chart on the strength of airplay alone. Achieved no.2 on the R&B singles chart and no.14 on the Hot 100 – however, the lack of a commercial single almost certainly cost Michael a chart topper (no UK release).

BMI Urban Awards: Best Song.

Official Versions:
Album Version.   Michael A Cappella.
Eve A Cappella.   Master Mix Instrumental.
Track Masters Master Mix feat. Eve.

Original demo version recorded by Floetry was included on the duo's debut 2002 album, *FLOETRY*, as a bonus track.

BY THE TIME I GET TO PHOENIX

Song performed by the Jackson 5 as part of a medley – with *Danny Boy* and *Killing Me Softly With His Song* – during their Las Vegas shows in 1974. Also performed on *The Tonight Show* – hosted by Bill Cosby – in America in March 1974.

Hit versions:
Glen Campbell – no.26 in the States in 1967.
Isaac Hayes – no.37 in the States in1969.
Mad Lads – no.84 in the States in 1969.
Glen Campbell & Anne Murray – no.81 in the States in 1971.

CALIFORNIA GRASS

Song Michael cited he had written in his court disposition in November 1993 – remains unreleased.

CALL OF THE WILD

Song featured on the Jackson 5's album *MOVING VIOLATION*, released in May 1975 in the States and July 1975 in the UK.

Scheduled as the B-side of the cancelled single, *Body Language (Do The Love Dance)*, in the States.

CALL ON ME

Song recorded by Michael on 31st September 1973 and included, with added overdubs and remixed, on the solo compilation *FAREWELL MY SUMMER LOVE*, issued in May 1984 in the States and June 1984 in the UK.

B-side of *Farewell My Summer Love*.

Original 1973 recording released in the States in March 1995, on Michael's anthology series compilation *THE BEST OF...* (no UK release).

CALLING MICHAEL (UNITED FANS FOR MICHAEL)

Fans tribute to Michael, recorded by United Fans For Michael during his court appearances in 2005.

CAN I GET A WITNESS

Marvin Gaye hit the Jackson 5 recorded a version of – remains unreleased.

Hit versions:

Marvin Gaye – no.15 on the R&B singles chart and no.22 on the Hot 100 in the States in 1963.

Lee Michaels – no.39 on the Hot 100 in 1971.

CAN I LIVE

Song co-written by Sisqó and Teddy Riley.

Originally intended for Michael's album *INVINCIBLE*, until Sisqó recorded it for his second album, *RETURN OF DRAGON*, in 2001.

CAN I SEE YOU IN THE MORNING

Song included on the Jackson 5's album, *THIRD ALBUM*, issued in September 1970 in the States and February 1971 in the UK.

Also featured on a rare, six track EP of songs from the same album, issued with a picture sleeve in the States.

B-side of *Goin' Back To Indiana* in several continental European countries, including Holland, Germany, Portugal and Sweden.

Heard in the 'CinderJackson' episode of the Jackson 5's cartoon series in 1971.

Electric Sheep Mix featured on the album, *SOUL SOURCE – JACKSON 5 REMIXES 2*, released in Japan in 2001.

CAN YOU FEEL IT

Co-written by Michael with brother Jackie, opening track on the Jacksons' album, *TRIUMPH*, released in October 1980.

Third single lifted from the album, fared much better in Europe than in the States. Charted at no. 6 in the UK, but only achieved no.30 on the R&B singles chart and no.77 on the Hot 100, in the States.

Promoted with innovative short film *'Triumph – Can You Feel It'*, directed by Bruce Gowers and Robert Abel, and costing around $140,000. Michael and his brothers were cast as larger-than-life, demi-

God figures, who cast stardust on the world, as children gazed up with smiling faces.

Grammy nomination: Best Rhythm & Blues Vocal By A Duo, Group Or Chorus (the Jacksons lost out to the Manhattans, who took the award for *Shining Star*).

Song chosen to open the Jacksons' Triumph Tour concerts.

Live version, recorded at a concert at Madison Square Garden in September 1981, featured as the opening track on the Jacksons album, *LIVE*, issued in November 1981.

Performed by the Jacksons during the *Michael Jackson: 30th Anniversary Celebration, The Solo Years* concerts, staged at New York's Madison Square Garden on 7th and 10th September 2001.

Hit cover versions:
Raze & Champion Legend (two versions on different sides of one
    single) – no.62 in the UK in 1990.
V (double A-side with *Hip To Hip*) – no.5 in the UK in 2004.

Hip hop version, titled *Can U Feel Me*, featured on BLACKstreet's 1999 album, *FINALLY*.

Adaption – with new lyrics by Jim Dyke and Steven Gittleman about a woman with a chimney pot on her head – titled *Feel It*, recorded by the Italian combo, the Tamperer featuring Maya in 1998. Gave Michael his eighth chart topper as a song-writer in the UK – also hit no.1 in Ireland, but only registered at no.103 on the 'bubbling under' section of the Hot 100 in the States.

Sampled by:
Parkride on a 1998 track, also titled *Can You Feel It*.
Steps on their version of *My Best Friend's Girl*, featured on their 1999 album, *STEPACULAR*.
Female rapper, Charli Baltimore on her song, *Feel It*.
Swedish rap group, Snook, on their track, *Superfitta*.

Sorry, the second single lifted from Madonna's 2005 album, *CONFESSIONS ON A DANCE FLOOR*, was originally reported to sample *Can You Feel It*. However, although something very similar to the bass-line from *Can You Feel It* could be heard, *Sorry* didn't credit Michael and brother Jackie among the song-writers – charted at no.1 in the UK and no.58 on the Hot 100 in the States.

CAN YOU REMEMBER

Song recorded by the Jackson 5 on the 10th and 15th July 1969, and featured on the group's debut album, *DIANA ROSS PRESENTS THE JACKSON 5*, released in December 1969 in the States and March 1970 in the UK.

Performed live – as a medley with *Sing A Simple Song* – by the Jackson 5 during their first national TV appearance in the States, on ABC-TV's *The Hollywood Palace Special*, aired on 18th October 1969. Michael and his brothers were introduced by Diana Ross. Album titled *MOTOWN AT THE HOLLYWOOD PALACE*, including *Can You Remember*, followed in March 1970 (no UK release).

Originally recorded by the Delfonics, for their 1968 album, *LA LA MEANS I LOVE YOU*.

Michael and his brothers first met the Delfonics in the pre-Motown days. 'We used to do a lot of shows at the Regal Theater in Chicago, and at the Capitol Theater there,' recalled William Hart, of the

Delfonics. 'I remember they (the Jackson 5) didn't have a place to change clothes, and we had a big trailer and all… and they thought that was nice of me, to let them come in and change. I remember Michael saying, "Thank you! Thank you! Thank you!"'

CAN'T GET OUTTA THE RAIN

Written by Michael with Quincy Jones, and recorded by Michael – developed from the ending of *You Can't Win*, his only solo offering from his first movie *The Wiz*, with a slight lyric change from 'game' to 'rain'.

B-side of Michael's first duet with Paul McCartney, *The Girl Is Mine*, issued in 1982.

CAN'T GET READY FOR LOSING YOU

One of 19 'Rare & Unreleased' tracks on the fourth CD of the Michael/Jackson 5 box-set, *SOULSATION!*, issued in June 1995 in the States and July 1995 in the UK.

Recorded by Motown song-writer Willie Hutch for his 1973 album, *FULLY EXPOSED*.

CAN'T LET HER GET AWAY

Written and produced by Michael with Teddy Riley, for his solo album *DANGEROUS*, released in November 1991.

Featured in the film, *The Meteor Man* (1993).

CARAVAN

Song performed by the Jacksons, with special guest Caroll O'Connor, on their TV series in 1976, as a medley with *I Don't Get Around Much Anymore* and *Take The A Train*.

CARMINA BURANA

Instantly recognisable piece of classical music written by Carl Orff. Michael used *Oh Fortuna – Carmina Burana* to great effect, during his

Dangerous World Tour; the version used was as performed by the Prague Festival Orchestra & Chorus.

Featured on Michael's home video, *Dangerous – The Short Films*.

CAROL'S THEME

Short song written by Joe Hamilton, sang by Michael at one of his *Dangerous* concerts – used on *The Carol Burnett Show* as the show's theme song.

CAROUSEL

Song Michael originally recorded for his 1982 album, *THRILLER*, but failed to make the final track listing when *Human Nature* was chosen instead.

Also known as 'Circus Girl'.

Unreleased until October 2001, when an edited version was added to the expanded, special edition of *THRILLER* as one of three bonus tracks.

Full version by Michael can be found on writer Michael Sembello's official web-site; Sembello's version can also be heard on the site.

CENTIPEDE

Song written and produced by Michael, for eldest sister Rebbie's debut album of the same name, released in 1984. Michael also sang backing vocals on the track.

Issued as Rebbie's debut single, achieving no.4 on the R&B singles chart and no.24 on the Hot 100, in the States. Failed to chart in the UK, despite being released twice.

RIAA Gold Record (USA million seller).

Although she was the last Jackson sibling to enter the recording studio, Rebbie did tour with her brothers, and along with Janet and La Toya she joined them for their TV series. 'The first date I did with them,' she recalls, 'was in Vagas at The Grand hotel, which was nice... I sang on several number like *Midnight At the Oasis*, when we did a TV series in 1976, which Michael coached for me.'

Sampled by:
Kurupt on *Who Do U Be*, a track on their 1998 album, *KURUPTION*.
Brand Nubian on *Let's Dance*, released for their 1990 album,
    FOUNDATION – also featured Rebbie's vocals.

CHAINED

Song recorded by the Jackson 5 with producer Bobby Taylor, for their debut album, *DIANA ROSS PRESENTS THE JACKSON 5*, released in December 1969 in the States and March 1970 in the UK.

CHATTANOOGIE SHOE SHINE BOY

Song the Jacksons performed on the TV series in 1976, with special guest, Johnny Dark.

CHEATER

Song written by Michael with Greg Phillinganes, recorded in 1987 and originally slated to appear on Michael's album, *BAD* – failed to make the final track listing, despite being one of Michael's favourites at the time.

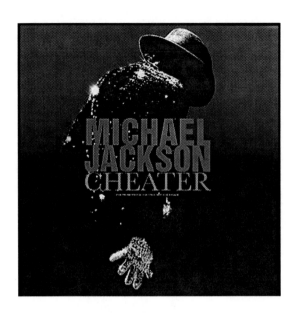

Demo version included on Michael's box-set, *THE ULTIMATE COLLECTION*, issued in November 2004.

One track promos released in 2005, to promote the box-set and as a potential single – full release cancelled.

CHICAGO 1945

Song written by Michael with Toto's Steve Pocaro.

'Years ago, Michael and I wrote a song called *Chicago 1945* – I did the music and Michael the lyrics,' Pocaro confirmed on Toto's web-site. 'He recorded the song twice, but never put it on an album… the instruments were played in a constant rhythm in the 16th note, which was called 'yada'. When I explained this to Michael, he liked it so much he gave me that nickname!'

In the film, *Moonwalker*, in an outdoor shot of Michael with Brandon Adams and Sean Lennon, a clapper-board with 'Chicago Nights' on it can be seen – possibly an alternate title.

Evolved into *Smooth Criminal*.

Cited by Michael in his court disposition in November 1993 – remains unreleased.

See also: *Smooth Criminal*.

CHILD OF INNOCENCE

Poem written by Michael – included in his book of poems and reflections, *Dancing The Dream*, published in 1992.

CHILDHOOD (Theme From 'Free Willy 2')

Written by Michael, and featured on his solo album HIS*TORY*, released in June 1995.

Theme song from the film, *Free Willy 2: The Adventure Home.*

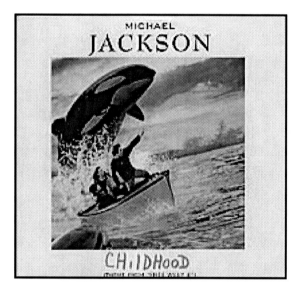

Michael has described *Childhood* as a reflection of his life:

> '*Our personal history begins in childhood and the song*
> '*Childhood' is a reflection of my life . . . it's about the pain,*
> *some of the joys, some of the dreaming, some of the mental*
> *adventures that I took because of the different lifestyle*
> *I had, in being a child performer. I was born on stage*
> *and 'Childhood', it's my mirror – it's my story.'*

B-side of Michael's duet with sister Janet, *Scream*, but listed alongside *Scream* on the Hot 100 in the States, where it debuted and peaked at no.5 – the highest ever new entry on the chart at the time (previous record holder, *Let It Be* by the Beatles, entered at no.6).

Instrumental version featured on the soundtrack album, *FREE WILLY 2: THE ADVENTURE HOME*.

Promo short film directed by Nick Brandt, shot in a fantasy forest. Filmed in Sequoia National Park, with ships filled with children (including the young star of the *Free Willy* films, Jason James Richter) floating over the treetops – paid homage to *Peter Pan*.

Official Versions:
Album Version.
Instrumental.

Scheduled performance by Michael, at the 1996 Grammy Awards, was cancelled.

CHILDREN OF THE LIGHT

Song recorded by the Jackson 5 for their album *LOOKIN' THROUGH THE WINDOWS*, released in May 1972 in the States and October 1972 in the UK.

Title track of a Jackson 5 compilation issued on the Spectrum record label in the UK in 1993.

CHILDREN OF THE WORLD

Poem written by Michael – included in his book of poems and reflections, *Dancing The Dream*, published in 1992.

CHILDREN'S CHRISTMAS SONG

Song the Jackson 5 recorded for their *CHRISTMAS ALBUM* circa 1970, but which failed to make the final track listing – remains unreleased.

The Supremes took the song to no.7 on Billboard's Christmas Singles chart in the States in 1965.

CHILDREN'S HOLIDAY

Written and produced by Michael, and recorded by Japanese children's choir, J-Friends.

Issued as a single in Japan – entered the singles chart at no.1.

All proceeds donated to a charity set up to aid the victims/families of the devastating earthquake that hit Kobe City, Japan, in January 1995.

CHILDREN'S HOUR, THE

Song Michael cited he had written in his court disposition in November 1993 – remains unreleased.

CHRISTMAS EVERYDAY

Song the Jackson 5 recorded for their *CHRISTMAS ALBUM* circa 1970, but which failed to make the final track listing – remains unreleased.

CHRISTMAS GREETINGS FROM MICHAEL JACKSON

Eight second greeting from Michael, originally included on a promo 7" single titled *Seasons Greetings From Motown Records*, sent to radio stations in the States circa 1971, so festive messages could be aired between the songs – also featured greetings from Jackie, Jermaine and Tito (but not Marlon), and other Motown artists.

Included on the 1995 festive compilation, *MOTOWN CHRISTMAS CAROL* – also featured the Jackson 5's *Santa Claus Is Coming To Town*, *I Saw Mommy Kissing Santa Claus*, *Frosty The Snowman* and *Have Yourself A Merry Little Christmas*.

See also: *Seasons Greetings From Motown Records*.

CHRISTMAS SONG, THE

Ever popular festive song recorded by the Jackson 5 – with Jermaine on lead vocals – for their *CHRISTMAS ALBUM*, issued in October 1970 in the States and December 1970 in the UK.

Released as a single in the Philippines.

Hit versions:
Nat 'King' Cole – no.80 in 1960, and no.65 in 1962, in the States;
 no.69 in the UK in 1991.
James Brown – no.12 on the Christmas Singles chart in the States
 in 1965.
Herb Alpert – no.1 on the Christmas Singles chart in the States in 1968.
Alexander O'Neal – no.30 in the UK in 1988.
Christina Aguilera – no.18 in the States in 2000.

CHRISTMAS WON'T BE THE SAME THIS YEAR

Another festive song the Jackson 5 recorded for *CHRISTMAS ALBUM*.

B-side of *Santa Claus Is Comin' To Town*, released in December 1970 in the States and two years later in the UK. Listed alongside *Santa Claus Is Comin' To Town* for one week only on Billboard's Christmas Singles chart.

CINDERELLA STAY AWHILE

Song Michael recorded for his fourth solo album, *FOREVER, MICHAEL*, released in January 1975 in the States and March 1975 in the UK.

CIRCUS GIRL

Alternate title for Michael's solo recording, *Carousel* – one of the bonus tracks added to the special edition of his *THRILLER* album, released in October 2001.

See also: *Carousel*.

CISCO KID, THE

One of five songs the Jackson 5 performed a medley of at the Grammy Awards ceremony on 2nd March 1974, to introduce the nominees for Best Rhythm & Blues Vocal Performance by a Group, Duo or Chorus.

Latin group War took the song to no.2 on the Hot 100 and no.5 on the R&B singles chart in the States. RIAA Gold Record Award (USA million seller).

The Jacksons performed *The Cisco Kid* on an episode of their TV series in 1976.

CLIMB E'VRY MOUNTAIN

Song from Rodgers & Hammerstein's musical *The Sound Of Music*, which starred Julie Andrews and Christopher Plummer.

First song Michael ever performed in public in August 1963, aged five years, at morning assembly at his school, Garnett Elementary. His *a cappella* rendition reduced his mother Katherine and her father-in-law, Samuel, to tears.

In his autobiography *Moonwalk*, Michael recalled, 'the reaction in the auditorium overwhelmed me. The applause was thunderous and people were smiling; some of them were standing... It was such a great feeling.'

Performed by Alex Burrall, who played the part of young Michael, in the TV mini-series, *The Jacksons: An American Dream*.

Hit versions:
Tony Bennett – no.74 on the Hot 100 in the States in 1960.
Shirley Bassey – no.1 in the UK in 1961.
Hesitations – no.90 on the Hot 100 in 1968.

CLOUD NINE

Temptations classic the Jackson 5 performed in concert in the early days.

Hit versions:
Temptations – no.2 on the R&B singles chart and no.6 on the Hot 100 in the States in 1968-69, and no.15 in the UK in 1969.
Mongo Santamaria – no.32 on the Hot 100 and no.33 on the R&B singles chart in 1968-69.

COLOUR OF MY SOUL

Song known to have been recorded by Michael; date uncertain – remains unreleased.

Michael's brother, Randy, is known to have recorded a demo – with an unidentified female singer – titled *Color Of Love*.

COME AND GET IT

Song the Jackson 5 recorded for Motown – remains unreleased.

(COME 'ROUND HERE) I'M THE ONE YOU NEED

Song the Jackson 5 recorded for their second album, *ABC*, issued in May 1970 in the States and August 1970 in the UK.

Featured in the 'Ray & Charles Superstars' episode of the Jackson 5 cartoon series in 1971.

Originally recorded by the Miracles for their 1966 album, *AWAY WE A GO-GO*. Single achieved no.4 on the R&B singles chart and no.17 on the Hot 100 in the States, and no.45 in the UK. Reissue hit no.13 in the UK in 1971.

COME TOGETHER

Lennon/McCartney cover Michael recorded, soon after his engineer was messing around with the song, and Michael realised it was his favourite Beatles song.

Filmed as the finale of Michael's 'movie like no other', *Moonwalker*, premiered in 1989 – co-starred, as one of the three children, Sean Lennon (son of John), and directed by Jerry Kramer.

Originally scheduled to get its first commercial release in 1990, on the *DAYS OF THUNDER* soundtrack, but Michael's record company refused to grant permission. Also scheduled to appear on Michael's cancelled greatest hits compilation, *DECADE 1980-1990*.

B-side of Michael's 1992 single *Remember The Time* in the UK (but not USA), where the full length version was featured. Listed alongside *Remember The Time* on the singles chart from the fourth week, peaking at no.10.

Made its album debut in June 1995, in an edited version, on Michael's HIS*TORY*.

Official Versions:
Album Edit.
Full Extended Version.

Live performance in Auckland, New Zealand, screened in that country as part of a *His*tory World Tour concert.

Other hit versions:
Beatles – no.1 in the States and no.4 in the UK in 1969 (double A-side with *Something* in the UK).
Ike & Tina Turner – no.57 in the States in 1970.
Aerosmith – no.23 in the States in 1978.

COMING HOME

One of 19 'rare & unreleased' tracks released on the Michael/Jackson 5 4CD box set *SOULSATION!,* issued in June 1995 in the States and July 1995 in the UK – demo version also known to exist.

(COMING) OUT OF THE CLOSET

Original title for Michael's hit, *In The Closet*, which he wanted to record with Madonna.

Demo version, featuring Michael and Madonna, may exist.

See also: *In The Closet*.

CONVOY

Song guest C.W. McCall performed on *The Jacksons* TV series in 1976, with Michael and his brothers singing backing.

C.W. McCall took *Convoy* to no.1 on the Hot 100 in the States and to no.2 in the UK. RIAA Gold Record (USA million seller).

CORNER OF THE SKY

Song originally written for Frankie Valli and the 4 Seasons, until his persistent no shows led to the Jackson 5 recording it for their album *SKYWRITER*, released in March 1973 in the States and July 1973 in the UK.

From the Berry Gordy financed musical *Pippin* – as well as a version by John Rubinstein, the Jackson 5's version of the song featured on the original cast album as a bonus track.

Performed by the Jackson 5 on *Soul Train* in 1972.

First single from *SKYWRITER* in the States (no UK release), charting at no.9 on the R&B singles chart and no.18 on the Hot 100.

COTTON FIELDS

One of many songs Michael recalls singing, with his mother and family, as a young boy in Gary, Indiana.

COULD IT BE I'M FALLING IN LOVE

One of five songs the Jackson 5 performed a medley of at the Grammy Awards ceremony on 2nd March 1974, to introduce the nominees for Best Rhythm & Blues Vocal Performance by a Group, Duo or Chorus.

The Spinners (known as the Detroit Spinners in the UK) took *Could It Be I'm Falling In Love* to no.1 on the R&B singles chart and no.4 on the Hot 100 in the States in 1973. RIAA Gold Record Award (USA million seller). Charted at no.11 in the UK.

Hit cover versions:
David Grant & Jaki Graham – no.5 in the UK in 1985, no.60 on the
    R&B singles chart in the States in 1986.
Worlds Apart – no.15 in the UK in 1994.

CRACK KILLS

Song Michael planned to record with rappers Run-DMC in the period 1986-87, for his album, *BAD*, but shelved as Michael didn't like Run-DMC's negative attitude towards him.

Cited by Michael in his court disposition in November 1993 – remains unreleased.

Unfinished lyrics, consisting of two verses and a drawing of a face in pencil, put up for auction in November 2005, and again on the internet auction site eBay, a year later.

CRY

Song Michael cited he had written in his court disposition in November 1993 – remains unreleased.

CRY

Song composed by R. Kelly, and recorded by Michael for his solo album, *INVINCIBLE*, issued in October 2001.

Officially premiered on Michael's web-site on 20th September 2001, and dedicated to the thousands of people who lost their lives in the 9/11 terrorist attacks in the States.

Initially released in the States at the same time as Michael's *You Rock My World*, as a limited, double A-sided 7" promo single. Briefly released to radio, but proved unpopular, so was quickly withdrawn and *Butterflies* distributed instead.

Promo short film, directed by Nick Brandt, was shot in six different locations (five in California and one in Nevada) – but didn't feature Michael at all, as he was in dispute with Sony over the promo's budget. Premiered in the UK on *Top Of The Pops* on 2nd November 2001.

Released as a single in the UK on the same day as sister Janet's *Son Of A Gun (I Betcha Think This Song Is About You)* – the first time Michael and Janet had gone head-to-head. Janet's single charted at no.13, Michael's at no.25 – his worse showing on the UK chart since 1993, when *Gone Too Soon* – the ninth single from *DANGEROUS* – stalled at no.33.

DADDY'S HOME

Solo single Jermaine Jackson promoted on *Soul Train* in 1972, with the rest of the Jackson 5 on backing vocals.

Featured on Jermaine's eponymous 1972 debut album. Released as a single – hit no.3 on the R&B singles chart and no.9 on the Hot 100 in the States, but wasn't a hit in the UK.

Live version featured on the Michael/Jackson 5's *LIVE!* album, issued in September 1988 in the UK (no USA release). All songs on the album were recorded at a concert on 30th April 1973, at the Osaka Koseinenkin Hall in Japan. Also included on the limited edition CD, *IN JAPAN!*, released by Hip-Select in 2004 – only 5,000 copies pressed.

Other hit versions:

Shep & The Limelites – no.2 on the Hot 100 and no.4 on the R&B singles chart in the States in 1961.

Chuck Jackson & Maxine Brown – no.46 on the R&B singles chart and no.91 on the Hot 100 in the States in 1967.

Cliff Richard – no.2 in the UK in 1981, no.23 on the Hot 100 in the States in 1982.

DANCE MIX 1

Megamix of Motown recordings by Michael and his brothers featured on the double CD, *THE MICHAEL JACKSON MIX*, issued in the UK in December 1987.

Featured songs: *ABC, I Want You Back, Get It Together, The Boogie Man, Just A Little Bit Of You, The Love You Save, Farewell My Summer Love, Love Is Here And Now You're Gone, Hallelujah Day, Skywriter* and *Lookin' Through The Windows*.

Promo edit featured: *ABC, I Want You Back, Get It Together* and *The Boogie Man*.

See also: *Dance Mix 2, Love Mix 1 & 2*.

DANCE MIX 2

Megamix of Motown recordings by Michael and his brothers featured on the double CD, *THE MICHAEL JACKSON MIX*, issued in the UK in December 1987.

Featured songs: *Sugar Daddy, Don't Let It Get You Down, Girl You're So Together, Mama's Pearl, My Girl, Dancing Machine, Shoo-Be-Doo-Be-Doo-Da-Day, Doctor My Eyes, Rockin' Robin* and *Little Bitty Pretty One*.

See also: *Dance Mix 1, Love Mix 1 & 2*.

DANCE ON THE CEILING

Incidental piece of music Michael composed with Nicholas Pike, for his short film, *Ghosts*, premiered in October 1996.

DANCING MACHINE

Song featured on the Jackson 5's album *GET IT TOGETHER*, released in September 1973 in the States and November 1973 in the UK.

Second single lifted from the album, following the title cut, and became the groups most successful single since *I'll Be There* in 1970.

No.1 for one week on the R&B singles chart in the States, but held at no.2 on the Hot 100 by Ray Stevens and his novelty smash, *The Streak*.

Sold over two million copies in the USA.

Promoted in the States by a host of TV appearances, including:

- *American Bandstand.*
- *The Bob Hope Special.*
- *The Tonight Show* (in April and November 1974 with host Johnny Carson, and in August 1974 with host Bill Cosby).

- *The Carol Burnett Show* (as part of the 'Salute to the Vocal Groups' medley).
- *The Jerry Lewis Telethon.*
- *The Merv Griffin Show* (in April 1974 and again in September 1974).
- *The Mike Douglas Show.*
- *The Sonny & Cher Comedy Hour.*
- *Soul Train.*
- *The Jacksons* TV series.

Failed to make the Top 50 singles chart in the UK, but registered at no.53 on the 'breakers' section of the chart.

Grammy Award nominations: Best R&B Song and Best R&B Vocal Performance by a Duo, Group or Chorus (it didn't win either).

Edited version featured on, and used as the title track of, the Jackson 5 album that followed *GET IT TOGETHER*.

Live performance by the Jacksons, at a concert in Mexico in 1976, included on the home video, *The Jacksons In Concert*, released in 1981 in the UK (no USA release). Also performed during the group's Destiny Tour – one concert was screened on BBC2 in the UK.

Song chosen to open the Jacksons' Destiny Tour concerts.

Remix by Nigel Martinez and Derek Marcil, with alternate vocals, featured on Michael's 1987 album, *THE ORIGINAL SOUL OF MICHAEL JACKSON*.

Second remix, with different alternate vocals, included on the 1992 TV soundtrack album, *THE JACKSONS: AN AMERICAN DREAM*.

Topless In Action Remixxx, as included on the Japanese album *SOUL SOURCE – JACKSON 5 REMIXES 2* in 2001, featured alternate vocals.

Other Remixes:
Dub Mix.
Extended Dance Mix.
Radio Remix.

Performed by the Jacksons and 'N Sync during the *Michael Jackson: 30th Anniversary Celebration, The Solo Years* concerts, staged at New York's Madison Square Garden on 7th and 10th September 2001.

Sampled on the B-side of M.C. Hammer's hit *U Can't Touch This* in 1990, which rose to no.1 on both the Hot 100 and R&B singles charts in the States, and achieved no.3 in the UK.

Also sampled on:
The Street Mix by Mag 7 – no.56 on the R&B singles chart and no.93 on the Hot 100 in 1998.
Dance Wit Me by Antuan & Ray Ray – no.66 on the R&B singles chart and no.125 on the 'bubbling under' section of the Hot 100 in 1998.
Dancin' by Vanilla Ice, from his 1990 album, *TO THE EXTREME*.

Appeared on the *INKWELL* movie soundtrack album, released on Warner Brothers in 1994.

DANGEROUS

Written by Michael with Bill Bottrell and Teddy Riley.

Developed from a song titled *Streetwalker*, which Michael wrote for his album *BAD*, and featured on the expanded special edition CD issued in October 2001.

Title track of Michael's solo album, released in November 1991.

'The genesis of the songs we co-wrote (for *DANGEROUS*),' said Bottrell, 'consisted of Michael humming melodies and grooves, and him then leaving the studio while I developed these ideas with a bunch of drum machines and samplers.'

Planned as an unprecedented 10th single release from *DANGEROUS*, but cancelled, after allegations of child molestation were made against Michael in August 1993.

Official Versions:
Album Version.   Roger's Dangerous Edit.
Roger's Dangerous Club Mix.   Roger's Rough Dub.
Early Version.

First performed by Michael when he opened the 20th annual American Music Awards ceremony, staged in Los Angeles on 25th January 1993. He went on to perform the song at the 25th Soul Train Anniversary Show, the MTV Video music Awards, on the popular German TV show, *Wetten Dass?*, and on the *American Bandstand* 50th anniversary special in Pasadena in April 2002.

Live performance in Auckland, New Zealand, screened in that country as part of a *His*tory World Tour concert. Different live performance from the same tour screened by Sat 1 TV in Germany.

Short promo *Dangerous* teaser directed by David Lynch.

Dangerous Tour montage, directed by Joe Wilcots, featured on Michael's home video, *Dangerous – The Short Films* in 1993.

Subject of a court hearing in Colorado in February 1994, after songwriter Crystal Cartier accused Michael of stealing the song from her, claiming she had written, copyrighted and recorded the song in 1985, as part of another song, *Player*.

Michael testified how *Dangerous* grew out of a song titled *Streetwalker*, which he co-wrote with William 'Bill' Bottrell in 1985. His original demo version was played in court; Michael also gave *a cappella* performances of *Dangerous* and *Billie Jean*, and provided the court with a rare insight into his songwriting habits. As Cartier was unable to supply any original tapes to back up her claim, the judge found in Michael's favour, and his accuser was denied the chance to appeal.

Remix featured on Michael's *Blood On The Dance Floor* single in 1997.

Performed by Michael at his *Michael & Friends* concert in Munich, Germany, on 27th June 1999 – screened by ZDF TV.

Alternate version, plus a remix titled 'Roger's Rough Dub', both included on the first acetate version of the special, expanded edition of *DANGEROUS* – bonus disc later cancelled.

Early edited demo version featured on Michael's box-set, *THE ULTIMATE COLLECTION*, issued in November 2004. A different, longer version also exists, with Michael heard screaming at the beginning – after a sound protection wall fell on him as he was about to record.

DANGEROUS MEDLEY

Exclusive six minute medley of seven songs featured on Michael's *DANGEROUS* album: *Black Or White/Can't Let Her Get Away/ Dangerous/Who Is It/Remember The Time/Give In To Me/Heal The World*.

Released in May 1992 in the UK and continental Europe (but not the USA), as a Pepsi promo-only cassette single, with the previously unreleased solo recording, *Someone Put Your Hand Out*.

500,000 copies distributed as freebies, competition prizes, etc..

Released as a CD single in Japan only.

Included on the compilation, *SIGNATURE SERIES*, released in the States in 1992.

DANGEROUS NEW JACK MEDLEY

One of two promo medleys, released on 12" and CD as *The Medleys*, in Brazil in 1994.

Featured: *Remember The Time*, *In The Closet*, *Jam* and *Black Or White*.

DANNY BOY

Song performed by the Jackson 5 as part of a medley – with *By The Time I Get To Phoenix* and *Killing Me Softly With His Song* – during their Las Vegas shows in 1974.

Also performed on *The Tonight Show*, hosted by Bill Cosby, in America in March 1974.

DAPPER-DAN

Song featured on Michael's fourth solo album, *FOREVER, MICHAEL*, released in January 1975 in the States and March 1975 in the UK.

DARLING DEAR

Written by George Gordy (Berry's brother) and his wife Rosemary.

Featured on the Jackson 5's *THIRD ALBUM*, issued in September 1970 in the States and February 1971 in the UK – recorded on 24th May 1970.

B-side of *Mama's Pearl* in both the USA and UK.

Appeared on the promo *Third Album EP*, along with five further tracks, released with a picture sleeve in the States in 1970.

Heard on 'The Michael Look' episode of the Jackson 5's cartoon series in 1971.

Rejuvenated By MURO Mix, as included on the Japanese album *SOUL SOURCE – JACKSON 5 REMIXES* in 2000, featured slightly extended vocals.

Sampled by Mic Little featuring Ne-Yo, on their 2006 American R&B hit, *Put It In A Letter*.

Originally recorded by Smokey Robinson & The Miracles for their 1970 album, *A POCKET FULL OF MIRACLES*. As the B-side of *Point It Out*, listed for a solitary week at no.100 on the Hot 100 in the States.

DAY BASKETBALL WAS SAVED, THE

Previously unreleased track – with an introduction by Rosey Grier – featured in the *Goin' Back To Indiana* TV special in July 1971. Later included on the Jackson 5's album, *GOIN' BACK TO INDIANA*, released in September 1971 in the States (no UK release).

DAYDREAMER

Song written for, and performed by, the Jackson 5 on their TV special that aired in the States on 5th November 1972 – no official release.

DEAR MICHAEL

Song Michael recorded for his solo album, *FOREVER, MICHAEL*, issued in January 1975 in the States and March 1975 in the UK.

B-side of *Just A Little Bit Of You* in both the States and UK.

Issued as a single, b/w *Just A Little Bit Of You*, in Italy in 1975.

American TV actress, Kim Fields, recorded a cover version in 1984. Fields, who appeared in NBC's *Facts Of Life*, was a good friend of Michael's sister, Janet.

DESCENDING ANGELS

Incidental piece of music Michael composed with Nicholas Pike, for his short film, *Ghosts*, premiered in October 1996.

DESTINY

Song written by Michael with brothers Jackie, Marlon, Randy and Tito – Michael is on record as saying the song was written about him.

Title track of the Jacksons' third album, issued in December 1978.

Released as a single in the UK (but not USA), where it achieved a lowly no.39.

Promoted, during the group's European visit, on *Top Of The Pops*, and on the Jacksons' own *Midnight Special* in the States in 1979 (where Jermaine re-joined his brothers for this song). Also featured on a Destiny Tour concert screened on BBC2 in the UK.

DIDN'T I (BLOW YOUR MIND THIS TIME)

Song Jackie Jackson recorded for his 1973 eponymous, debut solo album, with his brothers including Michael on backing vocals.

Hit versions:
Delfonics – no.3 on the R&B singles chart and no.10 on the Hot 100 in the States in 1970, and no.22 in the UK in 1971.
Millie Jackson – no.49 on the R&B singles chart in 1980.

New Kids On The Block – no.8 on the Hot 100 and no.34 on the R&B singles chart in 1989, and no.8 in the UK in 1990.

DIFFERENT KIND OF LADY

Written by Michael with brothers Jackie, Marlon, Randy and Tito, for the Jacksons' album, *GOIN' PLACES*, released in October 1977.

Opening horns missing from the version included on the *GOIN' PLACES* picture disc released in the States.

B-side of *Find Me A Girl* in the States, and of *Even Though Your Gone* and *Heartbreak Hotel* in the UK.

DIRTY DIANA

Written and recorded by Michael for his solo album, *BAD*, released in September 1987.

Inspired by rock groupies, who follow musicians and artists around the tour circuit. Guest guitarist, Steve Stevens, was Billy Idol's lead guitarist.

'I got a call from Quincy Jones to do that,' said Stevens. 'I had an experience where I had worked with Diana Ross, where she wasn't in the studio. My prerequisite to him (Quincy) was that Michael had to be present when I was recording. He (Michael) was very receptive, and he made some sensible suggestions.'

Fifth single lifted from *BAD* – and the fifth single to hit no.1 on the Hot 100 in the States, a record breaking achievement. Also charted at no.5 on the R&B singles chart, and no.4 in the UK.

B-side featured an Instrumental version.

7" single version replaced the original on later pressings of *BAD*.

Official Versions:
Album Version.
Single Version.
Instrumental.

Performed at a Wembley concert attended by Diana, Princess of Wales – at her insistence. 'I took it out of the show in honour of Her Royal Highness,' Michael said. 'She took me away and said, "Are you gonna do *Dirty Diana*?" So I said, "No, I took it out of the show because of you". She said, "No! I want you to do it. Do it – do the song!"'

Promoted by Michael's first 'live' video, filmed at Long Beach, California – directed by Joe Pytka. Premiered on MTV on 14th April 1988.

World Music Award: Number One Video In The World (Michael accepted the award via a live satellite link).

Used by Diana Ross to open her 1989 concerts – snippet opened her *GREATEST HITS LIVE* album, released in 1989. Album also featured a live version of *Muscles*, which Michael wrote.

Eighth of Michael's 20 *'Visionary – The Video Singles'* reissues, with the music on one side of a Dual Disc and the accompanying short film on the other side. Issued in April 2006 in the UK – charted at no.17.

DMC MEGAMIX

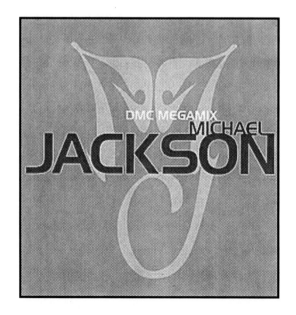

Fifteen minutes 40 seconds megamix of some of Michael's solo hits, released in various guises – including some formats of *Earth Song* – in 1995.

Songs featured: *Billie Jean, Rock With You, Bad, Thriller, Don't Stop 'Til You Get Enough, Black Or White, Remember The Time, Scream* and *Wanna Be Startin' Somethin'*.

Eleven minutes 18 seconds edit featured: *Billie Jean, Rock With You, Bad, Thriller, Don't Stop 'Til You Get Enough, Black Or White, Scream* and *Wanna Be Startin' Somethin'*.

DO I OWE

Song recorded by Jackie Jackson, with the Jackson 5 on backing vocals, for his only solo album for Motown, *JACKIE JACKSON*, issued in 1973.

Promo 7" single distributed to radio stations in the States.

DO THE BARTMAN

Song featured on the album *THE SIMPSONS SING THE BLUES*, issued in 1991.

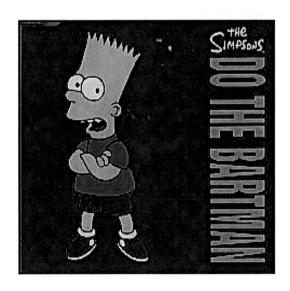

Includes the lyrics: 'If you can do the bart, you're bad like Michael Jackson' and 'Eat your heart out, Michael'.

Much speculation surrounded Michael's involvement in the song, before Simpsons' creator Matt Groening finally confessed at the second annual World Animation Celebration in Pasadena, USA, in February 1998, that Michael did in fact write and sing on the song.

Released as a single in the UK (but not USA), hitting no.1 for three weeks in February 1991.

Registered on the Hot 100 Airplay chart in the States, achieving no.11 during a nine week run.

DO THE FONZ

Song performed by the Jacksons on their CBS TV series in 1976.

DO WHAT YOU WANNA

Song Michael wrote with brothers Jackie, Marlon, Randy and Tito, for the Jacksons' album *GOIN' PLACES*, released in October 1977.

B-side of *Goin' Places* and *Blame It On The Boogie* in the States and UK.

DO YOU KNOW WHERE YOUR CHILDREN ARE

Song Michael cited he had written in his court disposition in November 1993 – remains unreleased.

DO YOU LOVE ME

Contours hit the Jackson 5 recorded a version of – remains unreleased.

Hit versions:
Contours – no.1 on the R&B singles chart and no.3 on the Hot 100 in the States in 1962.
Brian Poole & The Tremeloes – no.1 in the UK in 1963.
Dave Clark Five – no.11 on the Hot 100, and no.30 in the UK, in 1964.
Deep Feeling – no.34 in the UK in 1970.

Andy Fraser – no.82 on the Hot 100 in 1984.
Contours (reissue) – no.11 on the Hot 100 in 1988.
Duke Baysee – no.46 in the UK in 1995.

DO YOU LOVE ME

One of two songs Babyface revealed he had completed with Michael in late 1998, for a solo album by Michael scheduled for 1999, where they were aiming for a 'streeter' sound – remains unreleased.

DO YOU WANT ME

Song written by Sisqó and Dru Hill circa 1999, as a contender for Michael's album, *INVINCIBLE* – remains unreleased.

'I was driving when Michael Jackson called me on my cell phone,' said Sisqó. 'He wanted me to know how much he loved the record. We wanted to do a duet together. Next thing I did was to put my girlfriend on the phone, so she could also talk to Michael.'

DOCTOR MY EYES

Song the Jackson 5 recorded for their album, *LOOKIN' THROUGH THE WINDOWS* released in May 1972 in the States and October 1972 in the UK.

Released as a single in the UK – achieved no.9. No American release, as Jackson Browne's original version hit no.8 on the Hot 100 in early 1972.

DOES YOUR MAMA KNOW ABOUT ME

Track recorded by Jermaine Jackson, with the Jackson 5 on backing vocals, for his 1973 album, *COME INTO MY LIFE*.

A hit in the States in 1968 for Bobby Taylor & The Vancouvers, peaking at no.5 on the R&B singles chart and no.29 on the Hot 100.

DOGGIN' AROUND

Song Michael recorded for his solo album *MUSIC AND ME*, released in April 1973 in the States and July 1973 in the UK.

Scheduled to be issued as a single in the USA in February 1974, but cancelled – test pressings do exist.

Released as a single in Holland.

Hit versions:
Jackie Wilson (original version) – no.1 on the R&B singles chart and no.15 on the Hot 100 in the States in 1960.
Klique – no.2 on the R&B singles chart and no.50 on the Hot 100 in the States in1983.

DOIN' IT IN A HAUNTED HOUSE

Parody of Michael's *Thriller* by Yvonne Cage.

'I hope Michael won't be offended, I'm his number one fan and would love to meet him' said Cage. 'A lot of people have interpreted the song as being about sex, but I prefer to think about it as togetherness. I don't think it's vulgar – I think it's rather discreet.'

DOIN' THE JERK

Song the Jackson 5 performed regularly in the pre-Motown days, with Jermaine on lead vocals.

Performances included a department store at Glen Park, Chicago, in 1964, where Katherine Jackson hand-made the costumes her sons wore.

A hit in the States in early 1965 for the Larks (titled simply *The Jerk*), charting at no.7 on the Hot 100 and no.9 on the R&B singles chart.

DOING DIRTY

Song written by Michael with brother Marlon circa 1988-90, and considered for Michael's shelved greatest hits package, *DECADE 1980-1990* – remains unreleased.

DON'T KNOW WHY I LOVE YOU

Song featured on the Jackson 5's second album, *ABC*, released in May 1970 in the States and August 1970 in the UK.

Featured in the 'The Michael Look' episode of the Jackson 5 cartoon series in 1971.

Originally recorded by Stevie Wonder.

DON'T LET A WOMAN MAKE A FOOL OUT OF YOU

Song recorded by Joe 'King' Carrusco for his album, *SYNAPSE GAP (MUNDO TOTAL)*, issued in 1982.

Michael was standing in the corridor outside Studio 55 in Los Angeles, when Carrusco invited him in to sing backing on *Don't Let A Woman Make A Fool Out Of You*, and Michael readily agreed.

DON'T LET IT GET YOU DOWN

Song Michael originally recorded on 31st August 1973 – the same day he also recorded *Farewell My Summer Love* and *Girl You're So Together*.

Remained unreleased until May 1984, when an over-dubbed and remixed version was included on *FAREWELL MY SUMMER LOVE*.

Original recording featured on Michael's *THE BEST OF...* anthology series compilation, released in March 1995 in the States (no UK release).

DON'T LET YOUR BABY CATCH YOU

Song the Jackson 5 recorded for their album, *LOOKIN' THROUGH THE WINDOWS*, released in May 1972 in the States and October 1972 in the UK.

B-side of *The Boogie Man* in the UK (USA release cancelled, though promo copies with a picture sleeve were issued).

DON'T SAY GOODBYE AGAIN

Song featured on the Jackson 5's album, *GET IT TOGETHER*, released in September 1973 in the States and December 1973 in the UK.

Performed by the Jackson 5 on *Soul Train* in 1973.

DON'T STAND ANOTHER CHANCE

Song written by Marlon Jackson, for sister Janet's second solo album *DREAM STREET*, issued in 1984.

Backing vocals by Michael, Jackie, Marlon and Tito Jackson.

Released as a single in the USA (but not UK), achieving no.9 on the R&B singles chart and no.101 on the 'bubbling under' section of the Hot 100.

Official Versions:
Album Version.
Remixed Version.
Dub Version.

DON'T STOP

Fleetwood Mac hit Michael performed on stage at President Bill Clinton's Inaugural Gala on 19th January 1993, as part of an all-star choir.

Achieved no.3 on the Hot 100 in the States and no.32 in the UK for Fleetwood Mac in 1977.

DON'T STOP 'TIL YOU GET ENOUGH

Song written and recorded by Michael, for his first solo album after leaving Motown, *OFF THE WALL*, released in August 1979.

Lyrical content shocked his mother, Katherine Jackson, who pointed out the title could easily be misinterpreted – Michael asserted it wasn't a reference to sex, but that it could mean whatever people wanted it to mean.

Lead single from the album – heralded Michael's arrival as an adult solo performer, and paved the way for a new beginning to his musical career.

Promo short film, directed by Nick Saxton, premiered in October 1979.

Hit no.1 on the Hot 100 in the States, giving Michael his first chart topper since *Ben*, and gave him his first no.1 on the R&B singles chart. Also no.1 in Australia, New Zealand, Norway and South Africa, and no.3 in the UK.

Michael's first solo hit in Germany – it peaked at no.13.

Official Versions:
Album Version.	Roger's Underground Club Solution.
Masters At Work Remix.	Original Demo Recording.
7" Edit.	7" Edit w/Intro.
12" Version.	

Masters At Work Remix and Roger's remixes featured unreleased vocals and ad-libs, as the remixers were given access to the master tapes, which included vocals that didn't make the final album version of the song.

Live version, recorded at a concert at Madison Square Garden in September 1981, featured on the Jacksons album, *LIVE*, issued in November 1981. This version was included on the 12" single of Michael's *Beat It* in the UK.

Sampled by Baby Bump on *I Got This Feeling*, a no.22 hit in the UK in 2000.

Spliced with Q-Tip's *Breathe And Stop* by Mr On vs. Jungle Brothers, on *Breathe, Don't Stop* – registered with the BMI, but unofficial.

Michael recorded a version with Chris Tucker for the latter's movie, *Rush Hour 2*, in which Tucker was seen singing the song – remains unreleased.

Second of Michael's 20 *'Visionary – The Video Singles'* reissues, with the music on one side of a Dual Disc and the accompanying short film on the other side. Issued in February 2006 in the UK – charted at no.17.

DON'T WALK AWAY

Song written by Michael with Teddy Riley, Richard Stites and Reed Vertelney.

Featured on Michael's album *INVINCIBLE*, issued in October 2001.'

DON'T WANT TO SEE TOMORROW

Song the Jackson 5 recorded for their album, *LOOKIN' THROUGH THE WINDOWS*, released in May 1972 in the States and October 1972 in the UK.

DOWN BY THE OLD MILL STREAM

Song the Jacksons performed on their TV series in 1976, with their special guest star, Joey Bishop.

DREAM GOES ON, THE

Solo recording by Jermaine Jackson, included on the Jacksons TV soundtrack album, *THE JACKSONS: AN AMERICAN DREAM*, issued in October 1992 in the States and July 1993 in the UK.

Michael wasn't involved with the recording of this song, which was a tribute to the Jacksons.

DREAMER

Song the Jacksons recorded, with Michael on lead vocals, for their eponymous debut album, released in November 1976.

Cited by Michael in an interview in 1977 as one of his favourite tracks from the album to sing. 'I felt they (Kenneth Gamble & Leon Huff) could have written it with me in mind,' said Michael. 'I have always been a dreamer. I set goals for myself. I look at things and try to imagine what is possible, and then hope to surpass those boundaries.'

Issued as a single in the UK (but not USA), as a follow-up to the chart topping *Show You The Way To Go* – disappointingly peaked at no.22.

Promoted on the UK's premier TV music show, *Top Of The Pops*, with a promotional film clip (as very early music videos were called) filmed by the Jacksons, and performed by the group on *The Mike Douglas In Hollywood Show* and their own TV series in 1977.

DREAMS

Song written by Michael and registered with the BMI – remains unreleased.

DROP THE MASK

Song written by Diana Ross with Tim Tickner and Christopher Ward, and recorded by Diana as a bonus track on her 1999 album, *EVERY DAY IS A NEW DAY*.

Clearly aimed at Michael, the song opened with the lyrics:

> *Look in the mirror, who do you see?*
> *Where is the man that you used to be?*

Diana goes on to urge: 'Drop the mask – be yourself.'

95

D.S.

Song written by Michael, and featured on his album HIS*TORY*, issued in June 1995.

According to the lyric, 'Dom Sheldon is a cold man' – however, 'D.S.' is widely acknowledged to be a verbal attack on the State District Attorney, Thomas Sneddon, the man who led the criminal investigation against Michael in 1993 (and, indeed, the more recent investigation in 2004-05).

Live performance in Auckland, New Zealand, screened in that country as part of a *His*tory World Tour concert.

DUDE, THE

Song Quincy Jones recorded, with Michael on backing vocals, for his 1981 album of the same title.

EARTH SONG

Song written by Michael in a hotel room in Austria – evolved from a song titled, *What About Us*.

'I was feeling so much pain and so much suffering at the plight of the planet Earth,' said Michael. 'And for me, this is *Earth Song*, because I think nature is trying so hard to compensate for man's mismanagement of the Earth… and that's what inspired it. And it just suddenly dropped into my lap, when I was on tour in Austria.'

Included on Michael's album HIS*TORY*, released in June 1995, and issued as the follow-up to *You Are Not Alone* in most countries (but not the USA).

Shirley Caesar, of the Caesar Sisters, has confirmed Michael originally wanted her to be involved with the song. 'The studio technicians played the tape of the song Michael wanted me to consider,' she wrote in her book, *The Lady, The Melody & The Word*, 'but it didn't sound like something I'd sing. The name of it was 'Earth', and it dealt with environmental issues. I guess I felt that way because he had only rough taping of the song, but the finished product was awesome.' Caesar

96

withdrew from the project when the Church world became critical of her involvement with Michael. 'Let the record show, however,' she stated, 'that I love Michael Jackson, and I don't allow anyone to discuss him negatively in my presence.'

Michael's most successful single in both the UK and Germany – it topped the chart for six weeks in both countries. In the UK, it captured the coveted Christmas no.1 slot, and went on to shift over one million copies. In Germany, it gave Michael his first no.1 (for six weeks), and went on to become his only million seller.

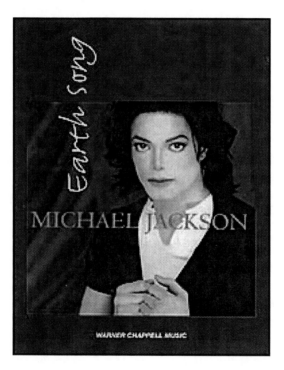

Official Versions:
Album Version.
Hani's Around The World Experience.
Hani's Extended Radio Experience.
Hani's Club Experience.
Hani's Radio Experience.
Radio Edit.

Promo short film shot by Nicholas Brandt was filmed on four different continents: South America (Amazon Rainforest), Africa (Tanzania), Europe (Croatia) and North America (New York).

Grammy nomination: Best Music Video, Short Form (the award went to the Beatles, for *Free As Bird* – one of the songs *Earth Song* kept out of the no.1 slot in the UK).

Genesis Awards: Doris Day Music Award (given for an animal sensitive music work).

French Film Awards: Best Video Award.

Promoted with three unusually high profile TV appearances: the German TV show, *Wetten Dass?* in 1995, The Brits awards ceremony in February 1996, and the World Music Awards in May 1996.

Michael, in his first British TV appearance since 1979, was named Artist Of A Generation at The Brits – Sir Bob Geldof presented him with the award. Michael's 'quasi-religious' performance upset some, including the lead singer of Britpop group Pulp, Jarvis Cocker, who invaded the stage halfway through the song, causing mayhem. Later, in a statement, Michael said: 'I am sickened, saddened, shocked, upset, cheated and angry, but was proud with how the cast remained professional.'

Live performance in Auckland, New Zealand, screened in that country as part of a *His*tory World Tour concert. Different live performance from the same tour screened by Sat 1 TV in Germany.

Opening piano bars used in the 'I bring you the future' advertisement, for the Esconic Video CD Player, in 1997.

Live performance at the *Michael Jackson & Friends* concerts, staged in Seoul, South Korea, on 25th June 1999, and in Munich, Germany, two days later.

Seventeenth of Michael's 20 *'Visionary – The Video Singles'* reissues, with the music on one side of a Dual Disc and the accompanying short film on the other side. Issued in June 2006 in the UK – charted at no.34, making it the least successful of all the reissues.

EASE ON DOWN THE ROAD

Song from Michael's first film, *The Wiz*, which he performed with Diana Ross and his co-stars. Featured on the accompanying soundtrack album, issued in September 1978 in the States and October 1978 in the UK.

Included in the original Broadway musical, on which the film *The Wiz* was based – the musical, which starred Stephanie Mills as Dorothy, scooped seven Tony Awards, including Best Musical and Best Score.

'I think the stage and MGM version (*The Wizard Of Oz*) kind of missed the point,' said Michael, comparing them to L. Fred Baum's original story; he felt the film *The Wiz* was much closer. 'The message (of the book) is that these people are looking for something they already have. It's inside them already, but they don't know it because they don't have that belief in themselves to realise it.'

Michael cited *Believe In Yourself*, by Lena Horne and Diana Ross, as his favourite song from the film. 'It's my favourite,' he said, 'because of what it says – I like what it says.'

Released as a single, credited to Diana Ross & Michael Jackson, achieved no.17 on the R&B singles chart and no.41 on the Hot 100 in the States, and no.45 in the UK.

Versions & Mixes:
Album Version #1.   Single Version.
Album Version #2.   12" Extended Mix.
Album Version #3.

One of three songs Michael sang a medley of, when he appeared on the *Kraft Salutes Disneyland's 25th Anniversary Show* TV special in 1980. The other two songs were *Follow The Yellow Brick Road* and *When You Wish Upon A Star*.

Performed by Michael and Diana Ross on her TV special, *diana!* in 1980.

Performed by Al Jarreau, Jill Scott, Monica and Deborah Cox during the *Michael Jackson: 30th Anniversary Celebration, The Solo Years* concerts, staged at New York's Madison Square Garden on 7th and 10th September 2001.

EAT IT

Parody of Michael's *Beat It*, written and recorded by Weird Al Yankovic, with Michael's blessing.

A no.1 smash in Australia; charted at no.12 in the States and no.36 in the UK.

'The only reason he (Michael) let me is that he has a sense of humour,' said Weird Al. 'It is heartening to find somebody that popular, talented and powerful, who can really take a joke.'

Grammy Award: Best Comedy Recording.

EATEN ALIVE

Song written by Michael with Barry and Maurice Gibb – two of the Bee Gees.

Originally written, and registered in March 1985, by Barry and Maurice Gibb. Michael heard their demo and felt it needed something else; Barry offered to share credit with Michael, if he wanted to supply what he thought was missing. Michael agreed and a second demo – recorded by Michael – was registered in July, with the note, 'words and music in the choruses have been completely rewritten'.

Both demo versions, recorded in Los Angeles, remain unreleased.

Recorded by Diana Ross in mid 1985 in Los Angeles, with Michael and the Gibb brothers on backing vocals, for her album of the same title, issued in September 1985.

Produced by Michael with Barry Gibb, Karl Richardson and Albhy Galuten. Michael was present during the recording of the instrumental tracks, and judged whether they were suitable by dancing to them in the studio. He also supervised the mixing, settling on one that Galuten wasn't too happy with.

Performed by Diana at the American Music Awards in 1986.

Issued as a single: charted at no.10 on the R&B singles chart and no.77 on the Hot 100 in the States, and no.71 in the UK.

Official Versions:
Album Version.   Instrumental.
Extended Remix.   Single Version Edited.

ECSTASY

Poem written by Michael – included in his book of poems and reflections, *Dancing The Dream*, published in 1992.

EKAN SATYAM (THE ONE TRUTH)

Song composed by popular Indian singer A.R. Rahman, with lyrics originally written by A.R. Parthasarathy in Sanskrit, with an English translation by Kanika Myer Bharat.

Rahman has confirmed the song, 'was penned especially for the *Michael Jackson & Friends* concert, which was held in Munich in June 1999.'

Michael (singing in English) and Rahman (singing in Sanskrit) recorded the song as a duet around September 1999. However, it failed to make Michael's *INVINCIBLE* album, and talk of the song being released as a single proved unfounded – remains unreleased.

ELIZABETH, I LOVE YOU

Song specially written by Michael for his close friend Elizabeth Taylor, and performed for her at her 65th birthday celebration, on 16th February 1997.

Birthday celebration, including Michael's performance, aired on ABC-TV in the States on 25th February 1997.

No official release, but bootleg recordings (taken from the TV special) are known to exist.

ELUSIVE SHADOW, THE

Poem written by Michael – included in his book of poems and reflections, *Dancing The Dream*, published in 1992.

E-NE-ME-NE-MI-NE-MOE (THE CHOICE IS YOURS TO PULL)

Song included on the Jackson 5's *LOOKIN' THROUGH THE WINDOWS* album, issued in May 1972 in the States and October 1972 in the UK.

ENJOY YOURSELF

Song featured on the Jacksons debut, self-titled album, released in November 1976.

Issued as the Jacksons' debut single, hitting no.2 on the R&B singles chart and no.6 on the Hot 100 in the States, and achieving no.42 in the UK.

Promoted in the States by the Jacksons on *The Mike Douglas In Hollywood Show*, *Sonny & Cher Show* and on their own TV series, and in Germany on *Beat Club* and *Muzik Laden*. Also featured on a Destiny Tour concert screened on BBC2 in the UK.

Promotional film clip (as very early music videos were called) filmed by the Jacksons.

RIAA Gold Record (USA million seller) – Michael and his brothers' first (Motown at this time wasn't affiliated to the RIAA, so the mega-sales of several Jackson 5 singles went unrecognised).

Alternate version featured on the 2004 compilations, *THE ESSENTIAL JACKSONS* (USA) and *THE VERY BEST OF THE JACKSONS* (UK).

Sampled by:
A+ on *Enjoy Yourself* – no.5 in the UK in 1999.
Backstreet Boys on *Let's Have A Party*, from their eponymous 1996 album.

ESCAPE FROM THE PLANET OF THE ANT MEN

Song recorded by Jermaine, with his brothers including Michael on backing vocals, for his solo album *JERMAINE JACKSON* (titled *DYNAMITE* in some countries, including the UK), released in May 1984.

One of three songs from the album featured on *Three Sides Of Jermaine Jackson*, a rare promo EP issued in the States.

Featured on the 12" release of Jermaine's duet with Pia Zadora, *When The Rain Begins To Fall*, in several countries.

E.T. THE EXTRA-TERRESTRIAL

Storybook album, produced by Quincy Jones, narrated by Michael, issued in November 1982 in the States and January 1983 in the UK.

Featured one new song by Michael, *Someone In The Dark*.

Charted at no.82 in the UK – remarkably high for a storybook album.

Grammy Award: Best Recording For Children. On collecting the Grammy, on a glittering evening he collected another seven for

THRILLER and its singles, Michael said, 'Of all the awards I've gotten, I'm most proud of this one.'

See also: *Someone In The Dark.*

ETERNAL LIGHT, THE

Song featured on the Jackson 5 album, *JOYFUL JUKEBOX MUSIC*, issued in October 1976 in the States and December 1976 in the UK.

First album released by Motown after Michael and his brothers (Jermaine apart) left for CBS/Epic, and credited to 'The Jackson 5 featuring Michael Jackson'.

EUPHORIA

Song Michael recorded for his solo album *MUSIC & ME*, released in April 1973 in the States and July 1973 in the UK.

EVEN THOUGH YOU'RE GONE

Song featured on the second Jacksons album, *GOIN' PLACES*, issued in October 1977.

Released as a single in the UK (but not USA, where *Find Me A Girl* was preferred) – charted at no.31.

Promotional film clip filmed by the Jacksons.

Official Versions:
Album Version.
Single Edit.

EVERYBODY

Written by Michael with brother Tito and Mike McKinney.

Recorded and produced by the Jacksons for their album *TRIUMPH*, released in October 1980.

EVERYBODY IS A STAR

One of 19 'Rare & Unreleased' tracks on the fourth CD of the Michael/Jackson 5 box-set, *SOULSATION!*, issued in June 1995 in the States and a month later in the UK – demo version also known to exist.

Lead vocal shared between Tito, Jackie, Jermaine and Michael.

Originally recorded by Sly & The Family Stone, and included on their *GREATEST HITS* compilation in 1970.

EVERYBODY'S SOMEBODY'S FOOL

Song Michael recorded for his second solo album, *BEN*, issued in August 1972 in the States and December 1972 in the UK.

Scheduled to be released as a single in the States in early 1973, but cancelled.

FACE

Song Michael considered including on his 1995 album, HIS*TORY*, but ultimately rejected – remains unreleased.

FALL AGAIN

Song Michael planned to complete and include on his 2001 album, *INVINCIBLE*, but when his son Prince was taken ill he didn't have time to finish it and it didn't make the album.

'We worked to the point that we were three-fourths of the way finished,' confirmed Walter Afanasieff in January 2000, 'then the incident happened when his son got very sick. We're going to have to reserve a little spot to finish the song.'

Demo version, recorded in 1999, released in November 2004 as one of the previously unreleased tracks on *THE ULTIMATE COLLECTION* box-set.

Recorded by Glenn Lewis – his version featured on the soundtrack album, *MAID IN MANHATTEN*, issued in late 2002.

Fake duet version by Michael and Glenn Lewis surfaced on the internet in 2005.

FAN LETTER TO MICHAEL JACKSON

Tribute song recorded by Rheostatics, for their 1995 album, *INTRODUCING HAPPINESS*.

FANFARE TRANSITION

Song written by Michael in 1992, and registered with the United States Copyright Office in August of the same year – remains unreleased.

Also known by the title, *Fanfare 1992*.

FANTASY

Song Michael cited he had written with brother Jermaine at his copyright hearing in 1993 – remains unreleased.

FAR, FAR AWAY

Song written by Michael, and cited by him at his copyright hearing in 1993; he couldn't originally recall whether he had written the song or not, but later confirmed he did – remains unreleased.

FAREWELL MY SUMMER LOVE

Song originally recorded by Michael on 31st August 1973 – the same day he also recorded *Don't Let It Get You Down* and *Girl You're So Together*.

Remained unreleased until May 1984, when it was one of nine previously unheard songs remixed and included on a 'new' Motown album, *FAREWELL MY SUMMER LOVE 1984* (the '1984' was quickly dropped).

Title track preceded the album as a single, and surpassed all expectations, charting at no.7 in the UK, no.37 on the R&B chart and no.38 on the Hot 100 in the States.

Official Versions:
Album version.
Extended version.
Single Version.
Original recording remains unreleased.

Cover version by Chaos peaked at no.55 in the UK in 1992.

FAT

Second parody of one of Michael's hits – this time *Bad* – by Weird Al Yankovic, released in 1988.

Failed to match the success of *Eat It*, struggling to no.80 in the UK and no.99 in the States.

Grammy Award: Best Concept Recording.

FEAR

Song written by Michael circa 1993, and considered for his album, HIS*TORY* – remains unreleased.

FEELIN' ALRIGHT

Song performed by the Jackson 5 with Diana Ross, for her 1971 TV special, *Diana!*, and included on the accompanying soundtrack album.

Serviced to DJs in the States as a promo 7" single with picture sleeve – today a great rarity, as disappointing airplay meant the planned single was cancelled.

Live version recorded at the Jackson 5's homecoming concert in Gary, Indiana, on 29th May 1971, included on their album, *GOIN' BACK TO INDIANA*, issued in September 1971 in the States (no UK release). Footage from the concert featured on the *Goin' Back To Indiana* TV special aired in the States on 19th September 1971.

Recorded by Dave Mason, for his 1972 album, *HEAD-KEEPER*.

FEVER

Classic song Rebbie Jackson performed on *The Jacksons* TV series in 1976, accompanied by brothers Michael and Marlon, who danced in the background.

Hit versions:
Little Willie John – no.24 in the States in 1956.
Peggy Lee – no.5 in the UK, no.8 in the States in 1958.
Helen Shapiro – no.38 in the UK in 1964.
McCoys – no.7 in the States, no.44 in the UK in 1965.
Rita Coolidge – no.76 in the States in 1973.
Peggy Lee – no.75 in the UK in 1992 (re-issue).
Madonna – no.6 in the UK in 1993.

FIND ME A GIRL

Song featured on the Jacksons album, *GOIN' PLACES*, released in October 1977.

Issued as a single in the States (but not UK) – failed to enter the Hot 100, but charted at no.38 on the R&B singles chart.

Official Versions:
Album Version.
Single Edit.

FINGERTIPS

Stevie Wonder song the Jackson 5 recorded a version of – remains unreleased.

Stevie – as Little Stevie Wonder – took the song to no.1 on the Hot 100 and R&B singles chart in the States in 1963.

FIRE IS THE FEELING

Original title of La Toya's debut hit, *Night Time Lover*, which Michael co-wrote with her – written with Donna Summer in mind.

See also: *Night Time Lover*.

FLAT FOOT FLOOGIE, THE

Song performed by Michael with siblings La Toya, Rebbie and Marlon, on *The Jacksons* TV series in 1976.

FLY AWAY

Song Michael cited he had written at his copyright hearing in 1994.

Recorded by Michael's sister Rebbie, for her 1998 album, *YOURS FAITHFULLY*, with Michael co-producing (with StoneBridge and Nick Nice) and singing backing vocals.

'That's simply a beautiful song,' said Rebbie, speaking about *Fly Away*. 'After he (Michael) wrote it, he said he could hear me singing it. It's about not wanting to lose a relationship".

Michael's own version of the song was finally heard in October 2001, when it was one of the bonus track added to the expanded, special edition reissue of his album *BAD*. Rebbie's version, compared to this version, has extra background vocals by Michael.

FOLLOW THE YELLOW BRICK ROAD

Originally from the Judy Garland film *The Wizard Of Oz*, one of three songs Michael sang a medley of, when he appeared on the *Kraft Salutes Disneyland's 25th Anniversary Show* TV special in 1980. The other two songs were *Ease On Down The Road* and *When You Wish Upon A Star*.

FOR ALL TIME

Song written by Michael Sherwood, David Paich and Steve Porcaro circa 1990, as a contender for Michael's album *DANGEROUS*, but it wasn't released at the time.

Surfaced on the internet towards the end of 2002 – no official release.

FOR ONCE IN MY LIFE

Stevie Wonder classic the Jackson 5 recorded a version of – remains unreleased.

Song the Jacksons sang the chorus of, as guest Sonny Bono performed a medley of *More Than You Know*, *Am I Blue*, *For Once In My Life* and *Try A Little Tenderness*, during their TV series in 1976.

Hit versions:
Tony Bennett – no.91 on the Hot 100 in the States in 1967.
Stevie Wonder – no.2 on the Hot 100 and R&B singles chart in the
    States, and no.3 in the UK, in 1968.
Jackie Wilson – no.70 on the Hot 100 in 1968.
Dorothy Squires – no.24 in the UK in 1969.

FOR THE GOOD TIMES

One of Katherine Jackson's favourite songs, which son Michael sang to her at her birthday party on 4th May 1984, staged at the Bistro Garden Restaurant in Beverley Hills.

Hit Versions:
Ray Price – no.11 on the Hot 100 in the States in 1970.
Perry Como – no.7 in the UK in 1973.

FOR THE REST OF MY LIFE

Track rumoured to have been recorded in late 1970 by the Jackson 5 with Diana Ross – never officially acknowledged by Motown.

FOREVER CAME TODAY

Supremes hit covered by the Jackson 5 on their album *MOVING VIOLATION*, released in May 1975 in the States and July 1975 in the UK.

Last Jackson 5 single issued whilst the group were still a Motown act, achieved no.6 on the R&B singles chart and no.60 on the Hot 100 in the States, but failed to chart in the UK.

Promo 7" singles on blue and red vinyl released in the States – now rare collectors items.

Promoted on *Soul Train*, *The Rich Little Show* and *The Carol Burnett Show* in 1976 – the latter was the group's first performance without

Jermaine (Marlon and Randy lip-synched his vocals). Also performed by the Jacksons on their own TV series in 1976.

Live performance by the Jacksons, at a concert in Mexico in 1976, included on the home video, *The Jacksons In Concert*, released in 1981 in the UK (no USA release).

Remixed 'Disc-O-Tech #3 Version' appeared on the album *DISC-O-TECH* in 1976 – this version was added to the '2 Classic Albums on 1 CD' re-issue of *DANCING MACHINE & MOVING VIOLATION*, released in the States in August 2001.

Original version by the Supremes, issued in 1968 on their album *REFLECTIONS*, achieved no.17 on the R&B singles chart and no.28 on the Hot 100 in the States, and no.28 in the UK.

FREE

Song Michael cited he had written at his copyright hearing in Mexico in 1993 – remains unreleased.

FROM THE BOTTOM OF MY HEART

Original title of Michael's charity recording, in aid of victims of Hurricane Katrina, in 2005 – title may have been changed because Stevie Wonder's new album featured a song with the same title.

Remains unreleased.

FROSTY THE SNOWMAN

Perennial Christmas favourite the Jackson 5 recorded for their *CHRISTMAS ALBUM*, released in October 1970 in the States and December 1970 in the UK.

B-side of *Mama's Pearl* in Turkey.

One of four songs from the album on the *Michael Jackson & The Jackson 5 Christmas EP*, issued in November 1987 in the UK.

GET AROUND

Song Michael cited he had written in his court disposition in November 1993 – remains unreleased.

Version crediting Rodney Jerkins, Fred Jerkins III and LaShawn Daniels considered for Michael's *INVINCIBLE* album – failed to make the final track listing and remains unreleased.

GET HAPPY

Song the Jacksons performed on their TV series in 1976.

GET IT

Michael's second duet with Stevie Wonder.

Michael completed the recording of his vocals whilst touring in Japan, the tapes of the songs having been personally delivered to him by Barry Betts, a fan who was hand-picked from the audience at one of Stevie's concerts.

Featured on Stevie's album *CHARACTERS*, released in 1988.

Disappointed as a single, peaking at no.4 on the R&B singles chart and no.80 on the Hot 100 in the States, and no.37 in the UK.

Official Versions:
Album Version.   Single Version.
12" Extended Mix.   12" Extended Mix Instrumental.

GET IT TOGETHER

Title track of an album the Jackson 5 released in September 1973 in the States and November 1973 in the UK.

Sold a respectable 700,000 copies as a single in the States, achieving no.2 on the R&B singles chart but a lowly no.28 on the Hot 100 – better than the UK, where it failed to chart at all.

Promo 7" red vinyl single released in the States.

Performed by the Jackson 5 in the States on *The Bob Hope Special*, *Soul Train* and *The Mills Brothers Special* in 1974, and by the Jacksons on their TV series in 1977.

Alternate version featured on the Jackson 5's 1986 compilation, *ANTHOLOGY*.

4Hereo Remix, as included on the Japanese album *SOUL SOURCE – JACKSON 5 REMIXES 2* in 2001, featured extended vocals.

GET ON THE FLOOR

Song written by Michael with Louis Johnson of the Brothers Johnson.

Developed from a song the Brothers Johnson were working on, for their *LIGHT UP THE NIGHT* album. Michael heard the incomplete song, put a melody to it, and recorded it himself.

Featured on Michael's first solo album for CBS/Epic, *OFF THE WALL*, released in August 1979.

Re-recorded by Michael in early 1980 – this newer version was included on new pressings of *OFF THE WALL*, in place of the original recording.

Newer version featured as the B-side of *Rock With You* in the UK and *Off The Wall* in the States.

GET READY

Temptations hit written and produced by Smokey Robinson, which the Jackson 5 often performed on the Chiltin' Circuit in the mid-to-late 1960s.

Performed by the Jackson 5, with the Temptations, in 1971 at the PUSH – Expo concert in Chicago.

Comedy version performed by the Jacksons on their TV series in 1976 – dressed in inflated, heavyweight suits, and billed as 'The Ton-Tations'.

The Temptations took the song to no.1 on the R&B singles chart, and achieved no.29 on the Hot 100, in the States in 1966. The single hit no.10 in the UK.

GHOSTS

Song written by Michael with Teddy Riley, developed after Michael was asked to write the theme to a new Addams Family film. He ultimately declined, and instead wrote his own short film (which became *Ghosts*), including the song he originally wrote for the film, *Is It Scary*.

Failed to make the final selection for Michael's HIS*TORY* album, and first heard in Michael's mini-movie *Ghosts*, which cost an estimated $7-9 million and premiered in Beverly Hills on 24th October 1996.

One of five previously unreleased songs featured on Michael's remix album, *BLOOD ON THE DANCE FLOOR*, issued in April 1997.

Double A-side single with His*tory* in most countries (but not the USA), charting at no.5 in the UK – Michael's eighth consecutive Top 5 single.

Official Versions:

Album Version.	Mousse T's Radio Rock.
Mousse T's Club Mix.	Mousse T's Radio Rock Singalong
Mousse T's Club Mix TV.	Remix.
Mousse T's Radio Edit.	Radio Edit.

Demo versions, with different backing vocals, sound effects and bass, leaked after they were used during the production of the final credits of the *Ghosts* short film (the final version of the song wasn't ready in time).

Title of a critically acclaimed 40 minute short film directed by Stan Winston, in which Michael played all the lead characters – written by Michael with Stephen King.

'We wrote it on the telephone, Stephen and I,' said Michael. 'He's a lovely guy – he's amazing. We wrote it on the phone, just talking together.'

Bob Fosse Award: Best Choreography in a Music Video.

GHOSTS – MEDLEY OF HIGHLIGHTS FROM 'BLOOD ON THE DANCE FLOOR – *HIS*TORY IN THE MIX'

Medley given away on promo cassette, as part of the *Ghosts* promotional pack, at the UK premiere of the short film in London in May 1997.

Tracks featured: *Stranger In Moscow (Tee's In-House Club Mix)*, *Blood On The Dance Floor*, *Scream Louder (Flyte Tyme Remix)*, *Ghosts*, *Earth Song (Hani's Club Experience)*, *You Are Not Alone (Classic Club Mix)* and His*tory (Tony Moran's History Lesson)*.

GIRL DON'T TAKE YOUR LOVE AWAY FROM ME

Song included on Michael's first solo album, *GOT TO BE THERE*, released in January 1972 in the States and May 1972 in the UK.

Featured in the 'Jackson And The Beanstalk' episode of the new Jackson 5 cartoon series in 1971.

GIRL IS MINE, THE

Written by Michael and recorded as a duet with Paul McCartney, for Michael's album *THRILLER*, issued in December 1982.

McCartney spent three days at Westlake Studios, Los Angeles, working on the song with Michael from 14th-16th April 1982 – the year after the pair first worked on *Say Say Say* and *The Man*, although it was the first Jackson/McCartney duet to gain a release.

Michael is on record as saying the duet is one of his most enjoyable recording moments:

'One of my favourite songs to record, of all my recordings as a solo artist, is probably *The Girl Is Mine*, because working with Paul McCartney was pretty exciting and we just literally had fun... it was like lots of kibitzing and playing and throwing stuff at each other and making jokes... and we actually recorded the track and the vocals pretty much live at the same time, and we do have footage of it, but it's never been shown – maybe one day we'll give you a sneak preview of it.'

Footage of Michael and Paul in the studio was screened at some venues during Paul's world tour in 1990.

Several demo versions known to exist, including a solo version by Michael, and others of him working on different keys for the melody of the song – some of these were played at the court disposition hearing in Mexico in 1993.

Lead single from *THRILLER*, hitting no.1 on the R&B singles chart and no.2 on the Hot 100 in the States, and no.8 in the UK. Cover photograph of Michael and Paul by the latter's late wife, Linda.

RIAA Gold Record (USA million seller).

Subject of two lawsuits, firstly Michael testified in a Chicago court on 6th December 1984, when Fred Sandford claimed it was the same as his song, *Please Love Me Now*. Secondly, in Mexico in 1993, after Robert Smith (*aka* Robert Austin), Reynaud Jones and Clifford Rubin claimed it infringed two of their songs, *Don't Let The Sunshine Catch*

You Crying and *Happy Go Lucky Girl*. In both cases, the judgement found in favour of Michael and his record company.

Sampled by Stevie Wonder – without credit – on *Fun Day*, from his 1991 album, *MUSIC FROM THE MOVIE JUNGLE FEVER*.

Cover version recorded by Yellowman.

'New edited version' – the original version minus rap by Michael and Paul – was released as a promo 7" single.

GIRL YOU'RE SO TOGETHER

Song Michael originally recorded on 31st August 1973 – the same day he recorded *Don't Let It Get You Down* and *Farewell My Summer Love*.

Remained unreleased until an up-dated version featured on Michael's solo album, *FAREWELL MY SUMMER LOVE*, issued in May 1984 in the States and June 1984 in the States.

Second and last single lifted from the album in many countries, including the UK (but not USA), where it charted at no.33.

B-side of *Touch The One You Love* in the States.

Original recording remains unreleased.

GIRLFRIEND

Written by Paul McCartney, and mentioned to Michael at a Hollywood party in 1978, as a song he might like to record. Nothing happened, so Paul recorded the song himself, for the Wings album, *LONDON TOWN*.

Brought to Michael's attention again by producer Quincy Jones, when they were looking for songs for Michael's first solo album as an adult. This time Michael did record the song, and included it on *OFF THE WALL*, released in August 1979.

Fifth single from the album in the UK (but not USA), where it gave Michael a then record fifth hit from one album, peaking at no.41.

GIRLS GIRLS GIRLS

Track Jay-Z recorded, with Kanye West producing, for his 2001 album, *THE BLUEPRINT* – one planned remix was to feature Michael singing a hook, but if recorded it remains unreleased.

'My Mom likes it,' commented Jay-Z, around the time of the planned remix, 'because she gets to see how successful her son is – you're working with Michael Jackson, you must be all right; you must be pretty good!'

GIVE IN TO ME

Written by Michael with Bill Bottrell, and recorded by Michael with special guest Slash – from Guns N' Roses – on guitar.

'He sent me a tape of the song that had no guitars other than some slow picking,' said Slash. 'I called him and sang over the phone what I wanted to do.'

Slash, at the time, was just leaving for Africa, so he and Michael managed to work it out so they could record Slash's contribution when he returned from Africa. 'I basically went in and started to play – that was it,' said Slash. 'Michael just wanted whatever was in my style. He just wanted me to do that – no pressure. He was really in synch with me.'

Featured on Michael's solo album, *DANGEROUS*, issued in November 1991.

One demo version is known to fans as *Love Is A Donut* – no official release.

Seventh single released from the album in the UK, where it charted at no.2. American release cancelled, and *Who Is It* issued instead, following Michael's *a cappella* rendition of the song during his televised interview with Oprah Winfrey.

Official Versions:
Album Version.
7" Version.
Instrumental.

No.1 in New Zealand and Zimbabwe.

Promo 'live in concert' short film, also featuring Slash, shot in just two hours in Munich, Germany. Directed by Andy Moharan, and premiered on 10th February 1993, on *Michael Jackson Talks... To Oprah* – an interview that attracted around 100 million viewers.

GIVE IT UP

Written by Michael with brother Randy, and recorded by the Jacksons for their album *TRIUMPH*, released in October 1980.

B-side of *Time Waits For No One* in the UK (no USA release).

GIVE LOVE ON CHRISTMAS DAY

Song recorded by the Jackson 5 for *CHRISTMAS ALBUM*, issued in October 1970 in the States and December 1970 in the UK.

Released as a single in the Philippines.

Promo CD single released in the States in 1986, to promote the release of *CHRISTMAS ALBUM* on CD for the first time.

GIVE ME HALF A CHANCE

Song originally recorded – but not released – by the Jackson 5 between 1970-73.

One of the 'Never-Before-Released Masters' included on *LOOKING BACK TO YESTERDAY*, an album credited to Michael solo, released in February 1986 in the States and May 1986 in the UK.

GLOVED ONE, THE

Song written circa 2001 by Sisqó, for Michael's *INVINCIBLE* album – remains unreleased.

GOD REST YE MERRY GENTLEMEN

Well known festive song the Jackson 5 recorded for their *CHRISTMAS ALBUM* circa 1970, but which failed to make the final track listing – remains unreleased.

GOIN' BACK TO ALABAMA

Song recorded by Kenny Rogers, with Michael and Lionel Richie on backing vocals, for his 1981 album, *SHARE YOUR LOVE*.

GOIN' BACK TO INDIANA

Song originally featured on the Jackson 5's *THIRD ALBUM*, issued in September 1970 in the States and February 1971 in the UK.

Released as a single in several European countries, excluding the UK, hitting no.1 in Sweden.

One of six tracks featured on *Third Album EP*, released with a picture sleeve in the States in 1970.

Live version recorded at the Jackson 5's homecoming concert in Gary, Indiana, on 29th May 1971, included on their album, *GOIN' BACK TO INDIANA*, issued in September 1971 in the States (no UK release).

Goin' Back To Indiana TV special recorded in the States on 9th and 10th July 1971, and included concert footage of the Jackson 5's success homecoming on 29th May, aired on ABC-TV on 19th September 1971.

Featured in the first episode – titled 'It All Started With' – of the Jackson 5 cartoon series, which aired weekly in the States, starting 11th September 1971. Version featured was an alternate mix, with a slower tempo, and minus the horns and strings.

Performed by the Jackson children at The Jacksons Family Honors concert, staged at the MGM Grand Garden, Las Vegas, on 19th February 1994.

GOIN' PLACES

Title track of the Jacksons second album, issued in October 1977.

Charted at no.8 on the R&B singles chart and no.52 on the Hot 100 in the States, and no.26 in the UK.

Promotional film clip filmed by the Jacksons.

Official Versions:
Album Version.
Single Edit.

GOIN' TO RIO

Song written by Michael with Carole Bayer Sager circa 1976, and considered for his album, *OFF THE WALL*. Cited by Michael in his court disposition in November 1993 – remains unreleased.

GONE TOO SOON

Song Michael recorded for his solo album, *DANGEROUS*, released in November 1991. Demo version featured different vocals and 'perfect sunflower' lyric – no official release.

Prelude composed, arranged and conducted by Marty Paich.

Written for and dedicated to the memory of Ryan White, a haemophiliac who was diagnosed with the AIDS virus aged eleven years, and who died just after turning eighteen in April 1990.

Ninth single lifted from the album in numerous countries, excluding the USA but including the UK, where it achieved no.33 – Michael's ninth

Top 40 hit from the one album, thus equalling his own record, set with *BAD*.

B-side featured an Instrumental version.

Promo short film – directed by Bill DiCicco – featured footage of Michael with Ryan White, as well as brief coverage of Ryan's funeral, which Michael, Elton John and Barbara Bush attended.

Performed by Michael on 19th January 1993, at *An American Reunion: The 52nd Presidential Inaugural Gala*, for the incoming President, Bill Clinton. Michael, as well as dedicating the song to his late friend Ryan, used the occasion to speak out in favour of funding AIDS-related research:

> *'He is gone, but I want his life to have meaning beyond his passing. It is my hope, President-elect Clinton, that you and your admin-istration commit the resources needed to eliminate this awful disease that took my friend, and ended so many promising lives before their time.'*

Following the tragic death of Diana, Princess of Wales on 31st August 1997, Michael permitted the inclusion of *Gone Too Soon* on an album titled *TRIBUTE*, with all proceeds from the sale of the album going to the Diana, Princess of Wales Memorial Fund. Michael also dedicated his Ostend concert to the memory of Diana and, speaking via Kingdom International, took a swipe at the world's paparazzi:

'As one who has been under scrutiny the majority of my life, I speak with authority when I say that I am horrified that the paparazzi, supported by the tabloids' animalistic behaviour, may be acceptable to the public. The world's acceptance of this practice, if continued, will accelerate tragedies of this magnitude.'

Performed, with guest Stevie Wonder, by Babyface during his MTV Unplugged in New York City show, which aired in the States on 21st November 1997. Subsequently included on Babyface's album, *MTV UNPLUGGED NYC 1997*.

GOOD TIMES

Song the Jacksons recorded for their debut, self-titled album, released in November 1976.

B-side of *Dreamer* in the UK.

Performed at the American Music Awards in 1977, where Michael also presented an award with Lola Falana to Chicago, for Favourite Rock/Pop Group. Also performed on *The Jacksons* TV series in 1977.

GOT THE HOTS

Song written by Michael with Quincy Jones, and cited by Michael in his court disposition in November 1993.

Included on the first acetate of the expanded, special edition reissue of *THRILLER* in 2001 – later withdrawn and remains unreleased.

GOT TO BE THERE

Title track of Michael's debut solo album, released in January 1972 in the States and May 1972 in the UK.

Originally intended for the Supremes, then the Jackson 5 – indeed, Michael's brothers do feature on backing vocals, as they did on many early songs credited to Michael alone.

Michael's debut solo single, and in releasing it he broke a Motown tradition, as he became the first Motown artist to go solo whilst still an active member of a group (Diana Ross, Smokey Robinson and David Ruffin all had to leave their respective groups before becoming solo artists).

Sold around 1.6 million copies in the States alone, where it achieved no.4 on both the Hot 100 and R&B singles chart, and charted at no.5 in the UK.

Promoted in the States on the *Hellzapoppin* TV show in 1972.

Featured in the 'Michael In Wonderland' episode of the new Jackson 5 cartoon series in 1971.

Live version featured on the Michael/Jackson 5's *LIVE!* album, issued in September 1988 in the UK (no USA release). All songs on the album were recorded at a concert on 30th April 1973, at the Osaka Koseinenkin Hall in Japan. Also included on the limited edition CD, *IN JAPAN!*, released by Hip-Select in 2004 – only 5,000 copies pressed.

Title given to a cassette-only budget compilation released in 1989.

Cover versions include one by Chaka Khan, which she recorded for her eponymous 1982 album. 'I actually didn't like the original much,' she admitted, 'but Arif Mardin (her producer) was adamant I cover it. It turned out fantastic, and gave me a new respect for Michael's version.'

Other cover versions by:
The Boys (featuring Stokley of Mint Condition) – from their 1990 album of the same name.
The Lovelites – from their 1990 album, *THE LOVELIGHT YEARS*.
Smokey Robinson & The Miracles – from their 2004 album, *THE LIVE COLLECTION*.

GOT TO FIND A WAY SOMEHOW

Song written by Michael in 1979, and registered with the United States Copyright Office in November 1984 – remains unreleased.

GOTTA DANCE

Snippet of a song Michael performed as part of a three song medley – also including *Putting On the Ritz* and *They Can't Take That Away From Me* – on *The Jacksons* TV series in 1976.

GRAMMY NOMINATIONS MEDLEY

Brief medley performed by Michael and his brothers (minus Jermaine), at the Grammy Awards ceremony on 2nd March 1974, to introduce the nominees for the Best Rhythm & Blues Performance, Duo or Group: *Could It Be I'm Falling In Love*, *The Cisco Kid*, *Midnight Train To Georgia*, *Love Train* and *Be What You Are*.

GRAMMY NOMINATIONS RAP

Short ditty performed by the Jacksons at the Grammy Awards ceremony, staged in the Hollywood Palladium on 19th February 1977, to introduce the nominees for Best Rhythm & Blues Performance, Female – Natalie Cole won the award for *Sophisticated Woman (She's A Different Lady)*.

GREAT SPECKLED BIRD, THE

One of numerous songs Michael recalls singing, with his mother and siblings, as a young boy – mentioned in Katherine Jackson's autobiography, *My Family, The Jacksons*.

GREATEST HITS CLASSIC MEGAMIX

Medley of Michael's hits: *Bad, Rock With You, Don't Stop 'Til You Get Enough, Thriller, Rock With You, Remember The Time, Billie Jean, Black Or White, Thriller, The Way You Make Me Feel, Wanna Be Startin' Somethin'* and *Thriller*.

GREATEST SHOW ON EARTH

Song featured on Michael's second solo album, *BEN*, issued in August 1972 in the States and December 1972 in the UK.

GROOVE OF MIDNIGHT

Written by Rod Temperton, and dating from the *BAD* era. Short demo version by Michael surfaced on the internet in 2003 – no official release.

Recorded by Siedah Garrett for her 1988 album, *KISS*.

GUESS WHO'S MAKING WHOOPEE WITH YOUR GIRLFRIEND

Song recorded by the Jackson 5, that evolved into *Mama's Pearl*, as Berry Gordy felt the lyrics of the original song were unsuitable for the group's wholesome image.

Remains unreleased, but does exist as a bootleg recording.

HALLELUJAH DAY

Song included on the Jackson 5's album, *SKYWRITER*, released in March 1973 in the States and July 1973 in the UK.

Lyrics celebrated the end of the Vietnam War.

First single on which Michael's voice could be heard to be breaking.

Sold a disappointing 250,000 copies in the States, achieving no.10 on the R&B singles chart and no.28 on the Hot 100. Charted at no.20 in the UK.

HAPPY BIRTHDAY

Song written and originally recorded by Stevie Wonder, for his album *HOTTER THAN JULY*, issued in 1980.

Hit cover version:
David Parton – no.4 in the UK in 1977.

Michael joined Stevie on stage on 17th July 1998, to sing the song to Nelson Mandela, at his 80th birthday celebration.

HAPPY BIRTHDAY, LISA

Track featured on the Simpsons album, *SONGS IN THE KEY OF SPRINGFIELD*, issued in 1997.

Featured in the Simpsons episode titled 'Stark Raving Dad', in which Michael guested.

For many years mystery surrounded Michael's involvement with the song, however, the albums sleeve credited copyright ownership of the song to Mijac Music – Michael's publishing company, which registered the song with the United States Copyright Office in September 1991.

It has been confirmed Michael – under the pseudonym John Jay Smith – voiced his character, but *Happy Birthday, Lisa* was sung by sound-a-like, Kipp Lennon – a member of the family band, Venice. Michael was present when Lennon recorded his vocal: 'This is kind of weird,' said Lennon at the time, 'he's right next to me and I have to do him in front of everyone, on command!'

Michael's version included on the first acetate version of the special, expanded edition of his album, *DANGEROUS* – bonus disc subsequently cancelled.

HAPPY (LOVE THEME FROM 'LADY SINGS THE BLUES')

Song written by Smokey Robinson and Michael Legrand, originally included on Michael's album *MUSIC & ME*, released in April 1973 in the States and July 1973 in the UK.

Didn't feature in the movie *Lady Sings The Blues*, in which Diana Ross gave an Oscar-nominated performance as the blues singer, Billie Holiday.

Live performance by the Jacksons, at a concert in Mexico in 1976, omitted from the home video, *The Jacksons In Concert*, released in 1981 in the UK (no USA release).

Issued as a single in 1983 in many countries (no USA release), to promote the TV advertised compilation *18 GREATEST HITS*, credited to Michael Jackson Plus The Jackson 5 – the album spent three weeks at no.1 in the UK.

Picture disc single and wrap-around poster sleeve helped the single to no.52 in the UK.

Smokey Robinson's version featured on his 1975 album, *A QUIET STORM*, along with *The Wedding Song* – which Smokey wrote especially for the wedding of Jermaine Jackson and Hazel Gordy.

HAVE YOURSELF A MERRY LITTLE CHRISTMAS

Song featured on the Jackson 5's *CHRISTMAS ALBUM*, issued in October 1970 in the States and December 1970 in the UK.

Released as a single in the Philippines.

B-side of Michael's Dutch release of *Little Christmas Tree* in 1973.

HE WHO MAKES THE SKY GREY

Written by Jermaine Jackson with Sheik Abdullah of Bahrain, with vocals by Michael – no official release.

'The track was done a while ago now and was called *He Who Makes The Sky Grey*, but has not been released to date and I don't know if it ever will be,' said backing vocalist, Kim Chandler. 'Michael's vocals were already down, so we didn't get to meet him, unfortunately. However, he did ring up during the session, to speak to the session conductor – she was pretty excited!'

HEAL THE WORLD

Song written and recorded by Michael for his solo album *DANGEROUS*, released in November 1991.

Prelude composed, arranged and conducted by Marty Paich.

'Heal The World is one of my favourite of anything I have ever recorded,' said Michael in 1996, 'because it is a public awareness song. It is something that I think will live in the hearts of people for a long time, because it is about something that is very special, and something that is very innocent and something that is very important.'

Fifth single lifted from the album in the States, sixth in the UK and elsewhere. Fared poorly in the States, peaking at no.27 on the Hot 100 and no.62 on the R&B singles chart, but hit no.2 in the UK – kept out of the top spot by Whitney Houston's mega-hit, *I Will Always Love You*.

Official Versions:
Album Version.
Album Version – with special message from Michael.
7" Edit.
7" Edit With Intro.

Anti-war promo short film, directed by Joe Pytka, didn't feature Michael, but instead focussed on impoverished children playing around armed soldiers and tanks.

Lyrics included in Michael's book of poems and reflections, *Dancing The Dream*, published in 1992.

Gave its name to Michael's Heal The World Foundation, which was officially launched on 30th September 1992 in Burcharest, Romania. A playground at an orphanage, and a medical mission to Romania by 12 qualified doctors/medical staff, were among the first projects the Foundation funded.

Live performance by Michael, at his Dangerous Tour concert in Bucharest, Romania, on 1st October 1992, featured on the DVD released as part of his box-set, *THE ULTIMATE COLLECTION*, issued in November 2004.

Version including a special message from Michael featured on the compilation, *SIGNATURE SERIES*, released in the States in 1992.

Cited by Michael in his 1993 Mexican disposition, where he explained unusually for him, when he created the song he wrote both the lyrics and music at the same time.

Performed by Michael on 19th January 1993, at *An American Reunion: The 52nd Presidential Inaugural Gala*, for the incoming President, Bill Clinton, and during the half time interval at the American Super Bowl Final twelve days later.

Live performances, as part of concerts staged during Michael's *His*tory World Tour, screened in Germany and New Zealand.

Short, impromptu live performance on 16th December 1998, when Michael attended the grand opening of The Royal Towers of Atlantis resort in the Bahamas – Michael was handed a microphone and asked to sing which, somewhat reluctantly, he did.

Performed by Monica, Deborah Cox, Mya, Rah Digga and Tamia during the *Michael Jackson: 30th Anniversary Celebration, The Solo Years* concerts, staged at New York's Madison Square Garden on 7th and 10th September 2001.

Fifteenth of Michael's 20 *'Visionary – The Video Singles'* reissues, with the music on one side of a Dual Disc and the accompanying short film on the other side. Issued in May 2006 in the UK – charted at no.27.

HEAL THE WORLD – WE ARE THE WORLD

Medley performed by Boyz II Men at the VH1 Honors Awards in 1995 – Michael joined in with *We Are The World*, and was presented with a Special Award for his charitable works by Boyz II Men .

HEARTBREAK HOTEL

Written by Michael and recorded by the Jacksons for their album, *TRIUMPH*, released in October 1980.

Nightmarish opening scream courtesy of Michael's sister, La Toya.

Most successful Jacksons single on the R&B chart in the States, where it spent five weeks at no.2. Also charted at no.22 on the Hot 100 and no.44 in the UK.

Promo footage, of the Jacksons dancing around a swimming pool, remains unreleased.

Official Versions:
Album Version.
Single Edit.

Re-titled *This Place Hotel* on later releases, to avoid any confusion with the Elvis Presley classic with the same title (this didn't stop Whitney Houston from recording yet another song titled *Heartbreak Hotel* in 1998, and turning it into a smash hit).

Live version, titled *This Place Hotel* and recorded at a concert at Madison Square Garden in September 1981, featured on the Jacksons album, *LIVE*, issued in November 1981. This version appeared on the B-side of Michael's single, *P.Y.T. (Pretty Young Thing)*, in the UK.

Live version, recorded at one of Michael's Bad World Tour concerts in Australia, included on the home video, *A Legend Continues...*, released in 1988 (1989 in the States). Another live version, from the same tour, was screened on Nippon TV in Japan.

Sampled on numerous recordings, including:
Quo's *Quo Funk* (released on Michael's MJJ Music label in 1996).

Ideal's *Creepin' Inn*, from their eponymous 1999 album.

Ma$e's *Cheat On You*, from his 1997 album, *HARLEM WORLD*.

Heavy D & the Boyz's *Peaceful Journey*, the title track of their 1991 album.

Kik Franklin & God's Property's *You Are The Only Ones*.

Lil' Kim's *The Games In Trouble*, from the 2006 reissue of her album, *THE NAKED TRUTH*.

HEARTBREAKER

Song written by Michael with Rodney Jerkins, Fred Jerkins III, LaShawn Daniels, Mischke Butler and Norman Gregg, and recorded for his solo album *INVINCIBLE*, issued in October 2001.

HEAVEN CAN WAIT

Written by Michael with Teddy Riley, Andra Heard, Nate Smith, Teron Beal, Eritza Laues and K. Quiller, and featured on his album *INVINCIBLE*, issued in October 2001.

Scheduled for release to radio stations across the States, but cancelled. Many R&B stations started playing it anyway, resulting in a no.72 placing on the R&B singles chart during a lengthy 16 week run.

Originally lined up to feature on BLACKstreet's 1999 album, *FINALLY* – Riley stated in 2006 he planned to re-make the song, for a new BLACKstreet album.

HEAVEN HELP US ALL

Stevie Wonder song the Jackson 5 recorded a version of – remains unreleased.

Stevie took the song to no.2 on the R&B singles chart and no.9 on the Hot 100, and to no.29 in the UK, in 1970.

HEAVEN IS HERE

Poem written by Michael – included in his book of poems and reflections, *Dancing The Dream*, published in 1992.

HEAVEN KNOWS I LOVE YOU, GIRL

Song included on the Jacksons album, *GOIN' PLACES*, released in October 1977.

HEAVEN'S GIRL

Song written by R. Kelly, originally intended for Michael's HIS*TORY* album, but eventually was recorded by R. Kelly himself in 1995, for the Quincy Jones album, *Q'S JOOK JOINT*.

HERE I AM (COME AND TAKE)

Song recorded on 6th June 1973, and released for the first time – in an up-dated version – on Michael's *FAREWELL MY SUMMER LOVE* album, issued in May 1984 in the States and July 1984 in the UK.

Title given to a reissue of *FAREWELL MY SUMMER LOVE*, originating from Germany.

Original version remains unreleased.

Originally recorded by Al Green, and featured on his 1973 album, *CALL ME*. Single achieved no.2 on the R&B singles chart and no.10 on the Hot 100 in the States.

HE'S MY BROTHER

Song La Toya Jackson recorded for her 1995 album, *BAD GIRL*, as a tribute to brother Michael – the song sampled a snippet of his hit, *Bad*.

HE'S MY SUNNY BOY

Supremes cover, re-titled *I'm Your Sunny Boy* as Michael could hardly sing 'He's my sunny boy', the Jackson 5 are known to have recorded – remains unreleased.

Original version featured on the 1968 Supremes album, *LOVE CHILD*.

HIGHER GROUND

Stevie Wonder song that Michael was scheduled to record with Donny Osmond, as confirmed by Donny in an interview with the UK's GMTV in late 2003 – remains unreleased.

Stevie's original topped the R&B singles chart and peaked at no.4 on the Hot 100 in the States, and no.29 in the UK, in 1973.

*HIST*ORY

Written by Michael with James Harris III and Terry Lewis, and recorded for the album, HIST*ORY*, released in June 1995.
Backing vocals by Boyz II Men.

New pressings of HIST*ORY* in 1996 saw a slight modification to the opening of *History*, which used parts of Mussorgsky's *The Great Gates Of Kiev*.

Released as a double A-side single, with *Ghosts*, in many countries (no USA release). Charted at no.5 in the UK, where radio stations favoured *History* over *Ghosts*.

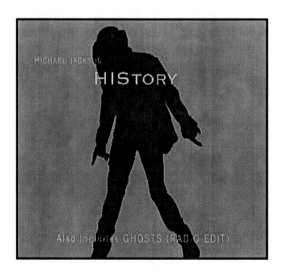

Official Versions:
Album Version.   The Ummah DJ Mix.
Album Version – different intro.   The Ummah Main Acappella.

MARK!'s Future Dub.
MARK!'s Keep Movin' Dub.
MARK!'s Phly Vocal.
MARK!'s Radio Edit.
MARK!'s Vocal Club Mix.
MARK!'s Vocal Dub Mix.

The Ummah Radio Mix.
The Ummah Urban Mix.
Tony Moran's History Lesson.
Tony Moran's History Lesson Edit.
Tony Moran's Historical Dub.

Promoted with live footage filmed during Michael's *His*tory World Tour – directed by Jim Gable. Featured the Tony Moran Remix. Screened on *Top Of The Pops* and the Lottery show in the UK.

Short His*tory Teaser* directed by Rupert Wainright – filmed in Hungary.

Featured in an advert for Michael's isotonic drink, *Mystery*.

*HIS*TORY (album message)

Special message Michael recorded for inclusion on some pressings of his HIS*TORY* album, distributed in France, Germany and Holland. Michael said:

> *'Hi, this is Michael Jackson. I want to thank all my fans in (country) for their continuing support over all the years. I hope to come and visit you very, very soon and perform for you all. I look forward to seeing you. Until then I'd like to say goodbye. I love you. Take care. 'Bye.'*

*HIS*TORY BEGINS MEDLEY

Short (2 minutes 38 seconds) promo CD with a medley of hits featured on the first CD – titled '*His*tory Begins' – from Michael's album, HIS*TORY*, released in 1995.

Songs featured: *Thriller (Intro), Billie Jean, Black Or White, Rock With You, Bad, Beat It, Remember The Time, The Way You Make Me Feel, Man In The Mirror, Don't Stop 'Til You Get Enough* and *Thriller*.

H.M.S. PINAFORE

Spoof performed by the Jackson 5 on the *Sandy In Disneyland* TV special in the States in April 1974, where they also performed a medley of their hits.

HOLD ON! I'M A COMIN'

Sam & Dave hit the Jackson 5 often performed on the Chitli' Circuit in the mid-to-late 1960s, as confirmed by their father Joseph, in an interview with *Blues & Soul* magazine in 1978.

Sam & Dave took the song to no.1 on the R&B singles chart and no.21 on the Hot 100 in the States in 1966 – not a hit in the UK.

HOLIDAY INN

Song written by Michael in 1976, and registered with the United States Copyright Office in November 1984 – remains unreleased.

HONEY CHILE

Song recorded by the Jackson 5 for their album, *MAYBE TOMORROW*, issued in April 1971 in the States and October 1971 in the UK.

Featured in the 'Farmer Jackson' episode of the Jackson 5's cartoon series in 1971.

Originally recorded by Martha Reeves & The Vandellas, and featured on their 1968 album, *RIDIN' HIGH*. Single charted at no.5 on the R&B singles chart and no.11 on the Hot 100 in the States, and no.30 in the UK.

HONEY LOVE

Song on the Jackson 5's *MOVING VIOLATION* album, released in May 1975 in the States and July 1975 in the UK.

HOT FEVER

Michael's original title for his hit, *The Way You Make Me Feel*, written in 1985 and registered with the United States Copyright Office in October that year – remains unreleased.

See also: *Way You Make Me Feel, The*.

HOT STREET

Song written by Rod Temperton that failed to make Michael's album, *THRILLER*, as Temperton and Quincy Jones didn't feel it was strong enough. Michael, however, said at his Mexican disposition hearing that he liked the song – remains unreleased.

Early demo version titled *Slapstick*.

HOW CAN YOU MEND A BROKEN HEART

Song recorded by the Bee Gees for their 1971 album, *TRAFALGAR*, which Michael sang a few lines from during an interview in 2004.

'And "How can you stop the rain from falling down?" sang Michael. 'I love that. "How can you stop the sun from shining? What makes the world go 'round?"' sang Michael, joined by film/music video director, Brett Ratner. 'I love that stuff! And when they (the Bee Gees) did *Saturday Night Fever*, that did it for me. I said, "I gotta do this – I know I can do this"… And I just started writing songs. I wrote *Billie Jean*, I wrote *Beat It*, *(Wanna Be) Startin' Somethin'*. Just writing – it was fun.'

HOW FUNKY IS YOUR CHICKEN

Song included on the Jackson 5's *THIRD ALBUM*, issued in September 1970 in the States and February 1971 in the UK.

Released as a single in Holland and Sweden.

Featured in 'The Winners Circle' episode of the Jackson 5's cartoon series in 1971.

HOW MUCH DO YOU GET FOR YOUR SOUL

Song recorded by the Pretenders, for their 1986 album, *GET CLOSE* – allegedly written as a swipe at Michael, following his massive sponsorship deal with Pepsi.

HOW SWEET IT IS (TO BE LOVED BY YOU)

Marvin Gaye hit the Jackson 5 recorded a version of – remains unreleased.

Hit versions:
Marvin Gaye – no.49 in the UK in 1964; no.4 on the R&B singles chart and no.6 on the Hot 100 in the States in 1965.
Jr. Walker & The All Stars – no.3 on the R&B singles chart and no.18 on the Hot 100, and no.22 in the UK, in 1966.
James Taylor – no.5 on the Hot 100 in 1975.
Tyrone Davis – no.36 on the R&B singles chart in 1980.

HUM ALONG AND DANCE

Song the Jackson 5 recorded for their album, *GET IT TOGETHER*, released in September 1973 in the States and November 1973 in the UK. Lead vocals – such as they were – by Jackie and Tito Jackson.

Originally recorded by the Temptations, for their 1970 album, *PSYCHEDELIC SHACK* – also recorded by another Motown act, Rare Earth, for their 1973 album, *MA*.

All three versions – including the Jackson 5's – produced by Norman Whitfield.

Rare Earth's version charted at no.95 on the R&B singles chart, and at no.110 on the 'bubbling under' section of the Hot 100, in the States in 1973.

Essentially an instrumental track, with scatting and improvised vocals – the song's chorus states, 'ain't no words to this song, you just dance and hum along.' Michael, in the Jackson 5 version, on hearing the song's chorus can be heard saying: 'Ain't no words? What you mean?' – to which Tito responds, 'we ain't had time to write none!'

Performed by the Jacksons on their TV series in 1976.

United Future Organization Mix issued to dance clubs in Japan in 1999, with release on the album, *SOUL SOURCE – JACKSON 5 REMIXES*, the following year.

Uncut version, clocking in at nearly 15 minutes, featured as a bonus track on the two albums on one CD reissue of *JOYFUL JUKEBOX MUSIC & BOOGIE*, issued in 2004 in the States (no UK release).

HUMAN NATURE

Written by Steve Porcaro and John Bettis. Porcaro recorded a rough demo on a cassette, which fellow Toto band David Paitch put three songs on for Quincy Jones to listen to, as possibles for *THRILLER*. Quincy didn't like Paitch's songs, but he did like the rough demo of *Human Nature* at the end of the tape, and asked if he could use it.

Last song selected for *THRILLER*, issued in December 1982 – it ousted *Carousel* from the final track listing.

Released as a single in most countries, but not the UK, where it was the B-side of *Leave Me Alone*. Charted at no.7 on the Hot 100 and no.27 on the R&B singles chart in the States.

Alternate version, with a slight difference in the short instrumental segment mid-way through the song, featured on the Japanese 3" CD single, *Thriller*.

Official Versions:
Album Version.
Edit.
Alternate Version.

Live performance by Michael, at his Dangerous Tour concert in Bucharest, Romania, on 1st October 1992, featured on the DVD released as part of his box-set, *THE ULTIMATE COLLECTION*, issued in November 2004.

Different live performance screened on Nippon TV in Japan, as part of one of Michael's concerts.

Sampled on a remixed version of *Right Here*, by SWV: Sisters With Voices. Logged seven weeks at no.1 on the R&B singles chart in the States, and achieved no.2 on the Hot 100, in 1993 – charted at no.3 in the UK. RIAA Gold Record (USA half-million seller). Featured on the original soundtrack album, *FREE WILLY*. Sampled on *Thug Nature* by Tupac '2Pac' Shakur, featured on his 2001 album, *TOO GANSTA FOR RADIO*.

Sampled on numerous other recordings, including:
The Power Of Human Nature – a popular 1989 bootleg recording also featuring Snap's *The Power*.
It Ain't Hard To Tell by Nas, on his 1997 album, *ILLMATIC*.
Thug Nature by Tupac '2Pac' Shakur, featured on his 2001 album, *TOO GANSTA FOR RADIO* (samples SWV's *Right Here/Human Nature*).
Why Why, a track on BLACKstreet's 2003 album, *LEVEL II*.
A remix of the 2006 no.1 hit *So Sick*, by Ne-Yo featuring LL Cool J – featured on the latter's 2006 album, *TODD SMITH*.

Cover versions recorded by Boyz II Men, with Claudette Ortiz, for their 2004 album, *THROWBACK*, and by David Mead for his 2004 album, *INDIANA*.

HURT, THE

Song written by Michael with brother Randy in collaboration with Toto's David Paich and Steve Porcaro.

Recorded by the Jacksons for their *VICTORY* album, issued in July 1984.

I AIN'T GONNA EAT MY HEART OUT ANYMORE

One of seven previously unheard songs included on the Jackson 5's album, *BOOGIE*, released on the Natural Resources label in January 1979 in North America only.

Album quickly withdrawn, and not made available again until 2004, when it and *JOYFUL JUKEBOX MUSIC* were released on one CD (no UK release).

Original version by the Young Rascals featured on their eponymous 1966 album.

I AM LOVE

Longish song recorded by the Jackson 5 for their album *DANCING MACHINE*, issued in September 1974 in the States and November 1974 in the UK.

Lead vocals by Jermaine (later Marlon, after four of the Jackson 5 left Motown). Split into two halves for single release, with Parts 1 & 2 appearing on either side of the 7" single. Charted at no.3 on the R&B singles chart and no.15 on the Hot 100 in the States, but wasn't a hit in the UK.

Performed by the Jackson 5 on *The Cher Show* in 1975, and by the Jacksons on their TV series in 1977.

Live performance by the Jacksons, at a concert in Mexico in 1976, included on the home video, *The Jacksons In Concert*, released in 1981 in the UK (no USA release).

146

I CAN ONLY GIVE YOU LOVE

Song included on the Jackson 5's album, *LOOKIN' THROUGH THE WINDOWS*, issued in May 1972 in the States and October 1972 in the UK.

I CAN'T GET YOU OFF MY MIND

Song Michael worked on in the early 1970s, demo version/mono acetate known to exist – no official release.

I CAN'T HELP IT

Song written by Stevie Wonder and Susaye Greene, and recorded by Michael for his album *OFF THE WALL*, issued in August 1979.

B-side of the album's lead single, *Don't Stop 'Til You Get Enough*.

Sampled on:
De La Soul's *Breakadawn* in 1993 – no.30 on the R&B singles chart and no.76 on the Hot 100, and no.39 in the UK.
Mary J. Blige's *Sexy*, a track on her 1999 album, *MARY*.
Baby by Fabulous, from the 2004 album, *REAL TALK*.

Also recorded by Kashief Lindo and by Peebles.

Stevie Wonder, although he has performed the song many times in concert, including the UNCF Gala in January 2005, has never released a version of the song.

I CAN'T HELP MYSELF (SUGAR PIE, HONEY BUNCH)

Four Tops classic the Jackson 5 recorded a version of – remains unreleased.

Hit versions:
Four Tops – no.1 on the Hot 100 and R&B singles chart in the States, and no.23 in the UK, in 1965.
Four Tops (reissue) – no.10 in the UK in 1970.
Donny Elbert – no.11 in the UK, and no.14 on the R&B singles chart and no.22 on the Hot 100, in 1972.

Bonnie Pointer – no.40 on the Hot 100 and no.42 on the R&B singles chart in 1980.

Performed by the actors portraying the Jackson 5 in the TV mini-series, *The Jacksons: An American Dream*.

I CAN'T QUIT YOUR LOVE

Song featured on the Jackson 5's album, *SKYWRITER*, issued in March 1973 in the States and July 1973 in the UK.

B-side of *Whatever You Got, I Want* in the States, and of *Forever Came Today* in the UK.

Performed by the Jacksons on their TV series in 1977.

Originally recorded by the Four Tops, and featured on their 1972 album, *NATURE PLANNED IT*.

I DON'T GET AROUND MUCH ANYMORE

Song performed by the Jacksons, with special guest Caroll O'Connor, on their TV series in 1976, as a medley with *Caravan* and *Take The A Train*.

I DON'T KNOW

One of two songs written for Michael by Pharrell Williams, and recorded by Usher for his 2001 album, *8701*.

See also: *U Don't Have To Call*.

I DON'T LIVE HERE ANYMORE

Song written by Michael circa 2001, but failed to make the final selection for his *INVINCIBLE* album – remains unreleased.

Also known by the title, *I Don't Live Anymore*.

I FORGIVE YOU

Song Michael cited he had written in his court disposition in November 1993 – remains unreleased.

I FOUND A LOVE

Previously unheard demo from the pre-Motown days, that surfaced on the download only Jackson 5 compilation, *SOUL MASTERS*, made available in 2005.

I FOUND THAT GIRL

Song featured on the Jackson 5's *ABC* album, issued in May 1970 in the States and August 1970 in the UK. Lead vocals by Jermaine.

B-side of *The Love You Save* but, largely thanks to Jermaine's popularity with girls, listed alongside the A-side on many Billboard charts, including the Hot 100 and R&B singles chart – it hit no.1 on both charts. Achieved no.7 in the UK.

Featured in the 'Rasho Jackson' episode of the Jackson 5 cartoon series in 1971.

Promo red vinyl, double-sided 7" single released in the States.

I GOT A FEELING

Four Tops track the Jackson 5 recorded a version of – remains unreleased.

The Four Tops recorded the song for their 1966 album, *4 TOPS ON TOP*.

I GOT RHYTHM

Song Michael danced to on the Jacksons TV series in 1977, as female backing singers sang, 'He's got rhythm' – Michael sang the title only at the end of the song.

Written by George & Ira Gershwin, and performed by Gene Kelly in the 1951 film, *An American In Paris*.

I GOT THE FEELIN'

James Brown hit performed by the Jackson 5 during their pre-Motown days, and one of the songs performed at their Motown audition in 1968 – remains unreleased.

No.1 for James Brown in 1968 on the R&B singles chart in the States, and no.6 on the Hot 100, but failed to chart in the UK.

I HAVE THIS DREAM

Song Michael wrote with Carole Bayer Sager and David Foster – subject of a song-writing contest organised by Tonos Entertainment and AOL Music. A statement released by Tonos read:

> *'Music serves as a salve for what ails the human spirit and a remedy to the soul during troubled times. Now, these three musical icons have created an inspiring musical landscape entitled I Have This Dream, and they're asking AOL members to come up with an optimistic and uplifting lyric, to complete this anthemic song.'*

The contest attracted over 1,000 entries and was won by Ric Kipp, whose lyric 'best reflected our vision for the song'.

Widely expected to be included on Michael's album, *INVINCIBLE*, but didn't feature. Speaking to *TV Guide* in November 1999, Michael said: 'There's a song on the album called *I Have This Dream*. It's a millennium song about the world and the environment, that I wrote with Carole Bayer Sager and David Foster.'

Version, with numerous guest vocalists including R. Kelly, Snoop Dog, James Ingram, Shanice, the O'Jays and Michael's brother, Jermaine, slated for release in early 2006, in aid of the victims of Hurricane Katrina – again, failed to appear and remains unreleased.

I HAVE THIS LOVE OF ME

Song Michael cited he had written in his court disposition in November 1993 – remains unreleased.

I HEAR A SYMPHONY

Supremes cover recorded, when Michael suggested singing a male version of the song, by the Jackson 5 between 1970-73.

Remained unreleased until it was included on Michael's solo album, *LOOKING BACK TO YESTERDAY*, issued in February 1986 in the States and May 1986 in the UK – demo version also known to exist.

B-side of the promo 7" single *Love's Gone Bad*, issued in Canada only.

Version with alternate vocal take featured on the 1995 box-set, *SOULSATION!*.

The Supremes took the song to no.1 on the Hot 100 and no.2 on the R&B singles charts in the States, and no.39 in the UK, in 1965.

I HEARD IT THROUGH THE GRAPEVINE

Motown classic the Jackson 5 recorded a version of – remains unreleased.

Hit versions:
Gladys Knight & The Pips – no.1 on the R&B singles chart and no.2 on the Hot 100 in the States, and no.47 in the UK, in 1967.
Marvin Gaye (original version) – no.1 on both American charts in 1968, and no.1 in the UK in 1969.
King Curtis – no.83 on the Hot 100 in 1968.
Creedence Clearwater Revival – no.43 on the Hot 100 in 1976.
Roger – no.1 on the R&B singles chart and no.79 on the Hot 100 in 1981.
Slits – no.60 in the UK in 1979.
Marvin Gaye (reissue) – no.8 in the UK in 1986.
California Raisins – no.84 on the Hot 100 in 1988.

I JUST CAN'T STOP LOVING YOU

Song written by Michael for his album, *BAD*, released in September 1987.

Recorded as a duet with virtual unknown Siedah Garrett, after Whitney Houston and Barbra Streisand both turned down the opportunity to record the song with Michael. Siedah was unaware Quincy Jones wanted her to record the song as a duet with Michael, until she turned up for the actual recording session.

Lead single from the album, topping the Hot 100 and R&B singles chart in the States, where it was the no.3 best selling single of 1987.

RIAA Gold Record (USA million seller).

Also no.1 in Belgium, Ireland, Holland, Norway and the UK.

Spoken introduction edited from later pressings of *BAD*, plus greatest hits compilations, from HIS*TORY* onwards.

Official Versions:
Album Version (with spoken intro).   Spanish Version.
Album Version (minus spoken intro).   French Version (unreleased).
Anglo-Spanish version.

Performed live by Michael with Sheryl Crow during his Bad World Tour, and with Siedah Garrett during his Dangerous World Tour.

Live performance by Michael, at his Dangerous Tour concert in Bucharest, Romania, on 1st October 1992, featured on the DVD released as part of his box-set, *THE ULTIMATE COLLECTION*, issued in November 2004.

Different live performance aired as part of a concert screened by Nippon TV in Japan.

Performed by James Ingram and Gloria Estefan during the *Michael Jackson: 30th Anniversary Celebration, The Solo Years* concerts, staged at New York's Madison Square Garden on 7th and 10th September 2001.

Spanish and French language versions recorded by Michael and Siedah, titled *Toda Mi Amor Eres Tu* and *Je Ne Veux Pas La Fin De Nous*, respectively.

Spoken intro sampled by Sweetback, featuring Maxwell, on the track *Softly, Softly*, from Sweetback's eponymous debut album, released in 1996.

See also: *Je Ne Veux Pas La Fin De Nous, Toda Mi Amor Eres Tu.*

(I KNOW) I'M LOSING YOU

Song recorded by the Jackson 5 for their debut album, *DIANA ROSS PRESENTS THE JACKSON 5*, issued in December 1969 in the States and March 1970 in the UK.

Included on the *ABC* EP released in Portugal.

Originally recorded by the Temptations, and included on their 1967 album, *WITH A LOT 'O SOUL*. Single hit no.1 on the R&B singles chart and no.8 on the Hot 100 in the States, and no.19 in the UK.

I LIKE YOU THE WAY YOU ARE (DON'T CHANGE YOUR LOVE ON ME)

Song recorded by the Jackson 5 between 1970-73.

Remained unreleased until included on Michael's album, *LOOKING BACK TO YESTERDAY*, issued in February 1986 in the States and May 1986 in the UK.

I LOVE YOU

Words Michael sang when James Brown, the Godfather of Soul, called him up on stage at a concert staged at the Beverly Theater, Los Angeles, in September 1983. Brown, at Michael's insistence, then called Prince on stage, to introduce him to the crowd.

At the 3rd annual BET Awards in June 2003, Michael presented Brown with a long silver cloak, as he was given a Lifetime Achievement Award.

'I am extremely shocked and saddened by the death of my mentor and friend,' said Michael in an official statement, issued following James Brown's death on Christmas Day 2006. 'Words cannot adequately express the love and respect that I will always have for Mr. Brown. There has not been, and will never be, another like him. He is irreplaceable. I send my love and heartfelt condolences to his family.'

Michael attended the funeral in Augusta, Georgia. 'I don't care what the media says tonight, James Brown wanted Michael Jackson here with him today,' the Rev. Al Sharpton, who led the ceremony, told the 9,000 mourners. '(James Brown) said, "I love Michael… tell him, don't worry about coming home. They always scandalise those that have talent".'

I LOVE YOU, ALPHA BITS

Advertising jingles the Jackson 5 performed in 1971, to promote breakfast cereals – several different were shot, including:

- Airship No.1 – featured the Jackson 5 floating away in a balloon, while singing and talking about the breakfast cereal.

- Airship No.2 – featured the group singing *ABC*, with Michael saying, 'Can you dig it? Well, you got it – that's our smash hit, *ABC*!'

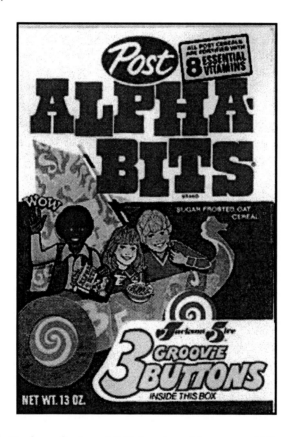

- Bunk Beds – featured Michael waking up, sliding down a fire pole, and joining his brothers at the breakfast table, singing, 'Give me a U, give me a P, getting up with Alpha Bits is E-Z!'

- Convertible Car & Park – featured the Jackson 5 running around in fast motion, with Michael singing, 'Give me an A, give me a B, gotta have my Alpha Bits with *ABC*!'

- Sugar Smacks – featured the Jackson 5 singing *I'll Be There*, with a cartoon character talking about the free records on the back of Super Sugar Crisp and Super Orange Crisp breakfast cereals.

A couple of other commercials are rumoured to have been made, but were probably not released: one with the Jackson 5 in a clubhouse, and the second with the group sitting around a piano and eating cereal. The latter also shows Michael's brothers rolling him around inside a giant cheerio (stills from this commercial are known to exist).

Three breakfast cereal packet designs featured the Jackson 5:

- Alpha Bits – version A: with song titles on cartoon flowers, no mention on the Jackson 5. Played one of three songs: 1. *Sugar Daddy*. 2. *Goin' Back To Indiana*. 3. *Who's Lovin' You*.

- Alpha Bits – version B: similar to version A. Played one of three songs: 1. *I'll Be There*. 2. *Never Can Say Goodbye*. 3. *Mama's Pearl*.

- Rice Krinkles – with a photo of the Jackson 5 standing off to the left. Played one of five songs: 1. *ABC*. 2. *I Want You Back*. 3. *I'll Bet You*. 4. *Darling Dear*. 5. *Maybe Tomorrow*.

I NEED YOU

One of 19 'Rare & Unreleased' tracks on the fourth CD of the Michael/Jackson 5 box-set, *SOULSATION!*, issued in June 1995 in the States and July 1995 in the UK. Credited to Jermaine Jackson.

I NEED YOU

Song recorded by Michael's nephews (brother Tito's three sons), 3T, for their debut album, *BROTHERHOOD*, issued in 1995.

Featured Michael on backing vocals.

Charted at no.3 in the UK (no USA release).

Official Versions:
Album Version.   Linslee Campbell Remix.
Christmas Mix.   Singalong Version.
Linslee Campbell Breakdown Mix.

I NEVER HAD A GIRL

B-side of *Let Me Carry Your Schoolbooks*, a single issued by Steel-Town Records in the States in 1971, credited to 'The Ripples & Waves + Michael' – a name the Jackson 5 reputedly used in the early days.

Nearly 20 years later Gordon Keith, founder and owner of Steel-Town Records, stated: 'The fine vocals were provided by another Gary, Indiana talent, Michael Rodgers' – not Michael Jackson.

Both songs featured on the Jackson 5 album, *PRE-HISTORY – THE LOST STEELTOWN RECORDINGS*, released in the States in June 1996 (no UK release). The sleeve notes implied, without actually saying, the Jackson 5 and the Ripples & Waves + Michael were one and the same group.

I NEVER HEARD

Written by Michael with Paul Anka, and recorded by Safire for her album, *I WASN'T BORN YESTERDAY*, issued in 1991 in the States (no UK release).

I ONLY HAVE EYES FOR YOU

Song Jermaine recorded, with the Jackson 5 on backing vocals, for his debut solo album, *JERMAINE*, released in 1972.

No.1 for Art Garfunkel in the UK, and no.18 on the Hot 100 in the States, in 1975.

I SAW MOMMY KISSING SANTA CLAUS

Song the Jackson 5 recorded for their *CHRISTMAS ALBUM*, issued in October 1970 in the States and December 1970 in the UK.

Released as a single in a limited number of countries (excluding the USA and UK), including New Zealand, where it charted at no.3, and the Philippines.

Lead song from a four track EP, *Merry Christmas From Michael Jackson With The Jackson 5*, released in the UK in 1987 – it charted at a lowly no.91.

Other hit versions:
Jimmy Boyd – no.1 in the States and no.3 in the UK in 1953.
Beverley Sisters – no.6 in the UK in 1953.
Billy Cotton & His Band – no.11 in the UK in 1953.
4 Seasons – no.19 on the Christmas singles chart in the States in 1964.

I SHOT THE SHERIFF

Eric Clapton hit the Jacksons performed on their TV series in 1976, along with War's *The Cisco Kid*.

Clapton took the song to no.1 on the Hot 100 in the States, and no.9 in the UK, in 1974.

I WANNA BE WHERE YOU ARE

Song Michael recorded for his debut solo album, *GOT TO BE THERE*, released in January 1972 in the States and May 1972 in the UK.

Written by Leon Ware and Arthur 'T-Boy' Ross – Diana's younger brother.

Issued as a single in the USA (but not UK), where it achieved no.2 on the R&B singles chart and no.16 on the Hot 100.

B-side of *Ain't No Sunshine* in the UK.

Featured in the 'Michael White' episode of the new Jackson 5 cartoon series in 1971.

Promoted by Michael on *American Bandstand* in 1971, and at a five day Black Expo – Save The Children concert, in Chicago in 1972.

Live version by the Jackson 5, recorded at the 'Black Expo' event, included on the double *SAVE THE CHILDREN* album issued in 1974.

Second live version featured on the Michael/Jackson 5's *LIVE!* album, issued in September 1988 in the UK (no USA release). All songs on the album were recorded at a concert on 30th April 1973, at the Osaka

Koseinenkin Hall in Japan. Also included on the limited edition CD, *IN JAPAN!*, released by Hip-Select in 2004 – only 5,000 copies pressed.

Performed by Monday Michiru remix featured on the album, *SOUL SOURCE – JACKSON 5 REMIXES*, released in Japan in 2000.

Recorded by Motown song-writer Willie Hutch for his 1973 album, *FULLY EXPOSED*.

Cover version by Jason Weaver featured on the album, *THE JACKSONS: AN AMERICAN DREAM*, issued in October 1992 in the States and July 1993 in the UK. Included on a three track promo CD single circulated to American radio stations, but no commercial release followed.

Numerous other covers versions recorded, including those by Marvin Gaye and the Fugees.

Song's hook used by the Fugees on a song unofficially titled *Wannabe*, which leaked in 2006.

I WANT TO BE FREE

Original title of the Jackson 5's debut hit, *I Want You Back*.

I WANT TO TAKE YOU HIGHER

Live recording by the Jackson 5, from their concert in Gary, Indiana, on 29th May 1971, included on the album *GOIN' BACK TO INDIANA*, issued in the States in September 1971 (no UK release). Footage featured on the group's *Goin' Back To Indiana* TV special, which aired on 19th September 1971.

I WANT YOU BACK

Song originally titled *I Want To Be Free*, and written for Gladys Knight & The Pips.

Recorded by the Jackson 5, as their debut Motown single and for their debut album, *DIANA ROSS PRESENTS THE JACKSON 5*, released in December 1969 in the States and March 1970 in the UK.

160

Hit no.1 on both the Hot 100 and R&B singles chart in the USA, and achieved no.2 in the UK.

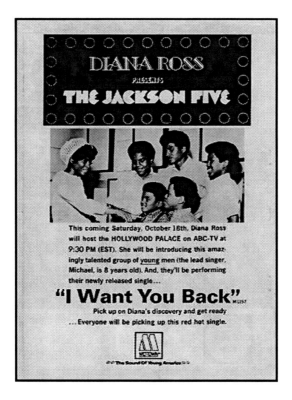

Promo 7" red vinyl single released in the States.

Promoted in the States on numerous TV shows, including: *Hollywood Palace Special* (where strings were added to the background music for the first time, pleasing Michael), *Ed Sullivan Show*, *Joey Bishop Show*, *American Bandstand*, *Andy Williams Show*, *Soul Train*, the *Goin' Back To Indiana* TV special and the group's own TV special.

Featured in the 'Drafted' episode of the Jackson 5's cartoon series in 1971 – alternate mix had Jackie ad-libbing rather than Jermaine.

Newly recorded version, with an introduction by Bill Cosby and Tommy Smothers, included on the Jackson 5's album, *GOIN' BACK TO INDIANA*, issued in September 1971 in the States (no UK release).

Previously unreleased live medley of *I Want You Back* and *ABC*, recorded at the Jackson 5's Los Angeles concert on 26th August 1972, featured on the TV soundtrack album, *THE JACKSONS: AMERICAN DREAM*, issued in October 1992 in the States and July 1993 in the UK.

Remixed in 1988 by Phil Harding, and credited to Michael Jackson with the Jackson 5. Promoted with the clip from the 'Drafted' cartoon episode. Achieved no.8 in the UK (no USA release).

Covered by numerous artists, including: the Newtrons (co-produced by Michael's eldest brother Jackie in 1990), Human Nature, Diana Ross, Graham Parker, David Ruffin, Martha Reeves, Incubus, Lauryn Hill, Red Hot Chilli Peppers and Jive Bunny & The Mastermixers.

Sampled by numerous artists, including:
Jermaine Jackson in 1991, on his *Word To The Badd!!* – charted at
  no.78 on the Hot 100 and no.88 on the R&B singles chart in the USA.
Kris Kross in 1992, on their global hit, *Jump* – no.1 on both American
  charts, and no.2 in the UK.
Nadanuf in 1997, on the track, *The Breaks Featuring Kurtis Blow*.
Tamia on her 1998 hit, *Imagination* – charted at no.12 on the R&B
  singles chart and no.37 on the Hot 100 in the States.
BLACKstreet & Maya's 'Want U Back Mix' of their 1998 hit, *Take Me
  There* – peaked at no.10 on the R&B singles chart and no.14 on the
  Hot 100 in the States, and no.7 in the UK.

Jay-Z on *Izzo (H.O.V.A.)* – peaked at no.4 on the Hot 100 and no.8 on the R&B singles chart in the States, and no.21 in the UK, in 2001.

Cover version by Cleopatra in 1998 – charted at no.4 in the UK.

Original Jackson 5 recording remixed by Sean 'Puffy' Combs in 1998, for the album *MOTOWN 40 – THE MUSIC IS FOREVER*. Featured added rap by Black Rob, with additional lyrics heard on the fade. Scheduled release as a single in the UK cancelled, following the success of Cleopatra's cover version – promo CD single issued.

Adaptation, featuring a studio recreated loop of *I Want You Back*, titled *My Baby* by Lil' Romeo (11 year old son of hip-hop artist Percy 'Master P' Miller) in 2001 – hit no.1 on the R&B singles chart and no.3 on the Hot 100 in the States, but only achieved no.67 in the UK.

Kei's Routine Jazz Party Mix, with alternate vocals, included on the Japanese album *SOUL SOURCE – JACKSON 5 REMIXES* in 2000, and the album *SOUL LEGENDS*. The former album also included the Readymade 5247 Mix.

Z-Trip Remix, on the album *MOTOWN REMIXED* in 2005, featured alternate vocals. The Australian version of the album featured alternate vocals on the Suffa 'Hilltop Hoods' Remix.

Other Official Versions:

Album Version.	12" Remix.
Remix Edit ('88).	PWL Remix ('88).
You Know We Got Soul Dub Mix.	Black Rob Club Mix ('98).
Black Rob Acappela ('98).	Black Rob TV Track ('98).
Black Rob Instrumental ('98).	
Clean Radio Edit w/rap ('98).	
Black Rob Radio Edit w/out rap ('98).	

Featured on an unreleased remix of 3T's *Sex Appeal*, which also featured Dealz – Jackie Jackson's son, Siggy.

Ranked no.9 on MTV and *Rolling Stone* magazine's poll in November 2000, to find the '100 Greatest Pop Songs' of all time.

Performed by the Jacksons during the *Michael Jackson: 30th Anniversary Celebration, The Solo Years* concerts, staged at New York's Madison Square Garden on 7th and 10th September 2001. *My Baby* performed by Lil' Romeo & Master P during the same concerts.

I WANT YOU BACK – ABC

Medley the Jackson 5 performed on the *Ed Sullivan Show* in 1970, at the Black Expo – Save The Children concert in 1972, on *Sandy In Disneyland* in 1974, and on their own TV series in 1976.

Previously unreleased live medley recorded at the Jackson 5's Los Angeles concert on 26th August 1972, featured on the TV soundtrack album, *THE JACKSONS: AMERICAN DREAM*, issued in October 1992 in the States and July 1993 in the UK.

I WANT YOU BACK – ABC – I'LL BE THERE – BEN – DADDY'S HOME – NEVER CAN SAY GOODBYE – THE LOVE YOU SAVE

Medley Michael and his brothers performed when they guested on the Mills Brothers' TV show in 1974.

I WANT YOU BACK – ABC – THE LOVE YOU SAVE

Medley the Jackson 5 performed on *The Flip Wilson Show* in 1971.

164

Live version featured on the Michael/Jackson 5's *LIVE!* album, issued in September 1988 in the UK (no USA release). All songs on the album were recorded at a concert on 30th April 1973, at the Osaka Koseinenkin Hall in Japan. Also included on the limited edition CD, *IN JAPAN!*, released by Hip-Select in 2004 – only 5,000 copies pressed.

Performed live by the Jackson 5, during their 1972 European Tour, at the Royal Command Performance in the UK – attended by HM The Queen Mother.

Second live performance by the Jacksons, at a concert in Mexico in 1976, included on the home video, *The Jacksons In Concert*, released in 1981 in the UK (no USA release).

Third live version, recorded at a concert at Madison Square Garden in September 1981, featured on the Jacksons album, *LIVE*, issued in November 1981.

I WANT YOU BACK – I'LL BE THERE – NEVER CAN SAY GOODBYE – THE LOVE YOU SAVE – DANCING MACHINE

Medley the Jackson 5 performed when they guested on Cher's TV show in 1974.

I WANT YOU BACK – THE LOVE YOU SAVE

Medley performed live by the Jacksons at *Motown 25: Yesterday, Today, Forever*, staged in the Pasadena Civic Auditorium on 25th March 1983.

Jermaine rejoined his brothers, to reform the Jackson 5, for the start of the medley, before young Randy came on stage as well – the six brothers also performed versions of *Never Can Say Goodbye* and *I'll Be There*.

I WANT YOU BACK – THE LOVE YOU SAVE – I'LL BE THERE

Medley Michael has performed live on numerous occasions, and screened on TV in the following countries:

- Japan (Nippon TV) – from the Bad World Tour.
- New Zealand – *His*tory World Tour.
- Germany (Sat 1) – *His*tory World Tour.

Live performance by Michael, at his Dangerous Tour concert in Bucharest, Romania, on 1st October 1992, featured on the DVD released as part of his box-set, *THE ULTIMATE COLLECTION*, issued in November 2004 – here, *I'll Be There* was listed as a separate song.

Known among fans as the 'Motown Medley'.

I WANT YOU TO COME HOME FOR CHRISTMAS

Song the Jackson 5 recorded for their *CHRISTMAS ALBUM* circa 1970, but which failed to make the final track listing – remains unreleased.

I WAS MADE TO LOVE HER

Stevie Wonder cover originally recorded between 1970-73 for a solo album by Michael, but remained unreleased until January 1979, when it was included on the Jackson 5's *BOOGIE* – issued in North America only, and quickly withdrawn.

Made available again, as a shorter edit with alternate vocal, on Michael's 1986 album, *LOOKING BACK TO YESTERDAY* – the same version was included on the Jackson 5's 1986 compilation, *ANTHOLOGY*.

Stevie took the song to no.1 on the R&B singles chart and no.2 on the 100 in the States in 1967, and no.5 in the UK.

I WILL FIND A WAY

Song the Jackson 5 recorded for the album, *MAYBE TOMORROW*, issued in April 1971 in the States and October 1971 in the UK.

B-side of *Maybe Tomorrow* in the States.

Featured in 'The Tiny Five' episode of the Jackson 5 cartoon series in 1971.

I WISH IT WOULD RAIN

Temptations hit – one of the songs the Jackson 5 performed at their Motown audition.

No.1 on the R&B singles chart for the Temptations in 1968, also no.4 on the Hot 100 and no.45 in the UK.

I YOU WE

Poem written by Michael – included in his book of poems and reflections, *Dancing The Dream*, published in 1992.

(IF I CAN'T) NOBODY CAN

Song known to have been recorded by Michael and his brothers for Motown – remains unreleased.

IF I DON'T LOVE YOU THIS WAY

Song featured on the Jackson 5's *DANCING MACHINE* album, issued in September 1974 in the States and November 1974 in the UK.

Michael, in an interview with Don Cornelius in 1974, stated he originally recorded the song for a solo album, but that it was included on *DANCING MACHINE* instead.

Performed solo by Michael on *Soul Train* in the States in 1974.

Originally recorded by the Temptations, and included on their album, *HOUSE PARTY*, released in 1974.

IF I HAVE TO MOVE A MOUNTAIN

Song the Jackson 5 recorded for *LOOKIN' THROUGH THE WINDOWS*, released in May 1972 in the States and October 1972 in the UK.

B-side of *Little Bitty Pretty One* in the USA (but not UK).

Featured on 'The Opening Act' episode of the new Jackson 5 cartoon series in 1971.

IF I TOLD YOU THAT

Song written by Rodney Jerkins, originally intended for Michael and Whitney Houston:

'That song was meant for Whitney and Michael,' Jerkins confirmed in 1998. 'We didn't make it happen and the next person was George Michael.'

Solo version recorded by Whitney, for her 1998 album, *MY LOVE IS YOUR LOVE*.

Duet version by Whitney and George Michael released as a single – achieved no.9 in the UK, and subsequently included on Whitney's compilation, *THE GREATEST HITS*, issued in 2000.

IF YOU DON'T LOVE ME

Previously unreleased recording by Michael, scheduled to be included on the expanded, special edition of *DANGEROUS* in 2001 – bonus CD shelved, so remains unreleased.

IF YOU REALLY LOVE ME

Stevie Wonder song the Jackson 5 recorded a version of – remains unreleased.

Stevie took the song to no.4 on the R&B singles chart and no.8 on the Hot 100 in the States, and to no.20 in the UK, in 1971.

IF YOU WANT HEAVEN

Song recorded by Michael and his brothers for Motown – remains unreleased.

IF YOU'D ONLY BELIEVE

Song featured on the Jackson album, *2300 JACKSON STREET*, issued in June 1989.

Michael wasn't involved with recording this track, however, he did join his family and other guests on stage, to sing it at the Jacksons Family Honours show in 1994.

IF'N I WAS GOD

Song recorded by Michael in the early-to-mid 1970s, unreleased until it appeared on his *LOOKING BACK TO YESTERDAY* album, issued in February 1986 in the States and May 1986 in the UK.

Longer version (a full minute longer), with alternate vocals, included on *THE BEST OF MICHAEL JACKSON*, released in the States in March 1995 as part of Motown's Anthology series (no UK release). On one version Michael sings, 'everyone needs...everyone', and on the other he sings, 'everyone...needs everyone'.

Originally recorded by Bobby Goldsboro, for his 1973 album, *SUMMER (THE FIRST TIME)*.

IGNITION

One of Michael's favourite R. Kelly songs – a short snippet of Michael singing the song featured in the documentary, *Living With Michael Jackson*, which first aired in the UK in February 2003.

R. Kelly took the song to no.2 on both American charts in 2002, and all the way to no.1 in the UK in 2003.

I'LL BE THERE

Song featured on the Jackson 5's *THIRD ALBUM*, released in September 1970 in the States and February 1971 in the UK.

Hastily re-worked by Willie Hutch, after Motown producer Hal Davis contacted him in the middle of the night: Motown boss Berry Gordy liked the title but not the song, and he wanted it finished for a recording session the following morning. Hutch stayed up all night, working on the song, before presenting it to Gordy at 8.00am; pleased with the new song, Gordy ordered Hutch into the studio, to arrange the vocals for the Jackson 5.

Issued as a single ahead of *Mama's Pearl*, when Berry Gordy decided a change of pace was called for.

Fourth no.1 from as many Motown releases on both charts in the States – a new record at the time. Achieved no.4 in the UK.

No.1 best selling single of 1970 in the States, ahead of Simon & Garfunkel's classic, *Bridge Over Troubled Water*.

Estimated global sales: 6 million – good enough, at the time, to make it the no.2 best selling Motown single of all time, after Marvin Gaye's *I Heard It through The Grapevine*.

Featured in the 'Pinestock USA' episode of the Jackson 5 cartoon series in 1971.

Cited by Michael, in the early 1970s, as one of his three favourite songs he had recorded for Motown, along with *ABC* and *Never Can Say Goodbye*.

Performed by the Jackson 5 on the *Jim Nabors Hour* in September 1970, and for a TV advertisement for Sugar Crisp breakfast cereal in the States.

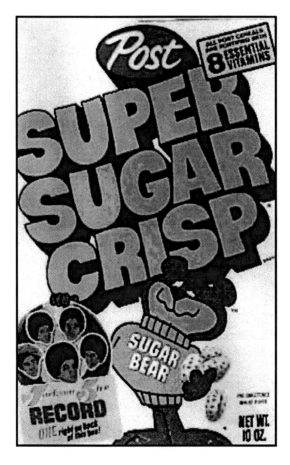

Used as the closing song for *The Jacksons* TV series in the States in 1976 and 1977.

Live version, recorded at a concert at Madison Square Garden in September 1981, featured on the Jacksons album, *LIVE*, issued in November 1981.

Live performance by the Jacksons, at a concert in Mexico in 1976, included on the home video, *The Jacksons In Concert*, released in 1981 in the UK (no USA release). Another performance, part of a Destiny tour concert, screened on BBC2 in the UK.

Performed live by the Jacksons at *Motown 25: Yesterday, Today, Forever*, staged in the Pasadena Civic Auditorium on 25th March 1983.

Title given to a budget cassette compilation released in the States in 1989.

Adult version scheduled to appear on the cancelled compilation, *DECADE 1980-1990* – remains unreleased.

Small Circle Of Friends Remix, as included on the Japanese album, *SOUL SOURCE – JACKSON 5 REMIXES* in 2000, featured alternate vocals.

Recorded by Willie Hutch for his 1973 album, *FULLY EXPOSED*.

Cover version by Mariah Carey, from a MTV Unplugged session and featuring uncredited vocals by Trey Lorenz, went all the way to no.1 on the Hot 100 in 1992 – also achieved no.11 on the R&B singles chart and no.2 in the UK. Featured on Mariah's third album, *MTV UNPLUGGED*, and was her sixth no.1 on the Hot 100.

Covered by numerous other artists, including Gloria Gaynor, Westlife, Temptations and Dane Bowers.

A cappella version recorded by Michael in 1993, for a Pepsi Cola commercial.

Previously unreleased version, with alternate lyrics and a longer, unfaded close, included on Michael's *LOVE SONGS* album, issued in the UK in January 2002 (no USA release).

I'LL BE THERE – FEELIN' ALRIGHT

Medley the Jackson 5 performed the *Diana!* TV special, first aired in the States on 18th April 1971.

Featured on the TV soundtrack album of the same title, released in March 1971 in the States and October 1971 in the UK.

See also: *Feelin' Alright*.

I'LL BET YOU

Song featured on the Jackson 5's *ABC* album, issued in May 1970 in the States and August 1970 in the UK.

Featured in the 'Mistaken Identity' episode of the Jackson 5 cartoon series in 1971.

Official Versions:
Album Version.
Edit.

The edited version featured on later vinyl copies of *ABC*.

Originally recorded by Funkadelic for their debut, eponymous album, issued in 1970.

I'LL COME HOME TO YOU

Song Michael recorded for his solo album, *FOREVER, MICHAEL*, released in January 1975 in the States and March 1975 in the UK.

I'LL TURN TO STONE

Four Tops hit the Jackson 5 recorded a version of – remains unreleased.

The Four Tops took the song to no.50 on the R&B singles chart and no.76 on the Hot 100 in the States in 1967.

I'M GLAD IT RAINED

One of 19 'Rare & Unreleased' tracks on the fourth CD of the Michael/Jackson 5 box-set, *SOULSATION!*, issued in June 1995 in the States and July 1995 in the UK.

I'M IN LOVE AGAIN

Song recorded by Minnie Riperton, with Michael on backing vocals – released in 1980, after her death, on her album *LOVE LIVES FOREVER*.

Michael paid tribute to Minnie on the back of the album sleeve: 'She was phenomenal – she did things with her voice that were incredible.'

I'M IN LOVE WITH MICHAEL JACKSON'S ANSWERPHONE

Novelty single recorded by Julie, released in the UK in October 1984 – not a hit. Name-checked several of Michael's hits, including *Beat It* and *Billie Jean*.

I'M MY BROTHER'S KEEPER

Song recorded by Jermaine Jackson, for his 1982 album, *I LIKE YOUR STYLE*.

Prevented from joining his brothers on their Triumph Tour, Jermaine instead went into the studio, to record a new album for Motown – including this song about Michael:

'When they went on the road,' said Jermaine, 'I went into the studio and did that song – I wanted to show how much I care about Michael.'

I'M SO HAPPY

Non-album recording by the Jackson 5.

B-side of *Sugar Daddy*, issued in November 1971 in the States and March 1972 in the UK.

Featured in the 'Groove To The Chief' episode of the new Jackson 5 cartoon series in 1971.

Made its first album appearance in October 2000, on the Jackson 5's double CD, *ANTHOLOGY* (no UK release).

IN OUR SMALL WAY

Song Michael recorded for his debut solo album, *GOT TO BE THERE*, issued in January 1972 in the States and May 1972 in the UK. Also included on Michael's second solo album, *BEN*, released in 1972.

Featured in the 'Groove To The Chief' episode of the new Jackson 5 cartoon series in 1971.

Included on the *Ben* EP released in Brazil.

IN THE BACK

Written and recorded by Michael between 1994-2004.

Scheduled to feature on Michael's 1997 album, *BLOOD ON THE DANCE FLOOR*, until *Superfly Sister* replaced it – early press releases listed it as one of the tracks on the album.

Remained unreleased until it was included on his box-set, *THE ULTIMATE COLLECTION*, issued in November 2004.

IN THE CLOSET

Written by Michael with Teddy Riley, and recorded by Michael for his album, *DANGEROUS*, issued in November 1991.

Originally titled *(Coming) Out Of the Closet*, and intended as a duet by Michael and Madonna. Demo version believed to exist – no official release.

Demo version also recorded by Michael solo, which has leaked on the internet – no official release. Other demo versions also known to exist.

'He (Michael) did a demonstration record for me,' said Riley, 'and he was the one who actually came up with the structure of how the song should come out. He would work out these string lines on the synthesiser, then he came up with these mouth sounds that were very percussive – sort of like a drum machine, but different. And it all worked.'

Credited to Michael and 'Mystery Girl' – whose identity was rumoured to be Madonna or Paula Abdul, but proved to be Princess Stephanie of Monaco.

Third single from *DANGEROUS*, released ahead of *Who Is It*, when Michael heard director Herb Ritts' ideas for the promo short film.

176

Promo premiered on 23rd April 1992. Co-starred supermodel Naomi Campbell – banned in South Africa because of its 'very sensual nature which could offend viewers.'

Hit no.1 on the R&B singles chart in the States, and charted at no.6 on the Hot 100 and no.8 in the UK.

RIAA Gold Record (USA million seller).

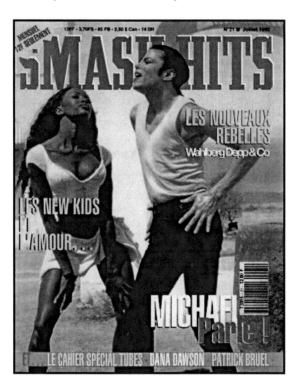

Official Versions:
Album Version.
Club Edit.
Club Mix.
Freestyle Mix.
KI's 12".
Mix Of Life.
Radio Edit.
The Mission.
The Mission Radio Edit.

The Newark Mix.
The Promise.
The Reprise.
The Vow.
Touch Me Dub.
Underground Dub.
Underground Mix.
7" Edit.

Live performances, as part of *His*tory World Tour concerts, televised in Germany and New Zealand.

Thirteenth of Michael's 20 *'Visionary – The Video Singles'* reissues, with the music on one side of a Dual Disc and the accompanying short film on the other side. Issued in May 2006 in the UK – charted at no.20.

IN THE LIFE OF CHICO

One of five songs hand-written by Michael circa 1979 – lyrics included in a personal notebook, with young actor Mark Lester on the cover, that formed part of a 10,000+ piece collection of Jackson memorabilia purchased by Universal Express and some of its entertainment partners, in November 2006.

IN THE STILL OF THE NITE (I'LL REMEMBER)

Boyz II Men recording featured in the TV mini-series, *The Jacksons: An American Dream*, and included on the accompanying soundtrack album, issued in October 1992 in the States and July 1993 in the UK.

Single release included *Snippets From The Jacksons: An American Dream*, and a live Jackson 5 medley of *I Want You Back* and *ABC*, lifted from the album.

Charted at no.3 on the Hot 100 and no.4 on the R&B singles chart in the States, and no.27 in the UK.

Other hits versions:
Five Satins – no.3 on the R&B singles chart and no.24 on the Hot 100 in the States in 1956.

See also: *Snippets From The Jacksons: An American Dream, Medley: I Want You Back – ABC (Live)*

IN THE VALLEY

Song Michael cited he had written in his court disposition in November 1993 – remains unreleased.

INVINCIBLE

Written by Michael with Rodney Jerkins, Fred Jerkins III, LaShawn Daniels and Norman Gregg.

Title track of Michael's album *INVINCIBLE*, issued in October 2001.

A lot of songs Michael worked on with Rodney Jerkins during the *INVINCIBLE* sessions remain unreleased, as Jerkins told *Cut* magazine:

'I really want people to hear some of the stuff we did together which never made the cut,' he said. 'There's a whole lot of stuff, just as good, maybe better. People have gotta hear it... Michael records hundreds of songs for an album, so we cut it down to thirty-five of the best tracks, and picked from there. It's not always about picking the hottest tracks, it's gotta have a flow, so there's a good album's worth of material that could blow your mind.'

IOWA

Piece of classical music written by Michael, as confirmed by his sister Janet, in an interview with *Q* magazine in 1993 – remains unreleased.

'He (Michael) has a song called *Iowa*, that he wrote – people will never hear that song,' said Janet. 'Just before he left to film *The Wiz*, he put all the songs he had written on to tape in the studio in our parents' house. Not one of them has been heard and those were songs to cry for. These are the things that he's written for orchestras, that are classical music – like something by Bach or Beethoven.'

IS IT SCARY

Written by Michael with James Harris III and Terry Lewis, and originally for the movie, *Addams Family Values* and a greatest hits compilation scheduled for late 1993 – cancelled.

First heard in Michael's mini-movie, *Ghosts* – originally, it was heard throughout the film, before Michael wrote and added the title song. One of five previously unreleased songs included on his album *BLOOD ON THE DANCE FLOOR*, issued in April 1997.

Promo CD and vinyl singles released in many countries.

Official Versions:
Album Version.
Deep Dish Dark & Scary Remix.
Deep Dish Dark & Scary Remix
  Radio Edit.
Deep Dish Double-O-Jazz Dub.
DJ Greek's Scary Mix.
Downtempo Groove Mix.
Eddie's Love Mix.
Eddie's Love Mix Radio Edit.
Eddie's Rub-A-Dub Mix.
Radio Edit.

IT ALL BEGINS AND ENDS WITH LOVE

Song featured on the Jackson 5's *DANCING MACHINE* album, issued in September 1974 in the States and November 1974 in the UK.

IT WAS A VERY GOOD YEAR

Song Michael performed, dressed as Frank Sinatra, on the *Diana!* TV special, broadcast in the States on 18th April 1971. Not included on the accompanying soundtrack album – remains unreleased.

Originally recorded in 1961 by the Kingston Trio. Sinatra's version charted at no.28 on the Hot 100 in the States in 1965, but wasn't a hit in the UK.

IT'S CHRISTMAS TIME

Song the Jackson 5 recorded for their *CHRISTMAS ALBUM* circa 1970, but which failed to make the final track listing – remains unreleased.

IT'S GREAT TO BE HERE

Song featured on the Jackson 5 album, *MAYBE TOMORROW*, released in April 1971 in the States and October 1971 in the UK.

Featured in the 'Bongo, Baby Bongo' episode of the Jackson 5 cartoon series in 1971.

Kenny Dope Remix, as included on the Japanese album *SOUL SOURCE – JACKSON 5 REMIXES* in 2000, featured alternate vocals.

A second remix, the Jungle Brothers Remix, was included on *SOUL SOUCE – JACKSON 5 REMIXES 2*, released in Japan in 2001.

Other remixes:
Remix.
Extended Remix.

Remix and Extended Remix versions released as a 12" single in the UK in 2003 by Disco Juice Records.

Sampled by:
702 on their single, *All I Want* – charted at no.33 on the R&B singles chart and no.35 on the Hot 100 in the States in 1997.
Mariah Carey on the 'So So Def Mix' of *Honey* – hit no.1 on the Hot 100 and no.2 on the R&B singles chart in the States, and no.3 in the UK, in 1997.
Puff Daddy & The Family on *It's All About The Benjamins*, from the 1997 album, *NO WAY OUT*.

IT'S NOT WORTH IT

Song Brady recorded, with Michael contributing background vocals, for her 2002 album, *FULL MOON*.

IT'S THE FALLING IN LOVE

Song Michael recorded for his *OFF THE WALL* album, released in August 1979 – featured guest vocals by Patti Austin.

B-side of *Billie Jean* in the UK.

Original version by co-writer Carole Bayer Sager featured on her 1978 album, *TOO*.

Also covered by Dionne Warwick and Dee Dee Bridewater.

IT'S THE SAME OLD SONG

Four Tops classic the Jackson 5 recorded a version of, with Jermaine singing lead – remains unreleased.

Hit versions:

Four Tops – no.2 on the R&B singles chart and no.5 on the Hot 100 in the States, and no.34 in the UK, in 1965.

Weathermen (*aka* Jonathan King) – no.19 in the UK in 1971.

KC & The Sunshine Band – no.30 on the R&B singles chart and no.35 on the Hot 100, and no.47 in the UK, in 1978.

Third World – no.77 on the R&B singles chart in 1989

IT'S TOO LATE TO CHANGE THE TIME

Song the Jackson 5 recorded for their *GET IT TOGETHER* album, issued in September 1973 in the States and November 1973 in the UK.

Performed on several TV shows in the States in 1974, including *The Merv Griffin Show*, *Mike Douglas In Hollywood* and *The Tonight Show* (hosted by Johnny Carson).

Released as a single in Italy.

Live performance by the Jacksons, at a concert in Mexico in 1976, omitted from the home video, *The Jacksons In Concert*, released in 1981 in the UK (no USA release).

IT'S YOUR THING

Song the Jackson 5 performed during their first ever TV appearance on the Miss Black America Pageant, staged at Madison Square Garden in New York, on 22nd August 1969 – clip included on Michael's home video, *The Legend Continues...*, released in 1988 (1989 in the States).

Recorded by the Jackson 5 for Motown on 7th August 1969.

Remained unreleased until June 1995, when it was one of 19 'Rare & Unreleased' tracks on the fourth CD of the Michael/Jackson 5 box-set, *SOULSATION!*

Box-set promoted in the States by the release of a seven track promo 12" single, featuring *It's Your Thing*.

Official Versions:
Album Version.   J5 In '95 Extended Remix.

A Cappella ('95)   J5 In '95 House Remix.
Instrumental ('95).

Hit versions:
Isley Brothers – no.1 on the R&B singles chart and no.2 on the Hot 100
   in the States in 1969, no.30 in the UK.
Señor Soul – no.39 on the R&B singles chart in 1969.
Salt-N-Pepa – no.4 on the R&B singles chart in 1988.

I'VE GOTTA BE ME

Sammy Davis, Jr. cover the Jackson 5 recorded for Motown – remains
unreleased. Sammy's version appeared on his 1968 album of the same
title.

Originally penned for the Broadway production, *Golden Rainbow*, as a
vehicle for the husband-wife team of Steve Lawrence and Eydie
Gorme.

J5 TALK & SING PERSONALLY TO VALENTINE READERS

Flexi disc given away on the front of the October 1972 issue of the
British teen magazine, *Valentine*.

As well as Michael and his brothers talking, featured snippets of *I Wanna Be Where You Are*, *I'll Be There*, *ABC* and *Never Can Say Goodbye*.

JACKSON 5 CARTOON THEME

Theme to the Jackson 5's cartoon series, which first aired on ABC-TV in the States on 11th September 1971, featuring the hits, *I Want You Back*, *ABC*, *The Love You Save* and *Mama's Pearl* – used to open and close the show.

JACKSON 5 MOTOWN MEDLEY, THE

Medley of *I Want You Back*, *The Love You Save*, *Dancing Machine*, *ABC* and *I'll Be There*.

B-side of the 12" promo of *Farewell My Summer Love*, issued in the States in June 1984, to coincide with the Jacksons Victory Tour.

JACKSON MAN

One of eight songs the Jackson 5 recorded for Steel-Town – said to be 'somewhat of a tribute to their father', Joseph Jackson.

One of two Steel-Town recordings that remain unreleased; the other is *Take My Heart*.

6.5" metal acetate, with *Take My Heart* on Side 1 and *Jackson Man* on Side 2, with title credits hand-written in green wax crayon. Acetate discovered by Adey Pierce in Indiana in 2000 – he purchased it from an ex-engineer who engineered all eight Jackson 5 recordings for Steel-Town.

Acetate value at £3,000 by *Record Collector* magazine, and sold on the internet auction site, eBay, for £4,200 in October 2006.

JACKSONS OPENING THEME SONG

Written by Michael with brothers Jackie, Marlon, Randy and Tito, as the opening theme for the group's TV series in the States in 1976 – registered with the BMI, but no official release.

JAM

Written by Michael with Teddy Riley, Bruce Swedien and Ivan Moore, and recorded for his *DANGEROUS* album, issued in November 1991.

Featured rap by heavy D.

Charted at no.3 on the R&B singles chart and no.26 on the Hot 100 in the States, and no.13 in the UK – hit no.1 in Zimbabwe.

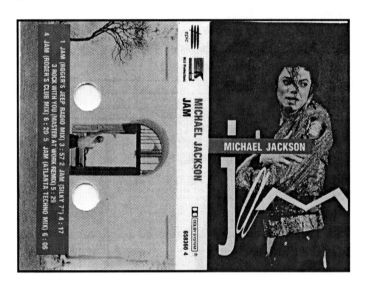

Official Versions:

Album Version.
Acappella Mix.
Atlanta Techno Dub.
Atlanta Techno Mix.
Roger's Club Dub.
E-Smoove's Jazzy Jam.
Maurice's Jammin' Dub Mix.
MJ Raw Mix.
More Than Enuff Dub.
More Than Enuff Mix.
Percapella.
Radio Edit.
Radio Edit w/out Rap.
7" Edit.

Roger's Club Mix.
Roger's Club Radio Mix.
Roger's Jeep Dub.
Roger's Jeep Mix.
Roger's Jeep Radio Mix.
Roger's Slam Jam Mix.
Roger's Underground Mix.
Silky Dub!
Silky 7".
Silky 12".
Teddy's Jam.
Teddy's 12" Mix.
Video Mix.
7" Edit w/out Rap.

'Jam' is a basketball term in the States, a theme Michael explored in the promo short film, which was directed by Michael and David Kellogg. Co-starred Michael Jordan of the Chicago Bulls basketball team, Heavy D and young rap duo, Kris Kross.

Song chosen to open Michael's Dangerous World Tour concerts.

Live performance by Michael, at his Dangerous Tour concert in Bucharest, Romania, on 1st October 1992, featured on the DVD released as part of his box-set, *THE ULTIMATE COLLECTION*, issued in November 2004.

Fourteenth of Michael's 20 *'Visionary – The Video Singles'* reissues, with the music on one side of a Dual Disc and the accompanying short film on the other side. Issued in May 2006 in the UK – charted at no.22.

JAM – BILLIE JEAN – BLACK OR WHITE

Medley Michael performed live during the half-time interval, at Superbowl XXVII, on 31st January 1993. Michael gave a short speech, before he performed *Heal The World*.

JAM SESSION

B-side of the Jackson 5's second single, *We Don't Have To Be Over 21 (To Fall In Love)*, released on Steel-Town Records circa mid-1968 (no UK release).

Finally released – titled Jam Session (Part 1) – on album in June 1996, on the pre-Motown compilation, *PRE-HISTORY – THE LOST STEELTOWN RECORDINGS* (no UK release).

Title of a pre-Motown compilation released on the Mastertone label in 1998.

JAM SESSION

Pre-Motown recording by the Jackson 5 – different to above – featured on the album, *BEGINNING YEARS 1967-1968*, issued in 1989 in the States and 1990 in the UK.

Album credit: The Jackson 5 And Johnny featuring Michael Jackson.

JAM SESSION (PART 1)

Re-titled version of song that originally appeared on the B-side of *We Don't Have To Be Over 21 (To Fall In Love)*.

Included on the pre-Motown compilation, *PRE-HISTORY – THE LOST STEELTOWN RECORDINGS* (no UK release).

JAM SESSION (PART 2)

Song previously titled, *Boys And Girls, We Are The Jackson Five (Jam Session)* – originally included on the pre-Motown compilation, *THE JACKSON FIVE FEATURING MICHAEL JACKSON*, released in the UK in September 1993 (no USA release).

Included on the pre-Motown compilation, *PRE-HISTORY – THE LOST STEELTOWN RECORDINGS* (no UK release).

JAMIE

One of 19 'Rare & Unreleased' tracks on the fourth CD of the Michael/ Jackson 5 box-set, *SOULSATION!*, issued in June 1995 in the States and July 1995 in the UK.

Originally recorded by Eddie Holland, for his eponymous 1962 album.

JE NE VEUX PAS LA FIN NOUS

French language version of Michael's *I Just Can't Stop Loving You*, recorded as a duet with Siedah Garrett – remains unreleased.

French lyrics written by Christine 'Coconut' Decriox. 'I met Quincy (Jones) in Los Angeles by friends of friends,' said Decriox. 'When I heard *I Just Can't Stop Loving You*, I said to Michael that he should sing it in French, because it is a harmonious language which is appropriate for this kind of romantic melodies. Quincy proposed to me to write the text – I did and Michael recorded it.'

Translation of French title: *I Do Not Want The End Of Us*.

See also: *I Just Can't Stop Loving You*

JINGLE BELLS

Festive favourite the Jackson 5 performed at the close of a benefit concert for the Foundation Of The Junior Blind in Los Angeles in late 1970, attended by 1,000 blind and partially sighted children aged 13-16 years old.

Recorded by Michael and his brothers for their *CHRISTMAS ALBUM* circa 1970, but which failed to make the final track listing – remains unreleased.

Hit versions:
Perry Como – no.74 on the Hot 100 in the States in 1957.
Ramsey Lewis – no.21 on the Christmas Singles chart in the States in 1965.
Booker T & The MG's – no.20 on the Christmas Singles chart in 1966.
Singing Dogs – no.1 on the Christmas Singles chart in 1971.
Judge Dread (medley) – no.64 in the UK in 1978.
Hysterics – no.44 in the UK in 1981.
Crazy Frog – no.5 in the UK in 2005.

JOHNNY RAVEN

Song Michael recorded for his *MUSIC & ME* album, issued in April 1973 in the States and July 1973 in the UK.

B-side of *Music And Me* in the UK.

JOY

Song Michael wrote the melody to, with a view to including it on his album, *DANGEROUS*. Tammy Lucas added lyrics but, ultimately, Michael wasn't happy with the song and didn't record it.

Recorded by Teddy Riley's BLACKstreet, for the group's eponymous debut album in 1994. Released as a single in 1995 – charted at no.12 on the R&B singles chart and no.43 on the Hot 100 in the States, and no.56 in the UK.

'Uptown Joy' remix sampled Michael's *I Can't Help It*.

JOY TO THE WORLD

Song the Jackson 5 recorded for their *CHRISTMAS ALBUM* circa 1970, but which failed to make the final track listing – remains unreleased.

JOYFUL JUKEBOX MUSIC

Title track of an album credited to 'The Jackson 5, Featuring Michael Jackson', issued by Motown in October 1976 in the States and December 1976 in the UK – after Michael and his brothers (minus Jermaine) had signed for CBS/Epic.

JUMP FOR JOY

Song the Jacksons recorded for their album, *GOIN' PLACES*, released in October 1977.

JUNK FOOD JUNKIE

Song the Jacksons performed, with special guest Mackenzie Phillips, on their TV series in 1976.

JUST A LITTLE BIT OF YOU

Song Michael recorded for his album, *FOREVER, MICHAEL*, issued in January 1975 in the States and March 1975 in the UK.

Achieved no.4 on the R&B singles chart and no.23 on the Hot 100 in the States, but failed to chart in the UK.

Performed by the Jackson 5 on *American Bandstand* and *Soul Train* in 1975, and by the Jacksons on their TV series in 1977.

JUST A LITTLE MISUNDERSTANDING

One of 19 'Rare & Unreleased' tracks featured on the fourth CD of the Michael/Jackson 5 box-set, *SOULSATION!*, issued in June 1995 in the States and July 1995 in the UK – demo version also known to exist.

Originally recorded by the Contours, and featured on their 1962 album, *DO YOU LOVE ME?*

JUST BECAUSE I LOVE YOU

Previously unreleased Jackson 5 recording included on the album, *BOOGIE*, released in North America only in January 1979 and quickly withdrawn.

JUST FRIENDS

Song Michael produced, and contributed backing vocals to, for Carole Bayer Sager – featured on her 1981 album, *SOMETIMES LATE AT NIGHT*.

JUST GOOD FRIENDS

Song Michael recorded as a duet with Stevie Wonder, for his album, *BAD*, released in September 1987.

Michael is a huge admirer of Stevie: 'Stevie Wonder is, you know – God, I've learnt so much from him by just sitting in on his sessions, and talking to him and listening... he's phenomenal... I had an interview with George Harrison in England, we did it together, and we were speaking of Stevie and he said, and these are his exact words, he said, Stevie Wonder makes him wanna retire. He said Paul (McCartney) feels the same way.'

Short film, suggesting there may have been plans to release the song as a single, believed to exist – remains unreleased.

Performed by Michael during his Bad World Tour in Sydney, Australia, on 20th November 1987, when Stevie made a surprise guest appearance on stage.

JUST SAY NO

Alternate title to Michael's *Morphine*, one of five new songs featured on his album, *BLOOD ON THE DANCE FLOOR*, issued in April 1997 – re-titled in some Far Eastern countries.

See also: *Morphine*.

KANSAS CITY

Song recorded in 1992 by Jason Weaver for the TV mini-series, *The Jacksons: An American Dream*, where it posed as the Jackson 5's debut single.

Featured on the soundtrack album of the same title, issued in October 1992 in the States and July 1993 in the UK.

KEEP HER

Previously unreleased bonus track included on the CD single of the Jacksons' *2300 Jackson Street*, issued in July 1989 in the States and August 1989 in the UK.

Michael had no involvement in recording this track.

KEEP OFF THE GRASS

Song recorded by the Jackson 5 for Motown in the early 1970s – remains unreleased.

KEEP ON DANCING

Song recorded by the Jacksons for their self-titled debut album, issued in November 1976.

Special Disco mix released as a single in Holland.

Performed by the Jacksons on their TV series in 1976, and featured in the Destiny Tour concert screened on BBC2 in the UK.

KEEP THE FAITH

Song written by Michael with Siedah Garrett and Glen Ballard, and recorded for his *DANGEROUS* album, released in November 1991.

Initially, Michael tried singing the first and second verses in the wrong key – then disappeared. 'I found him standing in the corner of his office, crying his eyes out,' recalls Bruce Swedien. 'He was absolutely heartbroken – cut to the quick.' Michael pulled himself together. 'We went in the studio,' said Swedien, 'cut a whole new demo and recorded a scratch vocal all the way through… we didn't leave the studio until dawn.'

Demo version featured completely different lyrics in some parts – no official release.

'I think he's an incredible singer,' said co-writer Ballard. 'He'll spend two years making a record, then go out and sing all the lead vocals in a week. He's got such confidence and ability. I've worked with him sitting at a piano and having him sing, and it's just a religious experience – the guy is amazing… he's expressive, has great pitch, does incredible backgrounds. His backgrounds are probably as good as anybody I've ever heard – they're textures unto themselves.'

KENTUCKY

Song Michael cited he had written in the mid-1970s in his court disposition in November 1993 – remains unreleased.

KENTUCKY ROAD

Song the Jackson 5 recorded for Motown – remains unreleased.

KICK IT

Song Michael worked on with Rodney Jerkins, Fred Jerkins III, LaShawn Daniels and Norman Gregg during the *INVINCIBLE* sessions, but failed to make the album – remains unreleased.

KILLING ME SOFTLY WITH HIS SONG

Song performed by the Jackson 5 as part of a medley – with *By The Time I Get To Phoenix* and *Danny Boy* – during their Las Vegas shows in 1974.

Also performed on *The Tonight Show*, hosted by Bill Cosby, in March 1974.

Hit versions:
Roberta Flack – no.1 on the Hot 100 and no.2 on the R&B singles chart in the States in 1973, no.6 in the UK.

Al B. Sure! – no.14 on the R&B singles chart and no.80 on the Hot 100 in 1988.

Fugees – no.1 in the UK in 1996.

K.I.S.S.I.N.G.

Song Siedah Garrett recorded for her 1988 album, *KISS* – although not credited, the vocal arrangement was reportedly by Michael.

KREETON OVERTURE

Song written by Michael with Marty Paich, Jai Winding and Pat Leonard in 1984, for the opening of the Jacksons Victory Tour.

Registered with the United States Copyright Office in October 1984 – remains unreleased.

L.A. IS MY LADY

Title track of an album Frank Sinatra released in 1984 – promo video included a brief appearance by Michael and his sister, La Toya.

LA ISLA BONITA

Song penned by Patrick Leonard, who worked with the Jacksons on their Victory Tour in 1984, with Michael in mind.

Michael passed, but Madonna wrote some lyrics for the song and recorded it for her 1986 album, *TRUE BLUE*. Issued as a single, it hit no.1 in the UK and charted at no.4 on the Hot 100 in the States.

LA LA (MEANS I LOVE YOU)

Delfonics cover the Jackson 5 recorded for their album, *ABC*, issued in May 1970 in the States and August 1970 in the UK.

Featured in the 'Jackson Island' episode of the Jackson 5 cartoon series in 1971.

Official versions:
Album Version.   Edit.

The edited version, with the beginning cut, featured on later vinyl releases.

The Delfonics took the song – from their album of the same title – to no.2 on the R&B singles chart and no.4 on the Hot 100 in the States in 1968, and to no.19 in the UK in 1971.

LADY IN MY LIFE, THE

Rod Temperton song Michael recorded for his album, *THRILLER*, released in December 1982.

Lyrics to an extra, unreleased verse appeared on the sleeve of original pressings of *THRILLER*. Cited by Michael as one of the most difficult tracks to cut for the album.

'We were used to doing a lot of takes, in order to get a vocal as nearly perfect as possible, but Quincy wasn't satisfied with my work on that song, even after literally dozens of takes,' said Michael. 'Finally, he took me aside late one session, and told me he wanted me to beg. That's what he said – he wanted me to go back to the studio and literally beg for it. So I went back in and had them turn off the studio lights, and close the curtain between the studio and the control room, so I wouldn't feel self-conscious. Q started the tape and I begged – the result is what you hear in the grooves.'

Included on a single for the first time when it featured on the UK release of *Liberian Girl*.

Sampled by LL Cool J, with Boyz II Men on backing vocals, on his single *Hey Lover*, issued in October 1995 in the States and January 1996 in the UK. Charted at no.3 on both American charts and at no.17 in the UK.

Also sampled by Trae featuring Hawk & Fat Pat, on the song *Swang*.

Cover versions include:
Marc Nelson – on his album *CHOCOLATE MOODS* in 1999.
Mya (re-titled *Man In My Life*) – included on her album *FEAR OF FLYING*, in 2000.
Silk – for their 2006 album, *ALWAYS & FOREVER*.

Versions also recorded by Lou Rawls and Diversiti.

LAST NIGHT

One of several songs written by Pharrell Williams and submitted for Michael's HIS*TORY* and *INVINCIBLE* albums, which were later recorded by Justin Timberlake, for his debut album *JUSTIFIED*, released in 2002.

LAVENDAR BLUE

Disney song recorded by the Jackson 5, exists as a bootleg – no official release.

Recording of the song by Burl Ives featured in the 1948 Disney film, *So Dear To My Heart*.

LEARNED MY LESSON

Song written by Michael in 1981, two versions of which were registered with the United States Copyright Office in January 1985 – both remain unreleased.

LEAVE ME ALONE

Song written by Michael, and included as a bonus track on the CD release of his album, *BAD*, issued in September 1987.

'I worked hard on the song, stacking vocals on top of each other like layers of clouds,' said Michael. 'I'm sending a simple message here: Leave me alone! The song is about a relationship between a guy and a girl, but what I'm really saying to people who are bothering me is: Leave me alone!'

Released as the eighth single from *BAD* in many countries, charting at no.2 in the UK (no USA release).

Promoted with a humorous, animated short film, directed by Jim Blashfield and Paul Diener – featured in Michael's 'movie like no other', *Moonwalker*. Included, a clip of Elizabeth Taylor's movie, *Cat*

On A Hot Tin Roof, plus footage of Michael's chimp, Bubbles, and his llama, Louise.

Grammy Award: Best Music Video, Short Form. *Moonwalker* also picked up a Grammy nomination, for Best Music Video, Long Form, but Michael's sister Janet took that award, for her *Rhythm Nation 1814*.

MTV Video Music Award: Best Special Effects in a Video.

Official Versions:

Album Version.	Extended Dance Mix.
Extended Dance Mix Radio Edit.	Dub Version.
Instrumental.	A Cappella.

Tenth of Michael's 20 *'Visionary – The Video Singles'* reissues, with the music on one side of a Dual Disc and the accompanying short film on the other side. Issued in April 2006 in the UK – charted at no.15.

LET IT BE

Beatles classic the Jackson 5 performed *a cappella* on *The Tonight Show*, hosted by Johnny Carson, in April 1974.

The Jackson 5's *ABC* deposed the Beatles single *Let It Be* from top spot on the Hot 100 on 25th April 1970.

Part of the Lennon-McCartney catalogue Michael bought from ATV Music in 1985, for a reputed $47.5 million – now valued at over $500 million.

Michael granted permission for a charity version of the song to be recorded, by Ferry Aid, to aid families of the victims of the Zeebrugge ferry tragedy in 1987. Ferry Aid included Paul McCartney. The project was promoted by *The Sun* newspaper, who publicly thanked Michael for his support.

Hits versions:
Beatles – no.1 on the Hot 100 in the States and no.2 in the UK in 1970.
Joan Baez – no.49 on the Hot 100 in 1971.
Ferry Aid – no.1 in the UK in 1987.

LET IT BE – SHORTNIN' BREAD

Medley the Jackson 5 performed on *The Jim Nabors Show* in the States in September 1970; *Let It Be* they sang *a cappella*, and they were joined by their host on *Shortnin' Bread*.

LET ME CARRY YOUR SCHOOLBOOKS

Single issued by Steel-Town Records in the States in 1971, credited to 'The Ripples & Waves + Michael' – a name the Jackson 5 reputedly used in the early days.

Nearly 20 years later Gordon Keith, founder and owner of Steel-Town Records, stated: 'The fine vocals were provided by another Gary, Indiana talent, Michael Rodgers' – not Michael Jackson.

Featured on the Jackson 5 album, *PRE-HISTORY – THE LOST STEELTOWN RECORDINGS*, released in the States in June 1996 (no UK release). The sleeve notes implied, without actually saying, the Jackson 5 and the Ripples & Waves + Michael were one and the same group.

LET'S HAVE A PARTY

One of 19 'Rare & Unreleased' tracks on the fourth CD of the Michael/Jackson 5 box-set, *SOULSATION!*, issued in June 1995 in the States and July 1995 in the UK.

LET'S TAKE A RIDE

One of several songs written by Pharrell Williams and submitted for Michael's HIS*TORY* and *INVINCIBLE* albums, which were later recorded by Justin Timberlake, for his debut album *JUSTIFIED*, released in 2002.

LETTER TO MICHAEL

Song about Michael by Leslie, released in early 1984 on the Stonehenge label.

LIBERIAN GIRL

Song originally titled 'Pyramid Girl', written and recorded by Michael for his album, *BAD*, issued in September 1987.

Spoken intro, in Swahili, by Letta Mbulla.

Promo video, directed by Jim Yukich, featured a host of stars, including: Brigitte Nielsen, Paula Abdul, Carl Weathers, Whoopi Goldberg, Quincy Jones, Jackie Collins, Rosanna Arquette, Olivia Newton-John, John Travolta, Steven Spielberg, Debbie Gibson, Weird Al Yankovic, Suzanna Somers, Don King, David Copperfield, Danny Glover, Dan Aykroyd, plus Michael himself and his chimp, Bubbles. Michael dedicated the promo to Elizabeth Taylor.

Ninth and last single lifted from *BAD*, charted at no.13 in the UK – set a new record of nine Top 30 singles from one album.

Official Versions:
Album Version.
Edit.
Instrumental.

Acetate surfaced circa 1989, including an unreleased instrumental version of the song.

Sampled on:

MC Lyte featuring Xscape's *Keep On, Keepin' On* – no.3 on the R&B singles chart and no.10 on the Hot 100, and no.39 in the UK, in 1996. Reissued in the UK a year later, when it charted at no.27.

'Darkchild' remix of Jennifer Lopez's *If You Had My Love* – no.1 on the Hot 100 and no.6 on the R&B singles chart, and no.4 in the UK, in 1999.

2Pac's *Letter 2 My Unborn* – no.21 in the UK, and no.64 on the R&B singles chart in the States, in 2001.

LIFE

Song written by R. Kelly that Michael wanted to record for his HIS*TORY* album, but Kelly persuaded him to record *You Are Not Alone* instead – which became the first single in Billboard's 55 year history to enter the Hot 100 at no.1.

Recorded by K-Ci & Jo-Jo – featured on their album, *IT'S REAL*, in 1999. Also appeared on the original soundtrack album *LIFE* in the same year.

LIFE OF THE PARTY, THE

Song the Jackson 5 recorded for their album, *DANCING MACHINE*, issued in September 1974 in the States and November 1974 in the UK.

Released as a single in the UK in November 1974 but failed to chart (no USA release).

Promoted on *The Sonny Comedy Revue* in 1974, on the *Carol Burnett Show* in 1975, and performed by the Jacksons on their TV series in 1977.

Live performance by the Jacksons, at a concert in Mexico in 1976, included on the home video, *The Jacksons In Concert*, released in 1981 in the UK (no USA release).

LIKE A VIRGIN – BILLIE JEAN

Medley performed by Madonna during her 1985 concert tour – featured on her first live home video, *Live – The Virgin Tour*, filmed in Detroit, Michigan.

LIKE I LOVE YOU

Song written for Michael by the Neptunes, for his *INVINCIBLE* album, but he didn't like the hook so rejected it.

Recorded by Justin Timberlake for his debut album, *JUSTIFIED* – single charted at no.2 in the UK and no.11 on the Hot 100 in the States in 2002.

LIME IN THE COCONUT

Song the Jacksons performed in their TV series in 1976, while dancing the 'limbo rock'.

LITTLE BITTY PRETTY ONE

Song the Jackson 5 recorded for their album, *LOOKIN' THROUGH THE WINDOWS*, issued in May 1972 in the States and October 1972 in the UK.

Charted at no.8 on the R&B singles chart and no.13 on the Hot 100 in the States, but wasn't a hit in the UK.

Featured in 'The Opening Act' episode of the Jackson 5 cartoon series in 1971.

Other hit versions:
Thurston Harris – no.2 on the R&B singles chart and no.6 on the Hot 100 in the States in 1957.
Bobby Day – no.57 on the Hot 100 in 1957.
Frankie Lymon – no.58 on the Hot 100 in 1960.
Clyde McPhatter – no.25 on the Hot in 1962.

LITTLE CHRISTMAS TREE

Festive offering written especially for Michael by Funkadelic's George Clinton.

Originally featured on the album, *A MOTOWN CHRISTMAS*, issued in September 1973 in the States and November 1976 in the UK.

Released as a single in Holland in 1973.

Added, as a bonus track, to the 2003 reissue of the Jackson 5's *CHRISTMAS ALBUM* – re-titled *20th CENTURY MASTERS – THE CHRISTMAS COLLECTION*.

LITTLE DRUMMER BOY, THE

Song recorded by the Jackson 5 for their *CHRISTMAS ALBUM*, issued in October 1970 in the States and December 1970 in the UK.

Released as a single in the Philippines and Venezuela.

Hit versions:
Harry Simeone Chorale – no.13 on the Hot 100 in the States, and no.13 in the UK, in 1959.
Beverley Sisters – no.6 in the UK in 1959.
Michael Flanders – no.20 in the UK in 1959.
Johnny Cash – no.63 on the Hot 100 in 1959.
Jack Holloran Singers – no.96 on the Hot 100 in 1962.
Johnny Mathis – no.11 on the Christmas Singles chart in the States in 1963.
Joan Baez – no.16 on the Christmas Singles chart in 1966.
Kenny Burrell – no.21 on the Christmas Singles chart in 1967.
Lou Rawls – no.2 on the Christmas Singles chart in 1967.
Royal Scots Dragoon Guards – no.13 in the UK in 1972.
Moonlion – no.95 on the Hot 100 in 1976.
David Bowie & Bing Crosby (medley) – no.3 in the UK in 1982.
RuPaul – no.61 in the UK in 1994.

LITTLE GIRLS

Song Michael cited he had written in his court disposition in November 1993 – remains unreleased.

LITTLE SUSIE

Song written and recorded by Michael for his album, HIS*TORY*, released in June 1995.

Michael cited he had written *Little Suzy* in his court disposition in November 1993 – this may or may not be the same song Michael later released as *Little Susie*.

One of five songs hand-written by Michael circa 1979 – lyrics included in a personal notebook, with young actor Mark Lester on the cover, that formed part of a 10,000+ piece collection of Jackson memorabilia purchased by Universal Express and some of its entertainment partners, in November 2006.

LIVING TOGETHER

Song the Jacksons recorded for their self-titled debut album, issued in November 1976.

Performed by the Jacksons on the TV series in 1977.

LLAMA LOLA

Song Michael mentioned he had written during his copyright hearing in Mexico in 1993 – remains unreleased.

(LONELINESS HAS MADE ME REALISE) IT'S YOU THAT I NEED

Temptations hit the Jackson 5 recorded a version of – remains unreleased.

The Temptations took the song to no.3 on the R&B singles chart and no.14 on the Hot 100 in the States in 1967.

LONELY BIRD

Song Michael cited he had written in his court disposition in November 1993 – remains unreleased.

LONELY HEART

Pre-Motown recording by the Jackson 5, first heard in 1989, when it was included on the album, *BEGINNING YEARS 1967-1968*.

Believed to originate from a demo tape recorded in the living room of 2300 Jackson Street or Tito's music teacher Shirley Cartman, which Cartman planned to pass on to Gordon Keith, founder and owner of Steel-Town Records – however, instead Keith accepted an invitation to hear the Jackson 5 play, and signed them soon after.

Cartman, after moving to Atlanta, had the demo tape transferred to more durable audiotape to preserve the recordings – it appears someone at the taping facility made an illegal copy of the tape, which led to its eventual release without Cartman's knowledge or permission.

Despite crediting Gordon Keith as song-writer, Cartman has confirmed she wrote *Lonely Heart*, as she felt the songs the Jackson 5 were performing at the time were a little too mature for them.

LONELY MAN

Song Michael cited he had written in his court disposition in November 1993 – remains unreleased.

LONELY TEARDROPS

Song written by Berry Gordy for one of Michael's idols, Jackie Wilson, who took it to no.1 on the R&B singles chart and no.7 on the Hot 100 in the States (not a hit in the UK).

Recorded between 1970-73 by Michael as a favour to Gordy, finally released on Michael's *LOOKING BACK TO YESTERDAY* album, issued in February 1986 in the States and May 1986 in the UK.

LOOK WHAT YOU'VE DONE

Tribute song recorded by a group of fans in Nottingham, England, on 4th May 1991 – coincidentally, the day Jackie Jackson and mother Katherine celebrated their birthdays.

LOOKIN' THROUGH THE WINDOWS

Title track of a Jackson 5 album released in May 1972 in the States and October 1972 in the UK.

Charted at no.5 on the R&B singles chart and no.16 on the Hot 100 in the States, and no.9 in the UK.

Promoted on several American TV shows, including *American Bandstand*, *Soul Train* and *The Sonny & Cher Comedy Hour*.

Performed on *Top Of The Pops*, whilst the Jackson 5 were in the UK, as part of their European concert tour.

Live version featured on the Michael/Jackson 5's *LIVE!* album, issued in September 1988 in the UK (no USA release). All songs on the album were recorded at a concert on 30th April 1973, at the Osaka Koseinenkin Hall in Japan. Also included on the limited edition CD, *IN JAPAN!*, released by Hip-Select in 2004 – only 5,000 copies pressed.

LOST CHILDREN, THE

Song written and recorded by Michael for his album, *INVINCIBLE*, issued in October 2001.

Featured Michael's four year old son, Prince, on narration.

One of three tracks on the album Michael chose as his personal favourites, during his Online Audio Chat appearance on 26th October 2001.

LOVE CALL

Song recorded by the Jackson 5 for Motown on 12th October 1971 – test pressings known to exist, but remains unreleased.

LOVE DON'T WANT TO WAIT

Jackie Jackson solo recording featured on the Jackson 5's album, *ANTHOLOGY*, issued in June 1976 in the States (not included on UK release).

LOVE FEELS LIKE FIRE

Four Tops track the Jackson 5 recorded a version of – remains unreleased.

The Four Tops recording featured on their 1965 album, *FOUR TOPS SECOND ALBUM*.

LOVE GO AWAY

Song the Jackson 5 recorded for Motown.

Lyrics appeared in the Winter 1984 issue, a Michael Jackson special, of *Rock & Soul* magazine – remains unreleased.

LOVE I SAW IN YOU WAS JUST A MIRAGE, THE

Song the Jackson 5 recorded for their *THIRD ALBUM*, released in September 1970 in the States and February 1971 in the UK.

Featured on the 'Wizard Of Soul' episode of the Jackson 5 cartoon series in 1971.

Original version by Smokey Robinson & The Miracles – from the album *MAKE IT HAPPEN* – charted at no.10 on the R&B singles chart and no.20 on the Hot 100 in the States in 1967.

LOVE IS HERE AND NOW YOU'RE GONE

Supremes cover Michael recorded for his debut solo album, *GOT TO BE THERE*, issued in January 1972 in the States and May 1972 in the UK.

B-side of *Rockin' Robin*.

Featured on the 'Jackson And The Beanstalk' episode of the new Jackson 5 cartoon series in 1971.

The Supremes original – lifted from the album *THE SUPREMES SING HOLLAND-DOZIER-HOLLAND* – charted at no.1 on both American charts, and no.17 in the UK, in 1967.

LOVE IS THE THING YOU NEED

Song featured on the Jackson 5's album, *JOYFUL JUKEBOX MUSIC*, issued in October 1976 in the States and December 1976 in the UK – originally recorded during the *SKYWRITER* sessions.

LOVE MIX 1

Megamix of Motown recordings by Michael and his brothers featured on the double CD, *THE MICHAEL JACKSON MIX*, issued in the UK in December 1987.

Featured songs: *Ben, Ain't No Sunshine, One Day In Your Life, Never Can Say Goodbye, Got To Be There, Happy (Love Theme From 'Lady Sings The Blues'), I'll Be There, We're Almost There* and *People Make The World Go Round.*

Promo edit featured: *Ben, Ain't No Sunshine* and *One Day In Your Life.*

See also: *Dance Mix 1 & 2, Love Mix 2.*

LOVE MIX 2

Megamix of Motown recordings by Michael and his brothers featured on the double CD, *THE MICHAEL JACKSON MIX*, issued in the UK in December 1987.

Featured songs: *Who's Lovin' You, I Was Made To Love Her, You've Really Got A Hold On Me, Music And Me, Call On Me, Lonely Teardrops, You've Got A Friend, Girl, Don't Take Your Love From Me, We've Got A Good Thing Going* and *I'll Come Home To You.*

See also: *Dance Mix 1 & 2, Love Mix 1.*

LOVE NEVER FELT SO GOOD

Song written by Michael with Paul Anka and Kathy Wakefield.

Recorded by Johnny Mathis for his 1984 album, *A SPECIAL PART OF ME*.

Demo version by Michael leaked on the internet in 2006 – no official release.

LOVE SCENES

One of 19 'Rare & Unreleased' tracks on the fourth CD of the Michael/ Jackson 5 box-set, *SOULSATION!*, issued in June 1995 in the States and July 1995 in the UK.

LOVE SONG

Non-album Jackson 5 recording.

B-side of *Lookin' Through The Windows*, released in June 1972 in the States and October 1972 in the UK.

Included of the Jackson 5's *ANTHOLOGY* collection, released in the States in October 2000 (no UK release).

LOVE TRAIN

One of five songs the Jackson 5 performed a medley of at the Grammy Awards ceremony in 1974, to introduce the nominees for Best Rhythm & Blues Performance by a Group, Duo or Chorus.

The O'Jays took the song to no.1 on both American charts, and to no.9 in the UK.

LOVE YOU SAVE, THE

Song the Jackson 5 recorded for their second album, *ABC*, issued in May 1970 in the States and August 1970 in the UK.

Hit no.1 on both American charts, and peaked at no.7 in the UK. Promo 7" red vinyl single released in the States.

Featured on the 'Winner's Circle' episode of the Jackson 5 cartoon series in 1971.

Performed by the Jackson 5 on the *Ed Sullivan Show* and *Jim Nabors Show* in 1970, and on their own TV series in 1976.

Title given to a budget cassette compilation released in the States in 1989.

Asakusa S.C. '01 Mix, as included on the Japanese album *SOUL SOURCE – JACKSON 5 REMIXES 2* in 2001, featured alternate vocals.

LOVELY ONE

Written by Michael with brother Randy, and recorded by the Jacksons for the album, *TRIUMPH*, released in October 1980.

Lead single from the album – charted at no.2 on the R&B singles chart and no.12 on the Hot 100 in the States, and no.29 in the UK.

Official Versions:
Album Version.   Single Edit.

Live version, recorded at a concert at Madison Square Garden in September 1981, featured on the Jacksons album, *LIVE*, issued in November 1981.

Performed solo by Michael during his Bad World Tour – one performance screened on Nippon TV in Japan.

LOVE'S GONE BAD

Song the Jackson 5 recorded at least three versions of, one in 1972 and two in 1973 – possibly for the album, *SKYWRITER*.

First version originally included on the album, *BOOGIE*, issued in North America in January 1979 and quickly withdrawn. This version also featured as a bonus track on the '2 Classic Albums on 1 CD' reissue of *SKYWRITER* & *GET IT TOGETHER*.

Alternate version included on Michael's *LOOKING BACK TO YESTERDAY* album, issued in 1986, and released as a promo 7" single in Canada only – a great rarity. This version was credited to Michael solo, but used the same vocal take as the first version, with some backing vocals omitted from the first verse.

Alternate take featured on Michael's 1995 Anthology series compilation, *THE BEST OF...* (no UK release). This take, by a much younger Michael, is much less polished than the other two versions.

LOVING YOU IS SWEETER THAN EVER

Four Tops hit the Jackson 5 recorded a version of – remains unreleased.

Hit versions:
Four Tops – no.12 on the R&B singles chart and no.45 on the Hot 100, and no.21 in the UK, in 1966.
Nick Kamen – no.16 in the UK in 1987.

LUCY IS IN LOVE WITH LINUS

Song Michael cited he had written in his court disposition in November 1993 – remains unreleased.

LULU

One of 19 'Rare & Unreleased' tracks on the fourth CD of the Michael/ Jackson 5 box-set, *SOULSATION!*, issued in June 1995 in the States and July 1995 in the UK.

LULU'S BACK IN TOWN

Song Michael performed a few bars of on a home-made video, filmed circa 1975 by brother Randy – remains unreleased.

Originally written for *Broadway Gondolier* in 1935.

MAGIC MICHAEL JACKSON MIX

Medley released on the Dutch *You Are Not Alone* CD in 1995.

Featured the songs: *Childhood, Jam, Off The Wall, Billie Jean, Wanna Be Startin' Somethin', Black Or White, Jam, Beat It, They Don't Care About Us, Scream* and *Ease On Down The Road.*

The medley rounded off with a special message from Michael.

MAGICAL CHILD

Poem written by Michael – included in his book of poems and reflections, *Dancing The Dream*, published in 1992.

MAKE A WISH

Song Michael cited in his court disposition in November 1993, however, he admitted he couldn't recall if he had written it or not – remains unreleased.

MAKE OR BREAK

Song Michael cited he had written with John Barnes in his court disposition in November 1993 – remains unreleased.

Also known by the alternate titles, *For God's Sake/Make Or Break* and *Make A Break.*

MAKE TONIGHT ALL MINE

Jackson 5 recording included on the album, *JOYFUL JUKEBOX MUSIC*, released in October 1976 in the States and December 1976 in the UK.

Alternate version included on Michael's 1995 Anthology series compilation, *THE BEST OF...* (no UK release).

MAMA I GOTTA BRAND NEW THING (DON'T SAY NO)

Song featured on the Jackson 5's album, *GET IT TOGETHER*, issued in September 1973 in the States and November 1973 in the UK.

Included on the *Get It Together* EP released in Brazil.

Originally recorded by the Undisputed Truth, and included on their eponymous 1970 album.

MAMA'S PEARL

Song the Jackson 5 recorded for their *THIRD ALBUM*, issued in September 1970 in the States and February 1971 in the UK.

Rarer single mix slightly different to album version, most noticeable on Tito's opening backing vocal – this mix would have been included on the album, had it been completed in time.

Broke the group's run of no.1s in the States; peaked at no.2 on both charts, prevented from topping the Hot 100 by *One Bad Apple* – performed in classic Jackson 5 style by the Osmonds.

No.1 on the sales-oriented Cashbox singles chart in the States, and achieved no.25 in the UK. Promo 7" red vinyl single released in the States.

Featured in 'The Rare Pearl' episode of the new Jackson 5 cartoon series in 1971.

Versions with alternate vocal takes featured on the Jackson 5's 1986 compilation, *ANTHOLOGY*, and on *THE JACKSONS STORY* compilation in 2004 (no UK release) – the latter featured the mono version 'folded' back into the stereo version.

Title given to a budget cassette compilation released in the States in 1989.

MAMA'S PEARL – WALK ON – THE LOVE YOU SAVE

Medley the Jackson 5 performed the *Diana!* TV special, first aired in the States on 18th April 1971. Featured on the TV soundtrack album of the same title, released in March 1971 in the States and October 1971 in the UK.

MAN, THE

Written by Michael with Paul McCartney, and recorded as a duet for Paul's album *PIPES OF PEACE*, released in November 1983.

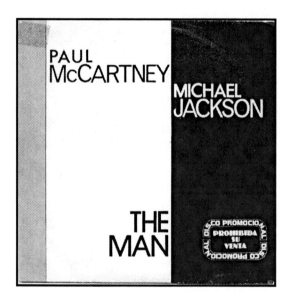

Planned as a follow-up to Michael and Paul's second collaboration, *Say Say Say*, until Michael's record company blocked its planned February 1984 release, fearing it would compete with releases from *THRILLER* – the 12" single was scheduled to feature an extended remix.

Officially released as a single in Peru, and made available as a promo only single in several other countries.

Also known by the title, *This Is The Man*.

MAN IN THE MIRROR

Song written by Siedah Garrett and Glen Ballard, and recorded by Michael for his album, *BAD*, issued in September 1987.

Hit no.1 on both American charts, but surprisingly struggled to no.21 in the UK.

Official Versions:
Album Version.
Single Mix.
Instrumental.

Promo short film, which didn't feature Michael, spliced footage of people who have endeavoured to 'make that change' with notorious figures – people like Martin Luther King, John F. Kennedy and Mother Teresa, plus Adolf Hitler and Idi Amin. Directed by Don Wilson.

Performed by Michael at the Grammy Awards ceremony at Radio City Hall, New York, in March 1988.

Grammy nomination: Record Of The Year (Bobby McFerrin's *Don't Worry, Be Happy* took the award).

Soul Trains Awards: Best R&B/Urban Contemporary Single, Male and Best R&B/Urban Contemporary Music Video.

Performed live – along with *What More Can I Give* – by Michael on 21st October 2001, at the 'United We Stand – What More Can I Give' concert, staged at Washington DC's RFK Stadium. Michael dedicated the song to the victims of the 9/11 terrorist attack and their families, saying: 'You are not alone. You are in our hearts, you are in our thoughts, and you are in our prayers.'

Montage of live performances opened Michael's 'movie like no other', *Moonwalker.*

Live performance by Michael, at his Dangerous Tour concert in Bucharest, Romania, on 1st October 1992, featured on the DVD released as part of his box-set, *THE ULTIMATE COLLECTION*, issued in November 2004.

Performed by 98°, Usher and Luther Vandross during the *Michael Jackson: 30th Anniversary Celebration, The Solo Years* concerts, staged at New York's Madison Square Garden on 7th and 10th September 2001.

Recorded by co-writer Siedah Garrett in 2003, for her solo album, *SIEDAH!*. 'This song is very special to me,' said Siedah. 'We (her and Glen Ballard) sat down and almost instantly, we came up with the music, lyric and melody for the first verse and chorus… we knew that afternoon that we had something special.'

Sampled by Rhythme Digital, featuring Redd Angel on vocals, on the track, *All Around The World.*

MAN OF WAR

Song featured on the Jacksons album, *GOIN' PLACES*, issued in October 1977.

B-side of *Music's Takin' Over* in the UK.

MARIA

Song the Jacksons recorded for their album, *2300 JACKSON STREET*, released in June 1989.

Michael wasn't involved in the recording of this track.

MARIA (YOU WERE THE ONLY ONE)

Song Michael recorded for his solo album, *GOT TO BE THERE*, issued in January 1972 in the States and May 1972 in the UK.

B-side of *Got To Be There*.

Featured on the 'Michael In Wonderland' episode of the Jackson 5 cartoon series in 1971.

MAYBE TOMORROW

Originally written for Sammy Davis, Jr. (who had just signed for Motown), recorded by the Jackson 5 for their album of the same title, released in April 1971 in the States and October 1971 in the UK.

Two different promo version issued in the States, one over a minute longer than the other; the shorter version is the rarer.

Charted at no.3 on the R&B singles chart and no.20 on the Hot 100 in the States (no UK release).

B-side of *Little Bitty Pretty One* in the UK.

Featured in the 'Groovatron' episode of the Jackson 5 cartoon series in 1971.

Newly recorded version, with an introduction by Tommy Smothers, performed on the *Goin' Back To Indiana* TV special included on the Jackson 5's album, *GOIN' BACK TO INDIANA*, issued in September 1971 in the States (no UK release).

Cover version by UB40 peaked at no.15 in the UK in 1987.

Sampled by Ghostface Killah on the track *All That I Got Is You*, from the 1996 album, *IRONMAN*.

MAYBE WE CAN DO IT

Song Michael co-wrote with Rodney Jerkins Sean 'P. Diddy' Combs, and recorded – featuring P. Diddy – during the *INVINCIBLE* sessions, but failed to make the album – remains unreleased.

In confirming his involvement, P. Diddy said: 'He (Michael) takes an insane amount of time to record a track, but that's just him, it's the way he works. I am, like, the norm and prefer to get the vocal arrangement, then work later on the production side. I got some harsh looks from Michael when I was in the studio, you can tell when he's not happy because he pulls these funny faces.'

MEDLEY OF HITS

11 minute medley of hits featured on side 1 of the Jackson 5 compilation, *MOTOWN SUPERSTAR SERIES VOL.12*, released in the States in September 1980.

Featured: *I Want You Back*, *ABC*, *The Love You Save*, *Never Can Say Goodbye*, *Dancing Machine* and *I'll Be There*.

B-side of a Four Tops/Temptations *Medley Of Hits*, released as a 12" single in the States in 1983.

MEDLEYS, THE

Two promo medleys released on 12" and CD in Brazil in 1994:

Back To The Past Medley: *Rock With You*, *Burn This Disco Out*, *Off The Wall*, *Don't Stop 'Til You Get Enough*, *Shake Your Body (Down To The Ground)*, *Blame It On The Boogie*, *Thriller* and *Billie Jean*.

Dangerous New Jack Medley: *Remember The Time*, *In The Closet*, *Jam* and *Black Or White*.

MELODIE

Song recorded on 15th January 1973, but remained unreleased until it appeared – newly mixed – on Michael's album, *FAREWELL MY SUMMER LOVE*, issued in May 1984 in the States and June 1984 in the UK.

Remix included on Michael's 1987 album, *THE ORIGINAL SOUL OF MICHAEL JACKSON* – scheduled release as a single in the States in October 1987 cancelled, and the album's one previously unheard recording, *Twenty-Five Miles*, issued instead.

Original 1973 version featured on Michael's *THE BEST OF...* compilation – part of Motown's Anthology series, released in March 1995 in the States (no UK release).

MEN IN BLACK

Song Michael recorded for the shelved greatest hits collection, *DECADE 1980-1990*, scheduled for release in 1990.

Included on an ultra rare promo titled 'Promo Flight Only', of which only ten copies exist, given to Sony Executives on their way to Neverland from Europe in 1991, as a teaser for tracks under consideration for Michael's album, *DANGEROUS* – the promo also featured the unreleased *Monkey Business*.

Remains unreleased.

MEPHISTO AND KEVIN

Song, with lyrical reference to Michael, recorded by Primus for the 1998 album, *CHEF AID: THE SOUTH PARK ALBUM.*

MICHAEL

Tribute song recorded by Back 2 Back, to show their support for Michael, following allegations of child molestation in 1993.

MICHAEL JACKSON

Track featured on Negativland's 1987 album, *ESCAPE FROM NOISE.*

MICHAEL JACKSON

Dance track echoing Michael's name, and sampling fans singing his name, recorded by Fat Boy Slim (*aka* Norman Cook) for his 1996 album, *BETTER LIVING THROUGH CHEMISTRY.*

MICHAEL JACKSON & FRIENDS MEDLEY

Medley Michael performed, with some of his friends including Slash (who came on stage for *Black Or White*), at his concerts in Munich and Seoul in June 1999.

Featured songs: *Don't Stop 'Til You Get Enough, The Way You Make Me Feel, Scream, Beat It* and *Black Or White*.

MICHAEL JACKSON MEDLEY

Medley of Michael's hits – solo and with the Jacksons – by Ashaye (*aka* Trevor Ashaye), featuring: *Don't Stop 'Til You Get Enough, Wanna Be Startin' Somethin', Shake Your Body (Down To The Ground)* and *Blame It On The Boogie*.

Extended 12" version also featured: *Rock With You, Billie Jean* and *Get On The Floor*.

Charted at no.45 in the UK in 1983.

Also known by the title: *Don't Stop 'Til You Get Enough*.

MICHAEL JACKSON MEDLEY

Five minute medley of some of Michael's hits, mixed by Wettbewerb von Andreas and Claus Friedrich, released exclusively on a six track promo CD single of *You Are Not Alone*, in Austria in 1995 – marked VIVA TV's Michael Jackson competition.

Tracks featured: *Beat It, P.Y.T. (Pretty Young Thing), Don't Stop 'Til You Get Enough, Working Day And Night, Man In The Mirror, Heal The World, Remember The Time, Black Or White, Billie Jean, In The Closet, Thriller, Bad, Smooth Criminal, Bad, Scream, Dangerous, Jam* and *Black Or White*.

MICHAEL JACKSON MEDLEY

Medley of Michael's hits by Unlimited Beat, featured: *You Are Not Alone, Don't Stop 'Til You Get Enough, Billie Jean, Thriller, Beat It, Bad, They Don't Care About Us, Black Or White* and *Earth Song*.

Released in 1998 but failed to chart; also featured on Unlimited Beat's album, *THE MEDLEYS VOL.1*.

MICHAEL JACKSON MEDLEY

Medley of *Thriller*, *Beat It* and *Smooth Criminal* performed by British boy band, Blue. Featured on their 2004 DVD, *Guilty – Live From London* and *THE PLATINUM COLLECTION*, released in 2006.

MICHAEL MANIA MEDLEY

Medley of Michael's hits – solo and with his brothers – by Replay, with the extended 12" single featuring: *Don't Stop 'Til You Get Enough* (twice), *Another Part Of Me* (twice), *Billie Jean*, *Working Day And Night*, *Bad*, *Blame It On The Boogie*, *Rock With You*, *I Want You Back*, *Shake Your Body (Down To The Ground)*, *The Way You Make Me Feel*, *Can You Feel It*, *Wanna Be Startin' Somethin'* and *Thriller*.

Released in 1988 but failed to chart.

MICHAEL McKELLAR

Song Michael cited he had written in his court disposition in November 1993 – remains unreleased.

MICHAEL THE LOVER

Pre-Motown recording by the Jackson 5, originally titled *Some Girls Want Me For Their Lover* and issued as the B-side of *You Don't Have To Be Over Twenty One To Fall In Love* (itself a reissue of *We Don't Have To Be Over 21 (To Fall In Love)*), released in March 1971 in the States (no UK release).

First appeared as *Michael The Lover* on the 1989 release, *BEGINNING YEARS 1967-1968*.

Title of a pre-Motown compilation released on the K-Point label in 1999.

MICHAEL'S IN A JAM

Michael inspired single by the Knight Crew, featuring Monica and Contrelle, released as a single in the States in 2004. Extended version included original material not on the single release.

MICHAEL'S MEDLEY

Instrumental medley of Jackson hits released by Patrick Adams on a 12" single in 1984 in the States. Songs featured: *I Want You Back, Got To Be There, ABC, Wanna Be Startin' Somethin', I'll Be There, Billie Jean, Ben, Beat It, Say Say Say* and *Thriller*.

B-side featured dub version: *I Want You Back, ABC, Billie Jean, Say Say Say* and *Thriller*.

MIDNIGHT RENDEZVOUS

Song featured on the Jacksons album, *2300 JACKSON STREET*, issued in June 1989.

Michael wasn't involved with the recording of this song.

MIDNIGHT TRAIN TO GEORGIA

One of five songs the Jackson 5 performed a medley of at the Grammy Awards ceremony in 1974, to introduce the nominees for Best Rhythm & Blues Vocal Performance by a Group, Duo or Chorus – this song, by Gladys Knight & The Pips, took the Grammy.

Charted at no.1 on both American charts, and achieved no.10 in the UK.

MIND IS THE MAGIC

Song written by Michael with Bryan Loren in 1989 – re-worked for German illusionists Siegfried & Roy, who had worked with Michael on his Bad World Tour, as the theme song for their 'Beyond Belief Show, staged in Las Vegas.

Remained unreleased until 1995, when Michael gave his permission for the song's inclusion on Siegfried & Roy's German album, *DREAMS & ILLUSIONS* (no USA or UK release), which featured music from their show and a TV special.

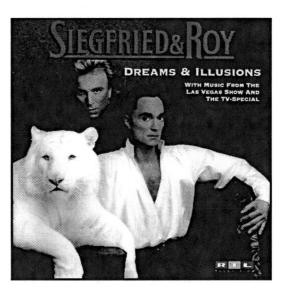

See also: *Siegfried & Roy*.

MIRRORS OF MY MIND, THE

Song the Jackson 5 recorded for their album, *DANICNG MACHINE*, issued in September 1974 in the States and November 1974 in the UK.

MISS LUCKY DAY

Song the Jackson 5 recorded for Motown – remains unreleased.

MJ MEGAMIX

Four minutes 58 seconds megamix of some of Michael's solo hits released on various formats in 1995, featured: *Thriller, Billie Jean, Bad, Don't Stop 'Til You Get Enough, Black Or White, Remember The Time, The Way You Make Me Feel, Wanna Be Startin' Somethin', Rock With You* and *Beat It*.

MJ MEGAREMIX

Ten minutes 33 seconds megaremix of some of Michael's solo hits released on various formats in 1995, featured: *Rock With You (Remix by Frankie Knuckles), Remember The Time (Remix by Steve 'Silk' Hurley), Don't Stop 'Til You Get Enough (Original Remix by Tony Moran & Ronnie Ventura), Billie Jean (Remix by Ronnie Ventura), Wanna Be Startin' Somethin' (Remix by Brothers In Rhythm), Black Or White (Remix by Clivilles & Cole)* and *Thriller (Remix by David Morales & Frankie Knuckles).*

Featured on Michael's home video, *History On Film Volume II*, accompanied by a montage of video clips.

MJ MELODY

Song written by Michael in 1982, and registered with the United States Copyright Office in November 1984 – remains unreleased.

MJ URBAN MEGAMIX

Four minutes 58 seconds urban megamix of some of Michael's solo hits, released on various formats in 1995, featured: *Rock With You, Billie Jean, Don't Stop 'Til You Get Enough, Remember The Time, The Way You Make Me Feel* and *Wanna Be Startin' Somethin'.*

226

MONEY

Written by Michael, and recorded for his HIS*TORY* album, issued in June 1995.

Track Sony wanted to issue as a single, ahead of *They Don't Care About Us* – Michael's choice.

Official Versions:
Album Version.
Fire Island Radio Edit.
Fire Island Radio Edit (different Intro).

MONEY HONEY

One of 19 'Rare & Unreleased' tracks on the fourth CD of the Michael/Jackson 5 box-set, *SOULSATION!*, issued in June 1995 in the States and July 1995 in the UK – demo version also known to exist.

Originally recorded in the mid 1950s by Clyde McPhatter & The Drifters.

MONEY (THAT'S WHAT I WANT)

Song heard in the TV mini-series, *The Jacksons: An American Dream* – it's possible the Jackson 5 performed this song in concert in the pre-Motown era

Hit versions:
Barrett Strong – no.2 on the R&B chart, and no.23 on the Hot 100, in the States in 1960.
Jennell Hawkins – no.17 on the R&B chart in 1962.
Bern Elliott & The Fenmen – no.14 in the UK in 1963.
Kingsmen – no.16 on the Hot 100 in 1964.
Jr. Walker & The All Stars – no.35 on the R&B chart, and no.52 on the Hot 100, in 1966.
Flying Lizards – no.5 in the UK in 1979, and no.50 on the Hot 100 in 1980.
Backbeat Band – no.48 in the UK in 1994.

MONKEY BUSINESS

Written by Michael with Bill Bottrell, and originally titled *Too Much Monkey Business*, recorded by Michael at Record One Studios and Westlake Studios in 1989.

First mentioned in 1991 in the British magazine *Revolution*, and cited by Michael in his court disposition in November 1993.

Included on an ultra rare promo titled 'Promo Flight Only', of which only ten copies exist, given to Sony Executives on their way to Neverland from Europe in 1991, as a teaser for tracks under consideration for Michael's album, *DANGEROUS* – the promo also featured the still unreleased *Men In Black*.

Scheduled to be included on the expanded, special edition of *DANGEROUS*, issued in 2001, before the bonus CD was cancelled.

Surfaced on the internet in 2002 – no official release until it was included on Michael's box-set, *THE ULTIMATE COLLECTION*, issued in November 2004.

MONOLOGUE – I WANT YOU BACK

22 second monologue – followed by *I Want You Back* – by Michael, talking about how Diana Ross 'discovered' the Jackson 5 and took them to Motown. Featured on *THE MOTOWN STORY* 10th anniversary box set, issued in the States in March 1971.

MOON IS WALKING, THE

Closing theme song to Michael's 1988 film, *Moonwalker*, performed by Ladysmith Black Mambazo.

MOONWALKER MEDLEY

Medley of 'retrospective' hits and clips featured as a montage in Michael's film, *Moonwalker*.

Songs featured: *Music And Me, I Want You Back, ABC, The Love You Save, 2-4-6-8, Who's Lovin' You, Ben, Dancing Machine, Blame It On*

The Boogie, Shake Your Body (Down To The Ground), Rock With You, Don't Stop 'Til You Get Enough, Can You Feel It, Human Nature, Beat It, Thriller, Billie Jean, State Of Shock, We Are The World, The Way You Make Me Feel, Dirty Diana and *Bad*.

Directed by Jerry Kramer, who also directed the *Man In The Mirror, Badder, Speed Demon, Leave Me Alone, Come Together* and *The Moon Is Walking* parts of the film.

MORE THAN I KNOW – AM I BLUE – FOR ONCE IN MY LIFE – TRY A LITTLE TENDERNESS

Medley of songs performed by guest, Sonny Bono, on the Jacksons' TV series in 1976 – Michael and his brothers sang the chorus.

MORNING GLOW

Song from the Broadway musical, *Pippin* – as well as a version by John Rubinstein & Chorus, Michael's version was included on the 1972 original cast recording album as a bonus track.

Included on Michael's album, *MUSIC & ME*, issued in April 1973 in the States and July 1973 in the UK.

Released as a single in the UK but failed to chart.

B-side of *With A Child's Heart* in the States.

MORPHINE

Written by Michael during the sessions for his HIS*TORY* album, but failed to make the final cut. First released as one of five new songs featured on his album, *BLOOD ON THE DANCE FLOOR*, issued in April 1997.

Re-titled *Just Say No* in some Far Eastern countries, which are especially strict when it comes to drugs and the law – the song, almost certainly, was inspired by Michael's dependency/addiction to prescribed drugs, around the time he wrote it.

MOTHER

Poem written by Michael – included in his book of poems and reflections, *Dancing The Dream*, published in 1992.

Edited version of the poem included in Katherine Jackson's autobiography, *My Family, The Jacksons*, published in 1990.

Registered with the US Copyright Office in June 1990, as *Mother Dear*.

MOVIE AND RAP

Excerpts of the Jackson 5's *I Want You Back* and *Never Can Say Goodbye*, and Michael's *Got To Be There*, featured on the Jacksons album, *LIVE*, issued in November 1981.

MOVING VIOLATION

Title track of the last album released by the Jackson 5, whilst they were still a Motown act, issued in May 1975 in the States and July 1975 in the UK.

Performed by the Jackson 5 on the TV shows, *Dinah* and *American Bandstand*, in the States in 1975, and by the Jacksons on their own TV series in 1977.

Also known by the title, *It's A Moving Violation*.

MTV MUSIC VIDEO AWARDS MEDLEY

Medley of hits Michael performed at the MTV Music Video Music Awards, staged at New York's Radio City Music Hall on 7th September 1995.

Featured songs: *Don't Stop 'Til You Get Enough, The Way You Make Me Feel, Jam, Scream, Beat It, Black Or White, Billie Jean, Dangerous* and *Smooth Criminal*.

Accompanied by Slash.

Michael also performed *Dangerous* and *You Are Not Alone*.

MUCH TOO SOON

Song Michael wrote circa 1981, and cited by him in his court disposition in November 1993 – remains unreleased.

Believed by some fans to be an early version of *Gone Too Soon* – unconfirmed.

MUSCLES

Song Michael wrote and produced for his long time friend, Diana Ross, and featured on her 1982 album, *SILK ELECTRIC*.

'I was coming back from England, after working on Paul McCartney's album, zooming along on Concorde,' said Michael, explaining how he wrote the song, 'and this song popped into my head. I said – hey, that's perfect for Diana! I didn't have a tape recorded or anything, so I had to suffer for like three hours. Soon as I got home, I whipped that baby on tape.'

Issued as a single in September 1982 in the States, and the following month in the UK – charted at no.4 on the R&B singles chart and no.10 on the Hot 100 in the States, and achieved no.15 in the UK.

Live version included on Diana's 1989 album, *GREATEST HITS LIVE*.

Cover versions recorded by the Weather Girls, for their 2005 album, *TOTALLY WILD*, and by Club 69 for their 1997 album, *STYLE*.

Sampled by Young Jeezy on *The Inspiration (Follow Me)*, a track on his 2006 album, *THE INSPIRATION*.

MUSIC AND ME

Song Michael recorded for his solo album, *MUSIC & ME*, issued in April 1973 in the States and July 1973 in the UK.

Released as a single in May 1974 in the UK – failed to chart (no USA release).

Live performance by the Jacksons, at a concert in Mexico in 1976, omitted from the home video, *The Jacksons In Concert*, released in 1981 in the UK (no USA release).

Album re-packaged, minus *Doggin' Around*, and reissued in the UK in 1993 – this album was originally issued in the States in 1985, as *MOTOWN LEGENDS*.

MUSIC'S TAKIN' OVER

Song the Jacksons recorded for their album, *GOIN' PLACES*, issued in October 1977.

Released as a single in March 1978 in the UK – failed to chart (no USA release).

MY CHERIE AMOUR

Stevie Wonder cover featured on the Jackson 5's debut album, *DIANA ROSS PRESENTS THE JACKSON 5*, issued in December 1969 in the States and March 1970 in the UK – lead vocals by Jermaine.

Featured on the 'Farmer Jackson' episode of the Jackson 5 cartoon series in 1971.

Stevie Wonder's original recording peaked at no.4 on both American charts and in the UK in 1969.

MY FAVOURITE THINGS

Song from *The Sound Of Music* the Jackson 5 recorded a version of for their *CHRISTMAS ALBUM* circa 1970, but which failed to make the final track listing – remains unreleased.

Hit version:
Herb Alpert – no.45 on the Hot 100 in the States in 1969.

MY GIRL

Temptations classic, written by Smokey Robinson, the Jackson 5 performed to win the City Wide Talent Show at Roosevelt High School in 1965.

Performed, in the early days, with Jermaine singing lead – before Michael took over as the Jackson 5's lead vocalist.

Pre-Motown recording by the Jackson 5 first heard in 1993, when it featured on a Japanese release, *BIG BOY*; later the same year, included on *THE JACKSON FIVE FEATURING MICHAEL JACKSON*, issued on the Stardust label in the UK/Europe.

Recorded by Michael for his solo album, *BEN*, issued in August 1972 in the States and December 1972 in the UK.

B-side of *Morning Glow* in the UK.

Title of a cassette-only compilation released in the States in 1989.

Hit versions:
Temptations – no.1 on both American charts, and no.43 in the UK, in 1965.
Otis Redding – no.11 in the UK in 1965.
Bobby Vee (medley) – no.35 on the Hot 100 in the States in 1968.
Eddie Floyd – no.43 on the R&B singles chart in the States in 1970.
Amii Stewart & Johnny Bristol (medley) – no.76 on the R&B singles chart in 1980.
Whispers – no.26 in the UK in 1980.
Daryl Hall & John Oates with David Ruffin & Eddie Kendrick (medley) – no.20 on the Hot 100 and no.40 on the R&B singles chart in 1985.
Suave – no.3 on the R&B singles chart and no.20 on the Hot 100 in 1988.
Temptations (reissue) – no.2 in the UK in 1992.

MY LITTLE BABY

Song the Jackson 5 recorded for their album, *MAYBE TOMORROW*, issued in April 1971 in the States and October 1971 in the UK.

B-side of *Doctor My Eyes* in the UK.

Featured in the 'Bongo, Baby Bongo' episode of the Jackson 5 cartoon series in 1971.

MYSTERY

Track written by Rod Temperton – turned down by Michael, then later recorded by Anita Baker for her 1986 album, *RAPTURE*.

Also the name of a peach flavoured isotonic drink Michael launched in 1996, and of a fan magazine dedicated to Michael.

NEITHER ONE OF US (WANTS TO BE THE FIRST TO SAY GOODBYE)

Gladys Knight & the Pips hit the Jackson 5 recorded a version of – remains unreleased.

Hit versions:
Gladys Knight & the Pips – no.1 on the R&B singles chart and no.2 on the Hot 100 in the States, and no.31 in the UK, in 1973.
David Sanborn – no.56 on the R&B singles chart in 1983.

NEVER CAN SAY GOODBYE

Song written by Clifton Davis originally intended for the Supremes, recorded by the Jackson 5 for their album, *MAYBE TOMORROW*, issued in April 1971 in the States and October 1971 in the UK.

Hit no.1 on the R&B singles chart and no.2 on the Hot 100 in the States, but stalled at no.33 in the UK.

Estimated USA sales: 1.6 million.

Early American copies released with special picture sleeve carrying the inscription: 'See The Jackson 5 on ABC-TV Special *Diana!* April 18th 1971'.

Promoted on the group's TV special and *The Flip Wilson Show* in the States in 1971, and performed by the Jackson 5 on *The Tonight Show* (hosted by Johnny Carson) in April 1974, and by the Jacksons on their own TV series in 1976.

Featured in 'The Rare Pearl' episode of the new Jackson 5 cartoon series in 1971.

Cited by Michael, in the early 1970s, as one of his three favourite songs he had recorded for Motown, along with *ABC* and *I'll Be There*.

Live version featured on the Michael/Jackson 5's *LIVE!* album, issued in September 1988 in the UK (no USA release). All songs on the album were recorded at a concert on 30th April 1973, at the Osaka Koseinenkin Hall in Japan. Also included on the limited edition CD, *IN JAPAN!*, released by Hip-Select in 2004 – only 5,000 copies pressed.

Live performance by the Jacksons, at a concert in Mexico in 1976, included on the home video, *The Jacksons In Concert*, released in 1981 in the UK (no USA release).

Performed live by the Jacksons at *Motown 25: Yesterday, Today, Forever*, staged in the Pasadena Civic Auditorium on 25th March 1983.

Adult solo version by Michael scheduled to feature on the shelved compilation, *DECADE 1980-1990* – remains unreleased.

236

Sub-title of the Jackson 5 compilation, *MOTOWN LEGENDS*, released in 1993.

Osawa 3000 Remix, as included on the Japanese album, *SOUL SOURCE – JACKSON 5 REMIXES* in 2000, featured extended vocals.

Other hit versions:

Isaac Hayes – no.5 on the R&B singles chart and no.22 on the Hot 100 in the States in 1971.

Gloria Gaynor – no.2 in the UK, and no.9 on the Hot 100 and no.34 on the R&B singles chart in the States, in 1974.

Communards – no.4 in the UK, and no.51 on the Hot 100 in the States, in 1987.

Yazz – no.61 in the UK in 1997.

Numerous other versions, including:

Johnny Mathis – for his album, *YOU'VE GOT A FRIEND*, in 1971.

Dennis Coffey & The Detroit Guitar Band – for the album, *GOIN' FOR MYSELF*, in 1972.

California Raisins – for the album, *SWEET, DELICIOUS & MARVELLOUS*, in 1990.

Dennis Brown – for his album, *MILK & HONEY*, in 1996.

Sheena Easton – for her album, *FABULOUS*, IN 2001.
Andy Williams – for his album, *I THINK I LOVE THE 70s*, in 2001.
Supremes – for their album, *70s ANTHOLOGY*, in 2002.
Vanessa Williams – for her album, *EVER LASTING LOVE*, in 2005.
Temptations – for their album, *REFLECTIONS*, in 2006.

Sampled by Lil' J. Xavier on the track *I Love My Music*, from his 2006 album, *YOUNG PRINCE OF THA SOUTH*.

NEVER HAD A DREAM COME TRUE

Stevie Wonder hit, recorded by the Jackson 5 for their *ABC* album, issued in May 1970 in the States and August 1970 in the UK.

Stevie's original – from his album *SIGNED, SEALED & DELIVERED* – charted at no.11 on the R&B singles chart and no.26 on the Hot 100 in the States, and no.6 in the UK, in 1970.

NEVERLAND LANDING

Song Michael cited he had written in his court disposition in November 1993 – remains unreleased.

Version, supposedly by Michael, surfaced on the internet – this was actually a song titled *Wayfaring Stranger*, performed live by Tom Fox.

NIGHT TIME LOVER

Written by Michael with sister La Toya, and recorded by La Toya for her debut, self-titled album in 1980, with Michael producing and singing backing vocals.

Originally titled *Fire Is The Feeling*, and written with Donna Summer in mind.

Issued as a single in the States in August 1980 – peaked at no.59 on the R&B singles chart, but failed to make the Hot 100 (no UK release).

NIGHTLINE / NITE-LINE

Originally written by Glen Ballard circa 1982, for Michael's *THRILLER* album, but failed to make the final track listing.

'When I found out it wasn't going to be on there, I just said, I'll be on the next one,' said Ballard in 1999. 'And the truth is, I got on the next two, which cumulatively sold over 50 million. It turned out to be good karma. I feel that if *Nite-Line* had been on *THRILLER*, I would never have written *Man In The Mirror*, which is an infinitely better song, and one of the best in my catalogue.'

Recorded as *Nightline* by the Pointer Sisters, for the original 1983 version of their album, *BREAK OUT* (on the second pressing *Nightline* was replaced by *I'm So Excited*); B-side of the group's hit single, *Automatic*.

Recorded by Ellen Foley for her 1983 album, *ANOTHER BREATH*, and by Randy Crawford for her album of the same title in 1994.

Known to have been recorded by Michael – no official release.

NIGHTMARE OF EDGAR ALAN POE, THE

Song believed to be written by Michael Jackson with Walter Afanasieff, circa 2000, for the shelved independently financed movie, *The Nightmare Of Edgar Alan Poe*, that Michael was slated to star in – remains unreleased.

Also known by the title, *Edgar Alan Poe*.

NO FRIEND OF MINE

Song by rapper Tempamental, featuring prominent backing vocals by Michael, made available in late 2006 on Tempamental's 'myspace' web page – originally titled, *Gangsta*.

NO NEWS IS GOOD NEWS

Song the Jackson 5 worked on with Stevie Wonder circa 1974 – remains unreleased.

NOBODY

Song the Jackson 5 recorded for their debut album, *DIANA ROSS PRESENTS THE JACKSON 5*, issued in December 1969 in the States and March 1970 in the UK.

Featured on the 'Groovatron' episode of the Jackson 5 cartoon series in 1971.

NONA

Song written by Jackie Jackson, for the Jacksons *VICTORY* album – failed to make the final selection.

NOT MY LOVER

Michael's original title for *Billie Jean*.

See also: *Billie Jean*.

NOTHIN' ELSE

One of several songs written by Pharrell Williams and submitted for Michael's HIS*TORY* and *INVINCIBLE* albums, which were later recorded by Justin Timberlake, for his debut album *JUSTIFIED*, released in 2002.

NOTHIN (THAT COMPARES 2 U)

Song featured on the Jacksons album, *2300 JACKSON STREET*, issued in June 1989.

Michael wasn't involved with recording this song.

NYMPHETTE LOVER

Song written by Michael in 1981, and registered with the United States Copyright Office in November 1984 – remains unreleased.

ODE TO SORROW

Song written by Michael in 1977, and registered with the United States Copyright Office in November 1984 – remains unreleased.

OFF THE WALL

Title track of Michael's first solo album for CBS/Epic, released in August 1979.

Written by Rod Temperton, who submitted three songs for the album. 'The one I thought would be their choice was *Off The Wall*,' he said. 'I tried to find out about Michael's character. I knew he liked Charlie Chaplin, and I thought *Off The Wall* would be a nice thing for Michael.'

Charted at no.5 on the R&B singles chart and no.10 on the Hot 100 in the States, and no.7 in the UK.

Official Versions:
Album Version.
Junior Vasquez Mix.

Live concert performance screened by Nippon TV in Japan.

Live version, recorded at a concert at Madison Square Garden in September 1981, featured on the Jacksons album, *LIVE*, issued in November 1981.

Sampled by Wisdome on *Off The Wall (Enjoy Yourself)* – charted at no.33 in the UK in 2000.

OFF THE WALL MEDLEY

Medley of *Rock With You*, *Off The Wall* and *Don't Stop 'Til You Get Enough*, from Michael's *OFF THE WALL* album.

Performed by Michael on his *His*tory World Tour – Auckland concert screened on TV in New Zealand.

OH, HOW HAPPY

Song the Jackson 5 recorded for their *THIRD ALBUM*, issued in September 1970 in the States and February 1971 in the UK.

One of six tracks from the album included on *Third Album EP*, released with a picture sleeve in the States in 1970.

Featured in the 'Wizard Of Soul' episode of the Jackson 5 cartoon series in 1971.

OH, I'VE BEEN BLESS'D

Song the Jackson 5 originally recorded for their debut album, *DIANA ROSS PRESENTS THE JACKSON 5*, but that failed to make the final cut.

Remained unreleased until it was included on *BOOGIE*, issued in North America only in January 1979, then quickly withdrawn.

ON MY ANGER

Song written by Michael with Teddy Riley circa 1999, and considered for Michael's album, *INVINCIBLE* – remains unreleased.

ON THE LINE

Written by Babyface, and originally recorded by Michael for the Spike Lee movie, *Get On The Bus*, but not featured on the soundtrack album.

Lead track of a 3-track 'minimax' CD single, released as part of the 'Deluxe Collector Box Set' of *Ghosts* in December 1997 in the UK (no USA release). Box set also included Michael's *Ghosts* mini-movie on home video and his *BLOOD ON THE DANCE FLOOR* album on CD.

Full length version included on Michael's *THE ULTIMATE COLLECTION* box-set, issued in November 2004.

Featured on a Columbia Pictures *Get On The Bus* promo CD, along with *Over A Million Strong* by the Neville Brothers, as a potential Oscar nominee, for Best Original Song.

ON THE WALL

Ditty performed by the Jacksons at the beginning of each episode of their *The Jacksons* TV series in 1976, to introduce their sisters, Rebbie, La Toya and Janet, as well as their special guest star, who would sign their name 'on the wall'.

ONCE WE WERE THERE

Poem written by Michael – included in his book of poems and reflections, *Dancing The Dream*, published in 1992.

244

ONE BAD APPLE

Song Berry Gordy rejected for the Jackson 5, only for it to be recorded in classic Jackson 5 style by the Osmonds – who held the no.1 spot on the Hot 100 in the States while the Jackson 5's own *Mama's Pearl* stalled at no.2.

'Did you know that record was ours at first?' Michael once asked. 'But Motown turned it down. George Jackson is the producer, and he came to Motown with it, and Motown turned it down because we were in a funky, strong track-type bag, with good melody. George's song was good, but too easy going – we were striving for something much stronger. So he went and gave it to the Osmonds. They sang it, and it was a smash – number one!'

ONE DAY I'LL MARRY YOU

Song recorded by the Jackson 5 between 1970-73, but unreleased until it was included on the album *BOOGIE*, issued in North America in January 1979 then quickly withdrawn.

ONE DAY IN YOUR LIFE

Song Michael recorded for his *FOREVER, MICHAEL* album, issued in January 1975 in the States and March 1975 in the UK.

Released as a single in the UK in April 1975 – failed to chart (no USA release).

Performed by Michael on *Dinah* and *Soul Train* in the States.

Live performance by the Jacksons, at a concert in Mexico in 1976, omitted from the home video, *The Jacksons In Concert*, released in 1981 in the UK (no USA release).

Re-activated by Motown in 1981, to cash-in on the success of Michael's *OFF THE WALL* album – stormed to no.1 in Australia, Belgium, Holland, Ireland, South Africa, the UK and Zimbabwe.

BPI Gold Disc (UK sales of 500,000) – Michael's first solo no.1 in the UK.

Achieved at no.42 on the R&B singles chart and no.55 on the Hot 100 in the States, where oldies rarely chart at all.

Green vinyl 7" single released in Ireland.

Album of the same title also released in 1981, credited to Michael, despite comprising tracks from two Jackson 5 albums, *GET IT TOGETHER* and *JOYFUL JUKEBOX MUSIC*.

ONE (FINALE)

Song the Jacksons performed on their TV series in 1976, with their special guest, Georgia Engel.

Originally featured in the 1975 Broadway musical, *A Chorus Line*.

ONE MORE CHANCE

Track featured on the Jackson 5's *ABC* album, issued in May 1970 in the States and August 1970 in the UK.

B-side of *I'll Be There*.

Released as a single, with picture sleeve, in Japan only.

Featured in the 'Rasho Jackson' episode of the Jackson 5 cartoon series in 1971.

Cover version by The One charted at no.31 in the UK in 1997.

ONE MORE CHANCE

Written by Randy Jackson, and recorded by the Jacksons *VICTORY* album, issued in July 1984.

One of sister Janet's favourite songs of all time – she even recorded a cover version, which featured on various formats of her 1993 single, *If.*

ONE MORE CHANCE

Only new song – written by R. Kelly – featured on Michael's compilation album, *NUMBER ONES*, issued in November 2003.

Charted at no.5 in the UK, and at no.40 on the R&B singles chart and no.83 on the Hot 100 in the States, in 2003.

Official Versions:

Album Version.	Paul Oakenfold Urban Mix.
Ford Remix.	R. Kelly Remix.
Metro Remix.	Ron G. Club Mix.
Night & Day Remix.	Ron G. Rhythmic Mix.
Night & Day R&B Remix.	Slang Remix.
Paul Oakenfold Mix.	Slang Electro Remix.
Paul Oakenfold Pop Mix.	

Promo short film shot in Las Vagas and edited, but not released by Sony, as a result of fresh allegations made against Michael (he was, of course, acquitted on all charges). A promo featuring a montage of concert footage was used to promote the song.

OOH BABY, BABY

Smokey Robinson & The Miracles cover the Jackson 5 recorded – remains unreleased.

Also know by the title, *Ooo (Oooh) Baby Baby.*

Hit versions:

Miracles – no.4 on the R&B singles chart and no.16 on the Hot 100 in the States in 1965.

Five Stairsteps – no. 34 on the R&B singles chart and no.63 on the Hot 100 in 1967.

Shalamar – no.59 on the R&B singles chart in 1977.

Linda Ronstadt – no.7 on the Hot 100 and no.77 on the R&B singles chart in 1979.

Romeo – no.67 on the R&B singles chart in 1987.

Zapp – no.18 on the R&B singles chart in 1989.

OOH, I'D LOVE TO BE WITH YOU

Song the Jackson 5 recorded for their *SKYWRITER* album, issued in March 1973 in the States and July 1973 in the UK.

Mistakenly included on the Michael/Jackson 5 box set, *SOULSATION!*, in place of the 'Rare & Unreleased' track *You're The Only One* – which remains unreleased.

OPUS ONE

Song the Jackson 5 performed, along with *Up The Lazy River*, with the Mills Brothers, on the *One More Time* TV special in the States in January 1974.

Also performed, as part of a 'Salute to the Vocal Groups' medley with *Bei Mir Bist Du Schon, Yakety Yak, Stop! In The Name Of Love*, an untitled Jackson 5 ditty and *Dancing Machine*, on *The Carol Burnett Show* in the States in January 1975.

Performed by the Jacksons on their TV series in 1977.

PAIN, THE

Song written by Rodney Jerkins, Jay Harvey Mason and Shawn Stockman, for Michael's album, *INVINCIBLE* – left off the album and remains unreleased.

PAPA WAS A ROLLIN' STONE

Temptations hit the Jackson 5 often performed live in the early days, and are known to have recorded a studio version of – remains unreleased.

Live recording featured on Michael & The Jackson 5's *LIVE!* album, issued in the UK in September 1988 (no USA release). Recorded at the Jackson 5's concert at Osaka Koseinenkin Hall, Japan, on 30th April 1973, with Jermaine singing lead. Album also known by the title, *IN JAPAN!* – included on the limited edition CD, *IN JAPAN!*, released by Hip-Select in 2004 – only 5,000 copies pressed.

Comedy skit performed by Michael and his brothers, dressed in inflated costumes as the 'Ton-Tations', on their TV series in 1976.

Live performance by the Jacksons at a concert in Mexico in 1976, with Marlon singing lead, included on the home video, *The Jacksons In Concert*, released in 1981 in the UK (no USA release).

Other covers versions include one by Bill Wolfer, with backing vocals by Michael, featured on Bill's 1980 album, *WOLF*.

Hit versions:
Temptations – no.1 on the Hot 100 and no.5 on the R&B singles chart in the States in 1972, and no.14 in the UK in 1973.
Undisputed Truth – no.24 on the R&B singles chart and no.63 on the Hot 100 in 1972.
Bill 'Wolf' Wolfer – no.47 on the R&B singles chart and no.55 on the Hot 100 in 1983.
Temptations (remix) – no.31 in the UK in 1987.
Was (Not Was) – no.12 in the UK and no.60 on the R&B singles chart in the States in1990.
George Michael (medley) – no.1 in the UK (as part of the *Five Live EP*), no.69 on the Hot 100 and no.88 on the R&B singles chart in 1993.

PENNY ARCADE

Song recorded by the Jackson 5 between 1970-73, but unreleased until it featured on the album *BOOGIE*, issued in North America in January 1979 but quickly withdrawn.

PEPSI GENERATION

Jingle based on *Billie Jean*, which accompanied Michael's first sponsorship deal with Pepsi Cola in 1984.

Pepsi campaign 'The Choice of a New Generation' launched at the Lincoln Center, New York, on 26th February 1984. Launch attended by 1,600 people; the programme for the evening came with a 7" promo of Michael's re-working of *Billie Jean*, for the advertising campaign.

Released as a promo 7" single, with 20 page booklet, in France in 1984.

Included on the album, *GREAT COLA COMMERCIALS VOLUME 2*, issued in the States in September 1998 – short and long versions featured.

Spoof of Michael's commercial by Bryan Stoller, titled 'The Shadow of Michael Jackson', released in 1984.

PEOPLE HAVE TO MAKE SOME SORT OF JOKE

Song Michael cited he had written, probably with one of his brothers, in his court disposition in November 1993 – remains unreleased.

PEOPLE MAKE THE WORLD GO ROUND

Stylistics cover Michael recorded for his solo album, *BEN*, issued in August 1972 in the States and December 1972 in the UK.

The Stylistics took the song to no.6 on the R&B singles chart and no.25 on the Hot 100 in the States in 1972.

Version by the Ramsey Lewis Trio included on Motown's various artist album, *SAVE THE CHILDREN*, released in 1974 in the States.

PEOPLE OF THE WORLD

Second song written and produced by Michael in 1998, for the Japanese children's choir, J-Friends – Japanese lyrics by Yasushi Okimoto.

Issued as a single in Japan (no USA or UK release).

PETALS

Song featured on the Jackson 5's *MAYBE TOMORROW* album, released in April 1971 in the States and October 1971 in the UK.

Featured in the 'Jackson Street USA' episode of the Jackson 5 cartoon series in 1971.

PETER PAN

Michael's favourite fictional character – he could be seen singing 'I'm Peter Pan' on the *Michael Jackson – Unauthorised* home video, released in the UK in 1992.

Song mentioned by Michael on *THE MICHAEL JACKSON INTERVIEW* CD released by Baktabak in 1993 – remains unreleased.

Speaking to *Life* magazine in 1997, Michael said he was planning a film version of *Peter Pan*, after he claimed he had been misled by Steven Speilberg, who he believed had reneged on an offer to cast him in *Hook* six years ago.

'I worked on the script, writing songs, for six months,' said Michael, 'and they let me down. I was so heartbroken. Steven Speilberg admitted later it was a mistake. I was torn. He put me through a lot. We're friends now, though.'

PLANET EARTH

Song considered by Michael for his album, *DANGEROUS* – remains unreleased.

Lyrics published as a poem in the booklet that accompanied *DANGEROUS*, and featured in Michael's 1992 book of poems and reflections, *Dancing The Dream*.

Copyright registered as *Planet Earth, I Love You*.

PLEASE COME BACK TO ME

Song recorded by the Jacksons, and included as a bonus track on one of the 12" singles of *2300 Jackson Street*, issued in August 1989.

Michael wasn't involved with the recording of this song.

POLITICAL SONG FOR MICHAEL JACKSON TO SING

Song recorded by Minutemen, for their 1984 album, *DOUBLE NICKELS ON THE DIME*.

'To sing, to sing – that's the most important part,' said the Minutemen's Mike Watt, 'because I did want him (Michael) to sing it. He never called.'

POP

Hit song featured on N'Sync's album, *CELEBRITY*, released in 2001.

Performed by N'Sync at the MTV Video Awards in September 2001, where they were joined on stage by Michael, who body-popped along to the song's beat.

POWER

Song written by Jackie Jackson, for the Jacksons 1984 album, *VICTORY* – failed to make the final selection and remains unreleased.

PRESSURE

Song written by Rodney Jerkins, LaShawn Daniels, Fred Jerkins III and Jay Harvey Mason, for Michael's album, *INVINCIBLE* – didn't make the final track listing and remains unreleased.

PRICE OF FAME

Song slated to appear on Michael's 1987 album *BAD*, and to be the theme for his new Pepsi Cola commercial, but it failed to make the album and was replaced by *Bad* on the commercial – remains unreleased.

Price Of Fame: Pepsi registered with the United States Copyright Office in March 1987.

PRIDE AND JOY

Song included on the Jackson 5 album, *JOYFUL JUKEBOX MUSIC*, issued in October 1976 in the States and December 1976 in the UK – originally recorded during the *GET IT TOGETHER* sessions.

Made its CD bow in 2000, on the UK compilation, *'RIPPLES AND WAVES' AN INTRODUCTION TO THE JACKSON 5* (no USA release). Album titled *THE UNIVERSAL MASTERS COLLECTION* in most continental European countries.

Originally recorded by Marvin Gaye – he took the song to no.2 on the R&B singles chart and no.10 on the Hot 100 in the States in 1963.

PRIVACY

Written by Michael with Rodney Jerkins, Fred Jerkins III, LaShawn Daniels and Bernard Bell.

Featuring on Michael's album, *INVINCIBLE*, issued in October 2001.

PRIVATE AFFAIR

Song included on the Jackson album, *2300 JACKSON STREET*, issued in June 1989.

Michael wasn't involved with recording this song.

PURPLE SNOWFLAKES

Song the Jackson 5 recorded for their *CHRISTMAS ALBUM* circa 1970, but which failed to make the final track listing – remains unreleased.

Originally recorded by Marvin Gaye for his festive Motown album.

PUSH ME AWAY

Written by Michael with brothers Jackie, Marlon, Randy and Tito, and recorded and produced by the Jackson for their album, *DESTINY*, issued in December 1978.

Performed solo by Michael on *American Bandstand*, and with his brothers on *Soul Train*, in the States in 1979.

B-side of Michael's *She's Out Of My Life* in the UK.

PUTTING ON THE RITZ

Snippet of a song Michael performed as part of a three song medley – also including *Gotta Dance* and *They Can't Take That Away From Me* – on *The Jacksons* TV series in 1976.

P.Y.T. (PRETTY YOUNG THING)

Song originally written by Michael with Greg Phillinganes, but totally re-done to a more up-tempo beat by Quincy Jones and James Ingram. Recorded by Michael for his album, *THRILLER*, issued in December 1982.

Sisters Janet and La Toya were the 'pretty young things' singing 'na na na' back at Michael.

Charted at no.10 on the Hot 100 and no.46 on the R&B singles chart in the States, and no.11 in the UK.

Michael's sixth Top 10 hit on the Hot 100 from six releases from *THRILLER* – a new record from one album.

Official Versions:
Album Version.
Demo Version.

Demo version by Michael sampled by Monica on her single, *All Eyez On Me* – charted at no.32 on the R&B singles chart and no.69 on the Hot 100 in the States in 2002. 'We used vocals from the song that didn't make the *THRILLER* album,' said Rodney Jerkins. 'He (Michael) had more vocals and ad-libs that were never heard, and we used the ones that were not heard.'

New vocals ('get it on, get it on'), recorded by Michael circa 2000, included on the track featured on the Japanese version of Monica's album, which was cancelled in the States/Europe.

Chorus sampled by rapper Memphis Bleek, on *I Wanna Love U* – sung by Donell Jones. Featured on Bleek's 2003 album, *M.A.D.E.*.

Demo, recorded between April and October 1982, included on Michael's box-set, *THE ULTIMATE COLLECTION*, issued in November 2004.

QUANTUM LEAP

Poem written by Michael – included in his book of poems and reflections, *Dancing The Dream*, published in 1992.

QUICKSAND

Martha Reeves & the Vandellas hit the Jackson 5 recorded a version of – remains unreleased.

Martha & the Vandellas took the song to no.8 on both the Hot 100 and R&B singles chart in the States in 1964.

RAPPIN' WITH THE JACKSON 5

Question and answer interview with the Jackson 5, released on a 7" single in 1971 – available to buy via *TcB!* magazine in the States only.

Michael named his favourite Jackson 5 songs as *Can I See You In The Morning* and *I'll Be There*, while his favourite singers/groups at the time were Diana Ross, the Supremes and the Four Tops.

REACH IN

Song the Jackson 5 recorded for their *THIRD ALBUM*, issued in September 1970 in the States and February 1971 in the States.

One of six songs from the album included on *Third Album EP*, released with a picture sleeve in the States in 1970.

Featured in the 'CinderJackson' episode of the Jackson 5 cartoon series in 1971.

REACH OUT AND TOUCH (SOMEBODY'S HAND)

Song included in a book of Jackson 5 sheet music, published by Motown in 1970 – if the group recorded the song it remains unreleased.

Debut solo hit for Diana Ross, charting in 1970 at no.7 on the R&B singles chart and no.20 on the Hot 100 in the States, and no.33 in the UK.

Performed by Jason Weaver and Holly Robinson in the TV mini-series, *The Jacksons: An American Dream*, in 1992 – failed to make the accompanying soundtrack album.

REACH OUT I'LL BE THERE

Four Tops classic recorded by the Jackson 5 for their debut album, *DIANA ROSS PRESENTS THE JACKSON 5*, in 1970 – listed as the final track on early copies of the album released in the States, but didn't actually appear on the album.

Remained unreleased until it was one of 19 'Rare & Unreleased' tracks on the fourth CD of the Michael/Jackson 5 box-set, *SOULSATION!*, issued in June 1995 in the States and July 1995 in the UK.

Hit versions:
Four Tops – no.1 on both American charts, and in the UK, in 1966.
Merrilee Rush – no.79 on the Hot 100 in 1968.
Diana Ross – no.17 on the R&B singles chart and no.29 on the Hot 100 in 1971.
Gloria Gaynor – no.56 on the R&B singles chart and no.60 on the Hot 100, and no.14 in the UK, in 1975.
Four Tops (remix) – no.11 in the UK in 1988.
Michael Bolton – no.37 in the UK in 1993.

READY OR NOT (HERE I COME)

Originally titled: *Ready Or Not Here I Come (Can't Hide From Your Love)*.

Song featured on the Jackson 5's *THIRD ALBUM*, issued in September 1970 in the States and February 1971 in the UK.

One of six tracks from the album included on *Third Album EP*, released with a picture sleeve in the States in 1970.

Featured in the 'Jackson Island' episode of the Jackson 5 cartoon series in 1971.

Originally recorded by the Delfonics, for their 1969 album, *SOUND OF SEXY SOUL*.

Hit versions:
Delfonics – no.14 on the R&B singles chart and no.35 on the Hot 100 in the States in 1969, and no.41 in the UK in 1971.
Fugees – no.1 in the UK in 1996.
Course – no.5 in the UK in 1997.

'What I picked up on Michael Jackson, because I study people when I watch them,' observed Wyclef Jean of the Fugees, 'is the way that he counts his rhythm with his feet and his neck at the same time is crazy... so he's hearing multiple things at once – and I don't know anybody who does that.'

RED EYE

Song Michael cited he had written in his court disposition in November 1993 – remains unreleased.

REFLECTIONS

Diana Ross & Supremes cover the Jackson 5 recorded for their album, *GET IT TOGETHER*, issued in September 1973 and November 1993 in the UK.

Original recording achieved no.2 on the Hot 100 and no.4 on the R&B singles chart in the States, and no.5 in the UK, in 1967.

REMEMBER THE TIME

Written by Michael with Teddy Riley and Bernard Bell, and recorded for his album, *DANGEROUS*, issued in November 1991.

Riley told the *Los Angeles Times* in November 1996, he wrote the song after Michael told him about falling in love with Debbie Rowe: 'I don't know why he didn't marry her the first time around.'

Several demo versions known to exist – no official release.

Second single lifted from the album – dedicated to Diana Ross.

Hit no.1 on the R&B singles chart and no.3 on the Hot 100 in the States, and no.3 in the UK. Also achieved no.1 in New Zealand.

RIAA Gold Record (USA million seller).

Official Versions:
Album Version.
A Cappella.
Bonus Beats.
E-Smoove's Late Nite Mix.

New Jack Main Mix.
New Jack Mix.
New Jack Radio Mix.
Silky Soul Dub.

Maurice's Underground Mix.	Silky Soul 7".
Mo-Mo's Instrumental.	Silky Soul 12"
New Jack Main Jazz.	12" Main Mix.
E-Smoove's Late Nite Dub.	

Promo 9 minutes short film, directed by John Singleton, had an Egyptian theme. Co-starred Eddie Murphy as Pharaoh Ramses, supermodel Iman as Queen Nefertiti and pro-basketball star Magic Johnson as a slave. Michael shared his first on-screen kiss with Iman (Mrs David Bowie).

American Music Award: Favourite Soul/R&B Single, Male.

Performed by Michael at the *Soul Train* Awards in March 1993 – Michael twisted his ankle during rehearsals the day before, so sang from a wheelchair.

Twelfth of Michael's 20 *'Visionary – The Video Singles'* reissues, with the music on one side of a Dual Disc and the accompanying short film on the other side. Issued in May 2006 in the UK – charted at no.22.

RIDE WITH ME (IT'S NOT WORTH IT)

Instrumental Rodney Jerkins wrote for a CD titled *VERSITILITY* – aimed at up-and-coming artists, to help them create their own songs by adding lyrics.

Contained a sample of Michael, as did Brandy's *It's Not Worth It*, but not a new Michael Jackson song as some fans believe.

ROCK MY WORLD

Original title of Michael's hit, *You Rock My World*.

See also: *You Rock My World*.

ROCK WITH YOU

Song Michael recorded for his album, *OFF THE WALL*, issued in August 1979 – written by Rod Temperton.

'*Rock With You* was a rhythm section I'd had before,' said Temperton. 'I thought I'd go with this one because he's (Michael's) good at handling very melodic things.'

Hit no.1 on both American charts, and achieved no.7 in the UK.

RIAA Gold Record (USA million seller).

No.9 best selling single of 1980 in the States.

Promo short film, directed by Bruce Gowers, premiered in November 1979.

Michael recorded a slightly jazzed-up version in early 1980, which was included on new pressings of *OFF THE WALL*, replacing the original recording.

Official Versions:
Album Version.
Single Version.
Frankie's Favourite Club Mix.
Frankie's Favourite Club Mix Radio Edit.
Masters At Work Remix.

Masters At Work Remix and Frankie's remixes featured unreleased vocals and ad-libs not heard on the album version, as the remixers were given access to the master tapes of the song, which included additional vocals.

Performed by Michael on two TV specials in the States in 1980, the charity event *Because We Care* and *diana!* – on the latter, he sang the song twice, solo and as a duet with Diana Ross.

Live version, recorded at a concert at Madison Square Garden in September 1981, featured on the Jacksons album, *LIVE*, issued in November 1981. This version was released on the B-side of Michael's UK single, *Wanna Be Startin' Somethin'*.

Live performance part of a concert screened by Nippon TV in Japan.

Cover version recorded by Brandy, for Quincy Jones's 1995 album, *Q'S JOOK JOINT*.

Cover version by D'Influence charted at no.30 in the UK in 1998.

Version also recorded by Chuck Loeb.

Demo version included on the second acetate version of the expanded, special edition of Michael's *OFF THE WALL* album in 2001 – later withdrawn.

Third of Michael's 20 *'Visionary – The Video Singles'* reissues, with the music on one side of a Dual Disc and the accompanying short film on the other side. Issued in February 2006 in the UK – charted at no.15.

ROCKIN' ROBIN

Song Michael recorded for his debut album, *GOT TO BE THERE*, issued in January 1972 in the States and May 1972 in the UK.

Not intended to be released as a single, until DJs across the States began playing it – prompting Motown to issue it as the follow-up to *Got To Be There*.

Charted at no.2 on both American charts, and just one place lower in the UK.

Featured on the 'Who's Hoozis' episode of the new Jackson 5 cartoon series in 1971.

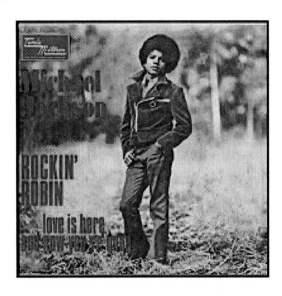

Promoted in the States by Michael on *American Bandstand* and *The Dating Game*, where Michael's chosen date was Latany Simmons.

Performed, during the group's European Tour in November 1972, by the Jackson 5 in the UK, on *Top Of The Pops* and at the Royal Command Performance – the latter was attended by HM The Queen Mother.

Performed by the Jacksons on their own TV series in 1977.

Live performance by the Jacksons, at a concert in Mexico in 1976, included on the home video, *The Jacksons In Concert*, released in 1981 in the UK (no USA release).

Sub-title of Michael's solo compilation, *MOTOWN LEGENDS*, released in 1993.

Hit versions:
Bobby Day (original version) – no.1 on the R&B singles chart and no.2 on the Hot 100 in the States, and no.29 in the UK, in 1958.

Rivieras – no.96 on the Hot 100 in 1964
Lolly – no.10 in the UK in 1999.

ROLLING THE DICE

Song written by Rod Temperton, which Michael worked on with Temperton and Quincy Jones during the *THRILLER* sessions.

Cited by Michael in his court disposition in November 1993 – remains unreleased.

RUDOLF THE RED-NOSED REINDEER

Festive favourite the Jackson 5 recorded for their *CHRISTMAS ALBUM*, issued in October 1970 in the States and December 1970 in the UK.

Hit versions:
Cadillacs – no.11 on the R&B singles chart in the States in 1956.
Gene Autry – no.70 on the Hot 100 in the States in 1957.
David Seville & The Chipmonks – no.21 on the Hot 100 in 1960.
Melodeers – no.71 on the Hot 100 in 1960.
Temptations – no.3 on the Christmas singles chart in the States in 1968.

RUNAROUND SUE

Dion hit Michael performed, with a whole host of other artists, as the finale for the Grammy Awards in early 1988 – he could be seen at the back, dancing and fooling around with Whitney Houston.

Michael owns the copyright to many of Dion's recordings, including *Runaround Sue*.

Dion took the song to no.1 in the States, and to no.11 in the UK, in 1961.

RYAN WHITE

Poem written by Michael – included in his book of poems and reflections, *Dancing The Dream*, published in 1992.

See also: *Gone Too Soon*.

SAD SOUVENIRS

Four Tops track the Jackson 5 recorded a version of – remains unreleased.

The Four Tops recording featured on their eponymous debut album, released in 1965.

SALUTE TO THE VOCAL GROUPS MEDLEY

Medley the Jackson 5 performed on *The Carol Burnett Show* in the States in January 1975, featuring: *Opus One, Bei Mir Bist Du Schon, Yakety Yak, Stop! In The Name Of Love, Dancing Machine* and *The Beat Goes On*.

Jackie, Jermaine and Randy performed *Bei Mir Bist Du Schon*, while Michael, Marlon and Tito did likewise on *Stop! In The Name Of Love*. Between *Stop! In The Name Of Love* and *Dancing Machine*, Michael and his brothers sang a short, untitled ditty about themselves.

Sonny & Cher's hit *The Beat Goes On* was performed by young Randy and even younger Janet Jackson; the Jackson 5 and hostess Carol

266

Burnett joined their siblings on stage towards the end of their performance.

SANTA CLAUS IS COMIN' TO TOWN

Another festive favourite the Jackson 5 recorded for their *CHRISTMAS ALBUM*, issued in October 1970 in the States and December 1970 in the UK.

Released as a single in the States in 1970 – at this time, Christmas singles were excluded from the mainstream Billboard charts. Hit no.1 on the special Christmas Singles chart in 1970 and 1971, and peaked at no.9 in 1973.

Charted at no.43 in the UK in December 1972.

One of four tracks from *CHRISTMAS ALBUM* featured on the *Merry Christmas From Michael Jackson With the Jackson 5 EP*, issued in the UK in 1987 – charted at no.91.

Other hit versions:
4 Seasons – no.23 on the Hot 100 in the States in 1962.
Carpenters – no.37 in the UK in 1975.
Bruce Springsteen – no.1 on the Christmas singles chart in the States, and no.9 in the UK, in 1985.
Bjorn Again – no.55 in the UK in 1992.

SATISFY

Written by James Harris III and Terry Lewis, and recorded by Mariah Carey – with Michael singing backing vocals – for her album, *CHARMBRACELET*, issued in 2002. Failed to make the final track listing and remains unreleased.

SATURDAY NITE AT THE MOVIES

Song the Jackson 5 often performed in concert in the pre-Motown days.

Remained unreleased until it appeared on the album, *BEGINNING YEARS 1967-1968*, issued in 1989.

Charted at no.18 on both the Hot 100 and R&B singles chart in the States in 1964, and at no.3 in the UK in 1972, for the Drifters.

SAVE ME

Song recorded by ex-Traffic guitarist Dave Mason, with Michael on backing vocals, for his solo album, *OLD CREST ON A NEW WAVE*, issued in June 1980 in the UK and July 1980 in the States.

'I was in one studio and he (Michael) was across the hall recording *THRILLER*,' said Mason. 'I had that song (*Save Me*), and thought it would be cool if someone could sing that really high part, so I thought I'd just go over there and ask him. I thought he'd just do this harmony part and he ended up doing this whole great thing and putting his own spin on it.'

Charted at no.70 on the R&B singles chart and no.71 on the Hot 100 in the States – not a hit in the UK.

SAVED BY THE BELL

Song Michael cited he had written with brother Jermaine in his court disposition in November 1993 – remains unreleased.

SAY SAY SAY

Written by Michael with Paul McCartney, and recorded as a duet for Paul's album, *PIPES OF PEACE*, issued in November 1983.

Michael and Paul first worked on the song, and their second duet on the Paul's album, *The Man*, during McCartney's 'War' sessions between May and September 1981. Song completed at Abbey Road studios in February 1983.

Produced by Beatles producer, George Martin, who said of Michael: 'He actually does radiate an aura when he comes into the studio, there's no question about it. He's not a musician in the sense that Paul is… but he does know what he wants in music and he has very firm ideas.'

Hit no.1 on the Hot 100, and no.2 on the R&B singles chart, in the States – achieved no.2 in the UK. Also no.1 in Canada, Finland, Italy and Norway.

Owed its success in the UK to *Top Of The Pops*, as it was outside the Top 10 and slipping down the chart, when a snippet of the promo video was featured as part of the American chart count down. Full length screenings on Noel Edmond's popular *Late, Late Breakfast Show* and Channel 4's cult music show *The Tube* followed, catapulting the single to no.2.

Official Versions:
Album Version.
Instrumental.
Jellybean Remix.

Michael's third single of 1983 to top the Hot 100, following *Billie Jean* and *Beat It* – together, they logged 16 weeks in pole position.

RIAA Platinum Record (USA two million seller).

Humorous short firm directed by Bob Giraldi, featured 'Mac & Jack' as travelling salesmen-cum-vaudeville artists, and co-starred Paul's wife Linda, Michael's sister La Toya, and Mr T (from *The A Team*). Filmed in Los Alamos, California, between 4th and 7th October 1983 – premiered in the UK on Channel 4's *The Tube* music programme on 28th October.

Cover version by Dutch group Hi-Tack, titled *Say Say Say (Waiting For U)*, hit no.4 in the UK in early 2006. Hi-Tack were also involved with BeatFreakz's hit remake of Rockwell's *Somebody's Watching Me*, also in 2006.

SCARED OF THE MOON

Song written by Michael circa 1985, as a contender for what became his *BAD* album, and cited in his court disposition in November 1993.

Demo version released on Michael's *THE ULTIMATE COLLECTION* box-set, issued in November 2004

SCREAM

Song written by Michael with sister Janet, James Harris III and Terry Lewis, and recorded as a duet with Janet for his album, HIS*TORY*, issued in June 1995.

'Sometimes, the only thing you can do is scream,' said Michael. 'You just wanna let it all out! People should listen, and decide for themselves.'

Lead single from the album, debuted at no.5 on the Hot 100 in the States – the highest ever new entry (the previous record holder, *Let It Be* by the Beatles, made its bow at no.6). Also achieved no.2 on the R&B singles chart and no.3 in the UK.

UK chart rules, which stated only three formats could be counted towards a chart placing, meant one 7" and two 12" singles charted independently, achieving no.43.

No.1 in Finland, Hungary, Italy, New Zealand, Spain and Zimbabwe.

270

Official Versions:

Album Version.
Clean Album Version.
Classic Club Mix.
Dave 'Jam' Hall's Extended Urban Remix.
Dave 'Jam' Hall's Urban Remix Edit.
Def Radio Mix.
D.M. R&B Extended Mix.
Scream Louder – Flyte Tyme Remix.
Single Edit.
Scream Louder – Flyte Tyme Instrumental.

Naughty Main Mix No Rap.
Naughty Radio Edit w/Rap.
Naughty Radio No Rap.
Naughty Pretty-Pella.
Pressurized Dub Pt.1.
Pressurized Dub Pt.2.
Naughty Acappella.
Naughty Main Mix.
Single Edit #2.

Futuristic short film, filmed in black and white, directed by Mark Romanek and cost $6 million – the most expensive music video ever. Premiered on 14th June 1995 on ABC-TV in the States.

Grammy Award: Best Music Video, Short Form.

Billboard Music Video Award: Video of the Year – Pop/Rock.

Short film nominated for 11 MTV Music Video Awards, but won only three: Best Dance Video, Best Choreography and Best Art Direction.

Song chosen to open Michael's *History* World Tour concerts.

Live performances screened in Germany and New Zealand, as part of concerts in Michael's *History* World Tour.

SCRUB, THE

Song written by Tito's music teacher, Shirley Cartman, who confirmed in her book, *A Teacher Remembers The Jacksons*, the Jackson 5 recorded it and other songs before they signed for Steel-Town Records – all remain unreleased.

SEASONS GREETING FROM MOTOWN RECORDS

Green label promo 7" single, sent by Motown to American radio stations and record distributors in 1973. Featured short messages from 14 Motown artists, including Michael, Jackie, Jermaine and Tito Jackson (but not Marlon).

Re-titled *Christmas Greetings From Michael Jackson*, when included on the 1995 festive compilation, *MOTOWN CHRISTMAS CAROL*.

SEDUCTION

Song written by Michael with Shelby Lee Myrick III, originally for his album, *INVINCIBLE* – failed to make the album and remains unreleased.

SEEING VOICES

Song written about 'signing' by Michael with veterans Ray Charles and Sidney Fine (who wrote *Lady* for Disney's *Lady & The Tramp* in 1955), and recorded by Michael and Ray Charles, with Ray's choir on backing vocals. Mentioned during the recording of Michael's *INVINCIBLE* album, but failed to make the final track listing – remains unreleased.

SEÑORITA

One of several songs written by Pharrell Williams and submitted for Michael's HIS*TORY* and *INVINCIBLE* albums, which were later recorded by Justin Timberlake, for his debut album *JUSTIFIED*, released in 2002.

SERIOUS EFFECT

Song written by Michael with Teddy Riley, and recorded by Michael, with rap by LL Cool J.

Scheduled to be included on the cancelled bonus CD of the expanded, special edition reissue of *DANGEROUS* in 2001.

Demo version by Michael solo known to exist.

Surfaced on the internet in 2002 – no official release.

SEVEN DIGITS

Song written by Michael with Bryan Loren – one of 20-25 songs they worked on together, for a new album, but ultimately not one of them appeared on *DANGEROUS* – remains unreleased.

SHAKE ME, WAKE ME (WHEN IT'S OVER)

Four Tops hit the Jackson 5 recorded a version of – remains unreleased.

The Four Tops took the song to no.5 on the R&B singles chart and no.18 on the Hot 100 in the States in 1966.

SHAKE YOUR BODY (DOWN TO THE GROUND)

Written by Michael with brother Randy, and recorded by the Jacksons for their album, *DESTINY*, issued in December 1978.

Early demo, recorded in 1978 and titled *Shake A Body*, included on Michael's box-set, *THE ULTIMATE COLLECTION*, issued in November 2004.

Song the Jacksons wanted to release as the lead single from *DESTINY*, but their record company insisted on issuing *Blame It On The Boogie* first instead.

274

Second single from the album – charted at no.3 on the R&B singles chart and no.7 on the Hot 100 in the States, and no.4 in the UK. Single version only half the length of the album version – extended Special Disco Remix also released.

RIAA Platinum Record (2 million copies in USA).

Performed by the Jacksons on *American Bandstand*, *Soul Train*, *The ABBA Special* (filmed in Switzerland), and their own *Midnight Special* – estranged brother Jermaine re-joined his brothers for the latter. *Soul Train* performance included on the home video, *Soul Searching*, released by Video Gems in the States in 1984 – also included *Think Happy* and Jermaine's *Let's Get Serious*.

Special Disco Version released on the 1979 Japanese promo album, *THE LEADER OF 80'S POP*, credited to Michael Jackson & The Jacksons.

Live version, recorded at a concert at Madison Square Garden in September 1981, featured on the Jacksons album, *LIVE*, issued in November 1981.

Performed by Michael during his Bad World Tour – one such concert screened on Nippon TV in Japan.

Performed by the Jacksons during the *Michael Jackson: 30th Anniversary Celebration, The Solo Years* concerts, staged at New York's Madison Square Garden on 7th and 10th September 2001.

Hit cover versions:
Full Intention – no.34 in the UK in 1997.
N-Trance (adaptation) – no.37 in the UK in 2000.

Sampled by Shaggy on *Dance & Shout* – no.19 in the UK in 2001, and registered at no.104 on the 'bubbling under' section of the Hot 100 in the States in 2000.

'Michael was really great in giving me the sample,' said Shaggy, 'because a lot of people tried to obtain a sample and couldn't get it… there were people that I've used sample with that just wanted everything. He basically was, like – hey, go ahead, man!'

Sampled by N-Trance on *Shake Ya Body* – charted at no.37 in the UK in 2000.

SHE

Song featured on the Jacksons album, *2300 JACKSON STREET*, issued in June 1989.

Michael wasn't involved with recording this track.

SHE DRIVES ME WILD

Written by Michael with Teddy Riley, and recorded for his album, *DANGEROUS*, issued in November 1991.

Percussion used on the track included motor sounds, trucks, cars screeching, motor bikes revving, car horns – and samples of Michael's tiger!

B-side of *Heal The World*.

SHE GOT IT

Song slated to appear on the bonus CD of the expanded, special edition reissue of *DANGEROUS* in 2001, before it was cancelled.

Snippets leaked on the internet in 2005, and some fans are known to have the full version of the song – no official release.

SHE SAY 'WANT'

Song the Jackson 5 recorded for Motown – remains unreleased.

Also known to fans by the title, 'She Say What'.

SHE WAS LOVING ME

Song Michael wrote with Mark C. Rooney for his album, *INVINCIBLE*, but failed to make the final track listing – remains unreleased.

SHE'LL BE COMING ROUND THE MOUNTAIN

Song Michael's mother Katherine has confirmed in her autobiography, *My Family, The Jacksons*, she used to sing with her young children in the late 1950s/early 1960s, in Gary, Indiana,

SHE'S A RHYTHM CHILD

Song featured on the Jackson 5's *DANCING MACHINE* album, issued in September 1974 in the States and November 1974 in the UK.

SHE'S GOOD

Song the Jackson 5 recorded for their album, *MAYBE TOMORROW*, issued in April 1971 in the States and October 1971 in the UK.

B-side of *Never Can Say Goodbye* – this version featured Jermaine singing solo, while the album version saw Jermaine backed by the Jackson 5.

Featured in the 'Jackson Street USA' episode of the Jackson 5 cartoon series in 1971.

SHE'S NOT A GIRL

Song Michael cited he had written in his court disposition in November 1993 – remains unreleased.

SHE'S OUT OF MY LIFE

Song Michael recorded for his solo album, *OFF THE WALL*, issued in August 1979.

Written by Tom Bahler – originally in E Flat, whereas Michael sang the song in E. Bahler couldn't play the song in E, 'so, Quincy recorded me playing it in my key and we made a tape for the pianist who was going to record it for the album. He took it home and studied it, in order to grasp whatever magic there was in my performance. When I listen to the record, I think – God, it sounds just like me!'

Inspired by Karen Carpenter, who broke up with Bahler, after she discovered he had fathered a child with another woman.

Every time he recorded the song, Michael cried, so producer Quincy Jones suggested a two week break – this changed nothing, so the emotional ending was left in. Numerous takes recorded, but Michael's first take made it on to his album.

Promo short film directed by Bruce Gowers – a simple affair with Michael sitting on a stool and singing, ended in tears as well.

Fourth single from the album – charted at no.3 in the UK, and no.10 on the Hot 100 and no.42 on the R&B singles chart in the States, making *OFF THE WALL* the first solo album to produce four Top 10 singles on both sides of the Atlantic.

RIAA Gold Record (USA million seller).

Performed by Michael during his Bad World Tour – at each concert, one lucky girl was allowed up on stage, to dance with Michael as he sang the song to her.

Live version, recorded at a concert at Madison Square Garden in September 1981, featured on the Jacksons album, *LIVE*, issued in November 1981. This version appeared on the B-side of the Jacksons single, *Wait*, in the UK.

Live performance by Michael, at his Dangerous Tour concert in Bucharest, Romania, on 1st October 1992, featured on the DVD released as part of his box-set, *THE ULTIMATE COLLECTION*, issued in November 2004.

Different live performance screened as part of a concert televised by Nippon TV in Japan.

Cover versions include:
Willie Nelson, for his 1984 album, *CITY OF NEW ORLEANS*.
98°, for their 1998 album, *98° AND RISING*.
Ginuwine, for his 1999 album, *100% GINUWINE*.
Mya (re-titled *Man Of My Life*), for her 2000 album, *FEAR OF FLYING*.

278

Josh Groban, as a bonus track for his 2003 album, *CLOSER*.
Patti LaBelle (re-titled *He's Out Of My Life*), for her 2005 album,
  CLASSIC MOMENTS.

Performed by Marc Anthony during the *Michael Jackson: 30th
Anniversary Celebration, The Solo Years* concerts, staged at New
York's Madison Square Garden on 7th and 10th September 2001.

SHE'S TROUBLE

Song – known to many fans by the title *Trouble* – written by Terry
Britten, Bill Livsey and Sue Shifrin, originally intended for Michael's
album, *THRILLER*, but didn't make the final track listing.

Bootleg version known to exist – no official release.

Versions recorded by Scott Baio, for his 1983 album, *THE BOYS ARE
OUT TONIGHT*, and by Musical Youth, for their 1983 album,
DIFFERENT STYLE. Musical Youth's version was a hit in the States,
peaking at no.25 on the R&B chart and no.65 on the Hot 100.

SHOO-BE-DOO-BE-DOO-DA-DAY

Stevie Wonder cover Michael recorded for his album, *BEN*, issued in August 1972 in the States and December 1972 in the UK.

Scheduled as the B-side of the planned follow-up to *Ben, Everybody's Somebody's Fool*, before it was surprisingly cancelled.

Sampled by Scanty Sandwich on *Because of You*, which rose to no.3 in the UK in January 2000.

Stevie Wonder's original version – from his 1968 album, *FOR ONCE IN MY LIFE* – topped the R&B singles chart, and achieved no.9 on the Hot 100, in 1968 – charted at no.46 in the UK.

SHORTNIN' BREAD

Song the Jackson 5 performed, as part of a medley with *Let It Be*, on the *Jim Nabors Show* in the States in September 1970.

Originally an Afro-American plantation song titled *La Manière Nègre*. Enjoyed a revival during the golden days of radio – made famous by Lawrence Tibbett, and later by Nelson Eddy. Shortnin' refers to all types of fat used in baking, e.g. butter, lard, margarine.

See also: *Let It Be – Shortnin' Bread.*

SHOUT

Written by Michael with Edward Riley, Claude Forbes, Roy Hamilton, Samuel Hoskins and Carmen Lampson, song originally scheduled to feature on Michael's *INVINCIBLE* album in 2001, before it was replaced by *You Are My Life*.

B-side of *Cry*, released in December 2001 in the UK (no USA release), and listed ahead of *Cry* and *Streetwalker* on the 12" single.

Version reportedly recorded by Backstreet boy, Nick Carter, for his debut solo album *NOW OR NEVER* in 2002, but failed to make the final selection. Bootleg versions of the Backstreet Boys performing the song in concert have appeared on the internet.

Sampled by independent artist, Kameko, on *Down And Out* – a track featured on his debut album, issued in 2006.

SHOW YOU THE WAY TO GO

Song the Jackson recorded for their eponymous debut album, issued in November 1976.

First Jackson single to hit no.1 in the UK, where it was promoted twice on *Top Of The Pops*, with one performance taken from *The Jacksons*

TV series. Also performed on the *Mike In Hollywood* show in the States, and during a Destiny Tour concert screened on BBC2 in the UK.

Single version featured slight alternate vocals. Charted at no.6 on the R&B singles chart and no.28 on the Hot 100 in the States.

Official Versions:
Album Version.
Single Edit.

Cover version by Danii Minogue (Kylie's sister) peaked at no.30 in the UK in 1992 – recorded for the charity album, *RUBY TRAX*.

Also covered by Men Of Vizion, for the *MONEY TRAIN* soundtrack and their debut album, *PERSONAL*, both released in 1996.

Sampled on the track *Party 2 Nite* by Ladae featuring Chubb Rock, from the 1996 album, *LADAE*.

SIEGFRIED & ROY

Written by Michael for illusionists Siegfried & Roy in 1989, two versions – vocal and instrumental – registered with the United States Copyright Office in January 1990 – remains unreleased.

Likely to be Michael's original title for *Mind Is The Magic*.

See also: *Mind Is The Magic*.

SIGNED, SEALED, DELIVERED I'M YOURS

Stevie Wonder classic the Jackson 5 recorded a version of – remains unreleased.

Hit versions:
Stevie Wonder – no.1 on the R&B singles chart and no.3 on the Hot 100 in the States, and no.15 in the UK, in 1970.
Peter Frampton – no.18 on the Hot 100 in 1977.
Boys Town Gang – no.50 in the UK in 1982.

282

Blue featuring Stevie Wonder & Angie Stone – no.11 in the UK in 2003.

Recorded by Jermaine Jackson for his 1981 album, *I LIKE YOUR STYLE*.

SILENT NIGHT

Festive favourite the Jackson 5 recorded for their *CHRISTMAS ALBUM* circa 1970, but which failed to make the final track listing – remains unreleased.

The song was written on Christmas Eve, 1818, by Father Joseph Mohr, the priest at a small church in Hallein, Austria – originally titled 'Song From Heaven'.

Best selling version recorded by Bing Crosby on 8th June 1942 (just ten days after he recorded *White Christmas*).

Other hit versions:
Mahalia Jackson – no.99 on the Hot 100 in the States in 1962.
Barbra Streisand – no.1 on the Christmas Singles chart in the States in 1966.
Temptations – no.7 on the Christmas Singles chart in 1969.
Dickies – no.47 in the UK in 1978.
Bros – no.2 in the UK in 1988.
Sinead O'Conner – no.60 in the UK in 1991.
Simon & Garfunkel (medley) – no.30 in the UK in 1991.

SILVER BELLS

Song the Jackson 5 recorded for their *CHRISTMAS ALBUM* circa 1970, but which failed to make the final track listing – remains unreleased.

Hit versions:
Bing Crosby & Carol Richards – no.78 on the Hot 100 in the States in 1957.
Al Martino – no.6 on the Christmas Singles chart in the States in 1964.
Earl Grant – no.3 on the Christmas Singles chart in 1966.

SINCE I LOST MY BABY

Temptations hit the Jackson 5 recorded a version of – remains unreleased.

Song also featured in the TV mini-series, *The Jacksons: An American Dream*, but not as performed by the Jackson 5.

Hit versions:
Temptations – no.4 on the R&B singles chart and no.17 on the Hot 100 in the States in 1965.
Luther Vandross – no.17 on the R&B singles chart in 1983.

SINCE YOU'VE BEEN GONE

Four Tops track the Jackson 5 recorded a version of – remains unreleased. The Four Tops recording featured on their 1965 album, *FOUR TOPS SECOND ALBUM*.

SING A SIMPLE SONG – CAN YOU REMEMBER

Medley the Jackson 5 performed on their first national TV appearance in the States, on 18th October 1969, on ABC-TV's *The Hollywood Palace Special*.

Included on the album, *MOTOWN AT THE HOLLYWOOD PALACE*, issued in the States in March 1970 (no UK release). The opening bar of the song was later used again on the Jackson 5's version of *Zip-A-Dee Doo-Dah*.

Sing A Simple Song, from their 1969 album *STAND!*, was a minor hit for Sly & The Family Stone on the Hot 100 in the States – it peaked at no.89 (as the flip-side of the chart topping *Everyday People*).

See also: *Can You Remember*.

SINGLES DISCO MIX

Rare, and very early, megamix of some of Michael's tracks (solo and with the Jacksons), released as a promo 12" single in 1983 in the UK – changed hands among avid collectors for up to £500 in 1983-84.

Featured hits: *Billie Jean (Intro)*, *Rock With You*, *Burn This Disco Out*, *Off The Wall*, *Don't Stop 'Til You Get Enough*, *Shake Your Body (Down To The Ground)*, *Blame It On The Boogie*, *Thriller* and *Billie Jean*.

SISTER SUE

Song Michael cited he had written in his court disposition in November 1993 – remains unreleased.

SKINNY LEGS AND ALL

Song the Jackson 5 performed in the mid-to-late 1960s, on the Chitlin' Circuit. Young Michael used to slide under tables, and mischievously lift the ladies skirts, before scurrying away – the audience invariably reacted by throwing money on stage, resulting in Michael and his brothers having pockets brimming with cash by the end of the gig.

SKY IS THE LIMIT, THE

Song Michael cited he had written with brother Jermaine in his court disposition in November 1993 – remains unreleased.

SKYWRITER

Title track of a Jackson 5 album issued in March 1973 in the States and July 1973 in the UK.

Second single, released with a rare picture sleeve, lifted from the album in the UK (no USA release) – charted at no.25.

Special advertisement shot by the Jackson 5, to promote the *SKYWRITER* album.

Song used by the Jackson 5, to open their Las Vegas Shows in April 1974.

Reissued in the UK in August 1977, as the lead track on the 3-track EP, *Jukebox Gem*.

SLAPSTICK

Song written by Rod Temperton, which Michael worked on during the *THRILLER* sessions – an early demo version of *Hot Street*.

Remains unreleased.

SLIPPED AWAY

Song Michael wrote with brother Marlon circa 1980 – failed to make the Jacksons album, *TRIUMPH*, and remains unreleased.

SMILE

Song recorded by Michael for his album, HIS*TORY*, issued in June 1995.

Scheduled for release as a single in the UK/Europe and other countries (not including the USA) in December 1997 – release cancelled, against Michael's wishes. Promo copies with shortened version issued, some featuring a rare and highly sought after picture sleeve depicting Michael dressed as Charlie Chaplin.

Promo short film, including footage of Charlie Chaplin, believed to have been shot – remains unreleased.

A Cappella snippet by Michael heard in his infamous interview with Martin Bashir, *Living With Michael Jackson*, first screened in the UK by ITV1 in February 2003.

Hit versions include:
Nat 'King' Cole – no.2 in the UK in 1954.
Tony Bennett – no.73 on the Hot 100 in the States in 1959.
Betty Everett & Jerry Butler – no.42 on both American charts in 1965.
Robert Downey, Jr. – no.68 in the UK in 1993.

SMOOTH CRIMINAL

Song written by Michael, and recorded for his *BAD* album, issued in September 1987 – evolved from another of Michael's songs, *Chicago 1945*.

Opening heartbeat heard on the song was Michael's, recorded by Dr Eric Chevlan, and digitally processed in a synclavier.

Seventh single lifted from the album – charted at no.2 on the R&B singles chart and no.7 on the Hot 100 in the States, and no.8 in the UK (where it gave Michael a record seventh Top 30 hit from one album).

No.1 in Belgium and Holland.

Official Versions:
Album Version.	Extended Dance Mix.
A Cappella.	Extended Dance Mix Radio Edit.
'Annie' Mix.	Instrumental.
Dance Mix Dub Version.	Single Version.

Featured in Michael's 'movie like no other', *Moonwalker*, which cost him an estimated $27 million, and premiered at the Cannes Film Festival in France on 18th May 1988.

Michael sang extra lines in the film version, compared with the album and single versions – it's believed these were part of the original studio version, but were taken out prior to the album's release (possibly to reduce the running time).

45 degree 'lean' in the short film achieved by using wires; in concert, Michael used an 'Anti-Gravity Illusion' device, to achieve the same effect.

Brit Award: Best Music Video of 1988.

People's Choice Awards: Favourite Music Video.

There are currently four alternate versions of the short film:

- Original *Moonwalker* version, as seen in the film.

- Edited *Moonwalker* version, as included on Michael's home video, His*tory On Film Volume II*.

- The Sped Up Video – as seen during the *Moonwalker* closing credits; this version was included on the *Visionary* reissue of *Smooth Criminal*.

- The Album Version – most commonly shown by music video stations; a version edited to be in-sync with the album version of the song.

Live performance by Michael, at his Dangerous Tour concert in Bucharest, Romania, on 1st October 1992, featured on the DVD released as part of his box-set, *THE ULTIMATE COLLECTION*, issued in November 2004.

Different live performances screened in Germany and New Zealand, as part of televised concerts.

Featured in the film, *American Pie 2* (2001).

Highly successful cover version by Los Angeles rockers, Alien Ant Farm, in 2001 which Michael approved: 'I fell in love with it,' he said. 'I heard it and gave it a triple A.' Promo video parodied several of Michael's short films. Single hit no.1 in Australia (for nine weeks), and charted at no.3 in the UK and no.23 on the Hot 100 in the States.

Dryden Mitchell, Alien Ant Farm's front-man, explained how the cover came about: 'We were playing a hometown show and Tye (Zamora, bassist) and Mike (Cosgrove, drummer) started playing it for three seconds, and a bunch of people in the crowd knew what it was. The next day, Mike went out and got the *BAD* tape, so I could figure out the lyrics and they could figure out the music. When we played it, we weren't proud of ourselves or anything, we were just like – this song is good, we like it!'

Opening sampled by Ashanti on the track, *Rescue*, from her eponymous album issued in 2002.

Ninth of Michael's 20 *'Visionary – The Video Singles'* reissues, with the music on one side of a Dual Disc and the accompanying short film on the other side. Issued in April 2006 in the UK – charted at no.19.

SNIPPETS FROM 'THE JACKSONS: AN AMERICAN DREAM'

Snippets of songs featured on *THE JACKSONS: AN AMERICAN DREAM* TV soundtrack album, issued on the Boyz II Men CD single, *In The Still Of The Nite (I'll Remember)*.

Featured snippets: *Who's Lovin' You (Live)*, *Kansas City* (by Jason Weaver), *I'll Be There, I Wanna Be Where You Are* (by Jason Weaver), *Dancing Machine (Remix), Jackson 5 Medley (I Want You Back/ABC (Live))*.

In The Still Of The Nite (I'll Remember) charted at no.3 on the Hot 100 and no.4 on the R&B singles chart in the States in 1992, and peaked at no.27 early the following year in the UK.

SO IN LOVE

Song Jermaine Jackson recorded, with the rest of the Jackson 5 on backing vocals, for his 1973 album, *COME INTO MY LIFE*.

SO SHY

Song Bill 'Wolf' Wolfer recorded, with Michael on backing vocals, for his 1982 album, *WOLF*.

SOLDIER'S ENTRANCE

Song Michael worked on circa 1999, with a view to recording it for his album, *INVINCIBLE* – remains unreleased.

SOME GIRLS WANT ME FOR THEIR LOVER

B-side of the Jackson 5's pre-Motown single *You Don't Have To Be Over Twenty One To Fall In Love*, issued in March 1971 in the States (no UK release) – A-side originally titled *We Don't Have To Be Over 21 (To Fall In Love)*.

Featured on the album, *GETTING TOGETHER WITH THE JACKSON 5*, also released in the States in 1971 (no UK release). Despite the title, the album only featured two songs by the Jackson 5.

Re-titled *Michael The Lover*, when included on the Jackson 5's album, *BEGINNING YEARS 1967-1968*, released in 1989.

It has been speculated *Some Girls Want Me For Their Lover* was actually recorded by Michael Rodgers, of the 'Ripples & Waves' fame, and not by Michael Jackson and his brothers – unconfirmed.

SOMEBODY'S WATCHING ME

Song Michael first heard at the Jackson family's Encino home in California, when Rockwell (*aka* Kennedy Gordy – son of Motown founder and owner, Berry Gordy) played him the demo.

'I played him the tape and the single stuck out in his mind,' said Rockwell. 'He asked if he and Jermaine could do the backing vocals. Michael really wanted to do the song because he identified so much with its message. He often feels like a fish in a bowl – always being watched by people wanting a piece of him.'

Rockwell often used to stand in the wings when the Jackson 5 were on stage, and was seen as a young boy in the 1971 TV special, *Diana!*

Michael missed the first recording session – he was at a theme park with one-time teen rival, Donny Osmond. The following evening, Michael recorded his vocals in just over an hour.

Rockwell used an alias to keep his identity secret from his father, and Michael's contribution went uncredited, as he was under contract to CBS/Epic and the single was issued by his previous record company, Motown.

Released in January 1984 – hit no.1 on the R&B singles chart and no.2 on the Hot 100 in the States, and no.6 in the UK. Also achieved no.1 in Belgium.

RIAA Gold Record (USA million seller).

Official Versions:
Album Version.
Edit.
Instrumental.

Cover version by Tru, titled *I Always Feel Like (Somebody's Watching Me)*, charted at no.42 on the R&B singles chart and no.71 on the Hot 100 in the States in 1997.

Sampled by the American trio, DC Talk, on *Somebody's Watching*, a track on their 2001 album, *SOLO*. In this instance, the song referred to God, who Christian rapper Toby McKeehan of DC Talk believed was constantly looking out for him.

Cover version by Dutch trio BeatFreakz, featuring a Michael Jackson sound-a-like, hit no.3 in the UK in 2006 – video, starring a pint-sized Michael, parodied Michael's *Thriller* short film. BeatFreakz also recorded a version of Michael's hit, *P.Y.T. (Pretty Young Thing)*.

SOMEDAY AT CHRISTMAS

Song the Jackson 5 recorded for their *CHRISTMAS ALBUM*, issued in October 1970 in the States and December 1970 in the UK.

Originally recorded by Stevie Wonder, for his festive album of the same title, released in 1967.

SOMEDAY WE'LL BE TOGETHER

Diana Ross & the Supremes hit Michael, his brothers and a host of Motown artists (past and present) performed, to welcome Motown founder, Berry Gordy, on stage at *Motown 25: Yesterday, Today, Forever* – celebration held at the Pasadena Civic Auditorium on 25th March 1983.

Last hit for Diana Ross & the Supremes, before Diana went solo – hit no.1 on both the Hot 100 and R&B singles chart in the States, and no.13 in the UK, in 1969.

SOMEONE IN THE DARK

Song Michael recorded for the storybook album, *E.T. THE EXTRA-TERRESTRIAL*, issued in November 1982 in the States and January 1983 in the UK.

Michael's record company, CBS/Epic, allowed him to recorded the storybook album – including one new song, *Someone In The Dark* – for MCA, on two conditions:

One: MCA must hold back the album until after Christmas 1982, so it wouldn't complete with Michael's new album, *THRILLER*.

Two: MCA must not release *Someone In The Dark* as a single.

MCA breached both conditions in the States, by releasing the album in November 1982, and by servicing radio stations with promo copies of *Someone In The Dark*.

Court action resulted in MCA having to withdraw the album, and being prohibited from releasing *Someone In The Dark* as a single – thus creating, arguably, Michael's rarest and most sought after promo single, with copies changing hands for £1,000+.

Scheduled to feature on Michael's cancelled compilation, *DECADE 1980-1990*.

Made its CD debut on the special, expanded version of *THRILLER*, released in 2001.

SOMEONE PUT YOUR HAND OUT

Written by Michael with Teddy Riley (who helped to change a verse in Michael's original composition), and recorded in April 1992, having failed to make it on to Michael's *DANGEROUS* album.

Released in the UK/Europe (but not USA) in May 1992, as a Pepsi exclusive, promo cassette single, to promote Michael's up-and-coming world tour. 500,000 copies made available by collecting Pepsi tokens, as competition prizes, etc.

Also released as a special Pepsi promo pack in June 1992, in the UK/Europe – the package included a poster, giant sticker, press file about Michael's world tour and the cassette single.

Issued as a promo CD single in Japan only.

Included on the compilation, *SIGNATURE SERIES*, released in the States in 1992.

Featured on the first acetate version of the special, expanded edition of Michael's *BAD* – later withdrawn.

Included on Michael's box-set, *THE ULTIMATE COLLECTION*, released in November 2004.

SOMEWHERE IN TIME

Song written by Michael in 1980, and registered with the United States Copyright Office in November 1984 – remains unreleased.

SONG FOR MICHAEL JACKSON TO $ELL

Song sub-titled *Magical Mystery Tour* – which it's a cover version of, with Beatles samples incorporated into the rave-up at the end. Recorded by Das Damen (German for 'The Ladies'), for their 1988 album, *MARSHMELLOW CONSPIRACY*.

Michael's representatives objected to the song, and forced its withdrawal – Das Damen therefore reissued their album minus this track.

SOUL JERK

Pre-Motown recording by the Jackson 5, first released in 1989 on the album, *BEGINNING YEARS 1967-1968*.

SOUND, THE

Ten and a half minute medley of hits featured on an official promo 12" single issued in France in 1988, including: *Don't Stop 'Til You Get Enough, Thriller, Bad, The Way You Make Me Feel, Beat It, Billie Jean* and *Rock With You*.

SPACE DANCE

Not a song as such, but part of the soundtrack of the videogame *Space Channel 5*, which was originally released for Sega Dreamcast in 2000 (and later for Playstation 2 in 2003). Michael featured in the last level of the game, as the character 'Space Michael'.

Michael's voice also featured on the Sega Dreamcast game, *Space Channel 5 Part 2*, released in Japan in 2002 and worldwide the following year – a computer generated, dancing Michael featured in a commercial for the game.

SPECIAL NONSTOP VERSION

Medley featuring *Blame It On The Boogie* and *Shake Your Body (Down To The Ground)*, released on the 1979 Japanese promo album, *THE LEADER OF 80'S POP*, credited to Michael Jackson & The Jacksons.

SPECIAL NONSTOP VERSION PART 1

Medley featuring *Rock With You*, *Off The Wall* and *Don't Stop 'Til You Get Enough*, released on the 1979 Japanese promo album, *THE LEADER OF 80'S POP*, credited to Michael Jackson & The Jacksons.

SPECIAL NONSTOP VERSION PART II

Medley featuring *Don't Stop 'Til You Get Enough*, *Rock With You* and *Working Day And Night*, released on the 1979 Japanese promo album, *THE LEADER OF 80'S POP*, credited to Michael Jackson & The Jacksons.

SPEECHLESS

Written by Michael, and recorded for his album, *INVINCIBLE*, issued in October 2001.

'Everything with Michael is a stand-out moment,' said engineer Bruce Swedien, prior to the release of *INVINCIBLE*, 'but an absolutely gorgeous piece of music called *Speechless* was really an event. Michael sings the first eight bars *a cappella*. At the end, he closes it off *a cappella* – it was Michael's idea to add the *a cappella* parts.'

One of three tracks Michael chose as his personal favourites from the album, during his on-line chat with fans on 26th October 2001.

'I was with these kids in Germany, and we had a big water balloon fight,' said Michael, 'and I was so happy after the fight that I ran upstairs in their house and wrote *Speechless*. Fun inspires me. I hate to say that, because it's such a romantic song, but it was the fight that did it. I was happy, and I wrote it in its entirety right there. I felt it would be good enough for the album. Out of the bliss comes magic, wonderment, and creativity.'

Cover version by Ghost featured on the 2002 album, *UNDER THE MOONLIGHT*.

SPEED DEMON

Written – reputedly after he picked up a speeding ticket – by Michael, and recorded for his *BAD* album, issued in September 1987.

Short film, mixing claymation with real life footage, included in Michael's film, *Moonwalker*.

Pencilled in for release as a single in 1989, before *Leave Me Alone* was chosen instead. Promo copies with a picture sleeve, featuring an edited version, issued in some countries, most notably Holland.

STAND

Sly & The Family Stone cover the Jackson 5 recorded for their debut album, *DIANA ROSS PRESENTS THE JACKSON 5*, issued in December 1969 in the States and March 1970 in the UK.

First song the Jackson 5 recorded, on 17th May 1969, for Motown. Performed by the Jackson 5 during their first appearance on *The Ed Sullivan Show* in the States in 1969.

Live version recorded at the Jackson 5's homecoming concert in Gary, Indiana, on 29th May 1971, included on their album, *GOIN' BACK TO INDIANA*, issued in September 1971 in the States (no UK release). Footage screened on the group's *Goin' Back To Indiana* TV special, aired in the States on 19th September 1971.

Title given to a budget price reissue of *GOIN' BACK TO INDIANA*, minus *Maybe Tomorrow*, released in the States in 1974 (no UK issue).

Sly & The Family Stone took the song to no.14 on the R&B singles chart and no.22 on the Hot 100 in the States in 1969 – failed to chart in the UK.

STAND TALL

Song written by Michael in 1982, and registered with the United States Copyright Office in December 1985 – remains unreleased.

STANDING IN THE SHADOWS OF LOVE

Four Tops cover the Jackson 5 recorded on 17th May 1969, for their debut album, *DIANA ROSS PRESENTS THE JACKSON 5*, issued in December 1969 in the States and March 1970 in the UK.

The Four Tops version hit no.2 on the R&B singles chart and no.6 on the Hot 100 in the States in 1966, and no.6 in the UK the following year.

STAR SPANGLED BANNER

America's national anthem.

Performed by the Jackson 5 – accompanied by the Leman Monroe High School Band – at the opening game of the baseball World Series at the Riverfront Stadium in Cincinnati, Ohio, on 10th October 1970. In a later interview, Michael and his brothers admitted they didn't know the words, and had to quickly learn them on the way to the stadium.

Hit versions:
José Feliciano – no.50 on the Hot 100 in the States in 1968.
Whitney Houston – no.20 on the Hot 100 in 1991.

STARLIGHT

Song Michael worked on during the *THRILLER* sessions, which turned into *Thriller* – referred to as 'Starlight Sun' by Michael, during his Mexican court disposition.

First heard by Michael when writer Rod Temperton brought a demo, with all the sounds programmed, to his Encino home for him to listen to.

Greg Phillinganes, Michael's keyboardist at the time, has confirmed he, Michael, Quincy Jones and Rod Temperton were in the studio, playing the song back, when Michael and Quincy started throwing ideas at each other – such as, changing certain chords to make the song sound darker, and adding the wolf howl. A day or so later, the song became *Thriller*.

Lyrics **Michael** sang during his court disposition: 'Starlight... Starlight sun... **Gimme some** starlight, for a new day has begun.'

Included **on the** second acetate version of the expanded, special edition of *THRILLER*, **but** later withdrawn – remains unreleased.

Also known **by** the title, *Give Me Some Starlight*.

STATE OF INDEPENDENCE

Jon & Vangelis song Donna Summer recorded, with Quincy Jones producing, for her eponymous 1982 album.

Backing vocals by an all-star chorus: Michael, Christopher Cross, James Ingram, Kenny Loggins, Lionel Richie, Dionne Warwick and Stevie Wonder.

Charted at no.14 in the UK, and no.31 on the R&B singles chart and no.41 on the Hot 100 in the States, in 1982.

No.1 in Holland.

Reissue peaked at no.45 in the UK in 1990, and a remixed version hit no.13 in the UK in 1996.

Jon & Vangelis's original recording belatedly charted at no.67 in the UK in 1984.

STATE OF SHOCK

Song written by Michael with 14 year old Randy Hansen. Recorded by the Jacksons with Mick Jagger, for their *VICTORY* album, issued in July 1984.

Lead single from the album, credited 'Lead vocals by Michael Jackson & Mick Jagger'. Dance Mix featured additional vocals; instrumental version also released.

Achieved no.3 on the Hot 100 and no.4 on the R&B singles chart in the States, but stalled at no.14 in the UK (the only country where it was issued as a picture disc).

RIAA Gold Record (USA million seller).

Jagger, it was reported, would join the Jacksons on stage on 4th or 5th August 1984, at Madison Square Garden, to perform the song during the group's Victory Tour – from this, a promo video was to have been made. Despite confirmation from Chuck Sullivan, tour promoter, Jagger never appeared.

Official Versions:
Album Version.   7" Version.
Dance Mix.   Instrumental.

One of three songs Michael worked on with Queen's lead vocalist, Freddie Mercury, in 1983 – the others were *There Must Be More To Life Than This* and *Victory*.

'I was going to be on *THRILLER*,' confirmed Freddie, before his death from an AIDS-related illness in November 1991. 'We had three songs in the can but, unfortunately, they were never finished.'

Demo version by Michael and Freddie surfaced on the internet in 2002 – no official release.

STAY

Song written by Michael with Bryan Loren circa 1988, during the *DANGEROUS* sessions – remains unreleased.

STAY WITH LOVE

Love theme from the TV mini-series, *The Jacksons: An American Dream*, recorded by Jermaine Jackson and Syreeta Wright – featured on the accompanying soundtrack album, credited to the Jacksons, issued in October 1992 in the States and July 1993 in the UK.

STEPPIN' OUT WITH MY BABY

Song the Jacksons performed on their TV series in 1976.

STILL IN LOVE WITH YOU

Written for the Jacksons album, *VICTORY* – lead vocal by Randy, but didn't make the album and remains unreleased.

STOP! IN THE NAME OF LOVE

Supremes hit the Jackson 5 sang as part of a 'Salute to the Vocal Groups' medley with *Opus One, Bei Mir Bist Du Schon, Yakety Yak,* an untitled Jackson 5 ditty and *Dancing Machine,* on *The Carol Burnett Show* in the States in January 1975 – clip included on the Vol.31 DVD of the show.

The Supremes took the song to no.1 on the Hot 100 and no.2 on the R&B singles chart in the States, and no.7 in the UK, in 1965.

STOP THE WAR

Song written by Michael with Carole Bayer Sager circa 1999 – remains unreleased.

STORMY MONDAY

Pre-Motown recording by the Jackson 5, first released in 1989 on the album, *BEGINNING YEARS 1967-1968*.

Remixed version featured on the albums, *BIG BOY*, released in Japan in 1993, and *THE JACKSON FIVE FEATURING MICHAEL JACKSON*, issued later the same year in the UK (no USA release). Bonus tracks on the albums included the previously unreleased, original version of *Stormy Monday*, recorded between 1965-67.

STRANGER IN MOSCOW

Written and recorded by Michael for his album, HIS*TORY*, issued in June 1995.

Written in a Moscow hotel room in September 1993, soon after the allegations of child molestation broke – 'a strange, eerie, lonely time', according to Michael. 'The lyrics are totally autobiographical,' he confirmed. 'When you hear lines like "here abandoned in my fame, Armageddon of the brain" – at the time, on the last tour when we were in Moscow, that's really how I felt… just all alone in my hotel, and it was raining – and I just started writing it.'

Charted at no.4 in the UK, but wasn't released in the States until nearly a year later, when a remixed version struggled to no.50 on the R&B singles chart and no.91 on the Hot 100.

Official Versions:
Album Version.	Spensane Vocal Remix (R&B).
Basement Boys 12" Club Mix.	Tee's Capella A Cappella.
Basement Boys Bonus Dub Beats.	Tee's Bonus Beats.
Basement Boys Danger Dub.	Tee's Freeze Mix.
Basement Boys Radio Mix.	Tee's Freeze Radio.
Basement Boys Lonely Dub.	Tee's Bonus Beats Dub.
Hani's Dub Hop Mix.	Tee's In-House Club Mix.
Hani's Extended Chill Hop Mix.	Tee's Light AC Mix.
Hani's Num Club Mix.	Tee's Mission Mix Club.
Hani's Num Dub.	Tee's Radio Mix.
Hani's Num Radio Mix.	TNT Frozen Sun Mix-Club.
Radio Edit.	TNT Danger Dub.

Charles 'The Mixologist' Roanne's Full R&B Mix.
Charles 'The Mixologist' Roanne's Full Mix W/Mute Drop

Promo short film, shot in black and white in an unused hanger in Van Nuys, California, directed by Nick Brandt – showed Michael walking in real time, while everything around him happened in slow motion.

Live performances screened in Germany and New Zealand, as part of televised concerts.

Nineteenth of Michael's 20 *'Visionary – The Video Singles'* reissues, with the music on one side of a Dual Disc and the accompanying short film on the other side. Issued in June 2006 in the UK – charted at no.22.

STREETWALKER

Written by Michael, song first mentioned in the British magazine *Revolution* in 1987, and cited by Michael in his court disposition in November 1993.

Remained unreleased until it was added to the expanded, special edition reissue of *BAD*, issued in October 2001. On the CD, Quincy Jones confirmed Michael wanted to include *Streetwalker* on the original release of *BAD*, while he favoured *Another Part Of Me* – which was finally chosen.

Included on the single release of *Cry* in the UK (no USA release).

Reputedly, Michael's song *Dangerous* evolved from *Streetwalker* – however, the similarities between the two songs are minimal.

STRENGTH OF ONE MAN

Song the Jacksons recorded for their self-titled debut album, issued in November 1976.

STYLE OF LIFE

Written by Michael with brother Tito, and recorded by the Jacksons for their self-titled debut album, issued in November 1976.

B-side of the Jacksons debut single, *Enjoy Yourself.*

Performed solo by Michael on *The Jacksons* TV series in 1977.

SUGAR DADDY

Song the Jackson 5 released as a single in November 1971 in the States and March 1972 in the UK.

Achieved no.3 on the R&B singles chart and no.10 on the Hot 100 in the States, but failed to chart in the UK.

Featured on the 'Michael White' episode of the new Jackson 5 cartoon series in 1971.

Performed by the Jackson 5 on *Hellzapoppin'* in the States in 1972, and by the Jacksons on their TV series in 1977.

Originally planned as the lead single from a new Jackson 5 album, but instead included on the Jackson 5's *GREATEST HITS* compilation, issued in December 1971 in the States and August 1972 in the UK.

SUNSET DRIVER

Written by Michael, and originally scheduled to appear on the expanded, special edition reissue of *OFF THE WALL* in 2001, but withdrawn.

Demo version, recorded in 1982, included on Michael's *THE ULTIMATE COLLECTION* box-set, issued in November 2004.

SUPERFLY SISTER

Written by Michael with Bryan Loren – one of 20-25 songs they worked on together, for a new album, but ultimately not one of them appeared on *DANGEROUS*.

'That song has always been one of my favourites,' said Loren, recalling *Superfly Sister*. 'Michael and I produced it fifty-fifty. Michael wrote the lyrics by himself but I came up with the title. I remember giving Michael a tape with the basic track, from there we wrote the melody together. A few days later, Michael came back with the lyrics to the song, and we basically recorded it right away.'

One of five previously unreleased songs included on Michael's album, *BLOOD ON THE DANCE FLOOR*, issued in April 1997.

SUPERSTAR

Female reply to Michael's *Billie Jean*, by Lydia Murdock – backing track based on *Billie Jean*, but changed sufficiently to deny Michael any song-writing credit.

'Michael was being provocative and ungentlemanly' said Murdoch. 'His record made good business sense, but mine came from the heart. For every man hurt in the '*Billie Jean*' syndrome, there are twelve girls left holding the baby.'

Charted at no.14 in the UK, and no.58 on the R&B singles chart in the States, in 1983.

SUPERSTITION

Stevie Wonder song the Jackson 5 often performed in concert in the early-to-mid 1970s.

Live recording featured on the Michael/Jackson 5's *LIVE!* album, issued in September 1988 in the UK (no USA release). All songs on the album were recorded at a concert on 30th April 1973, at the Osaka Koseinenkin Hall in Japan.

Included on the limited edition CD, *IN JAPAN!*, released by Hip-Select in 2004 – only 5,000 copies pressed.

Stevie took the song to no.1 on both American charts in 1972, and to no.11 early the following year in the UK.

SURPRISE SONG

Single made available to members of The Jacksons World Club in 1984, as part of a fan package – featured Michael and his brothers ad-libbing, rather than singing an actual song.

SUSIE

Song written by Michael in 1978, and registered with the United States Copyright Office in November 1984 – remains unreleased.

TABLOID JUNKIE

Written by Michael with James Harris III and Terry Lewis, and recorded for his HIS*TORY* album, issued in June 1995.

Nearly titled 'Tabloid Jungle' – the song was a response to the gutter press's constant hounding of Michael.

TAKE IT FROM HERE

One of several songs written by Pharrell Williams and submitted for Michael's HIS*TORY* and *INVINCIBLE* albums, which were later recorded by Justin Timberlake, for his debut album *JUSTIFIED*, released in 2002.

TAKE ME BACK

Song Michael recorded for his album, *FOREVER, MICHAEL*, issued in January 1975 in the States and March 1975 in the UK.

B-side of the 1981 reissue of *One Day In Your Life* in the UK – this version is different to the album version.

TAKE MY HEART

One of eight songs the Jackson 5 recorded for Steel-Town; one of two that remains unreleased – the other is *Jackson Man*.

6.5" metal acetate, with *Take My Heart* on Side 1 and *Jackson Man* on Side 2, with title credits hand-written in green wax crayon. Acetate discovered by Adey Pierce in Indiana in 2000 – he purchased it from an ex-engineer, who had engineered all eight Jackson 5 recordings for Steel-Town.

Acetate value at £3,000 by *Record Collector* magazine, and sold on the internet auction site, eBay, for £4,200 in October 2006.

TAKE THE A TRAIN

Song performed by the Jacksons, with special guest Caroll O'Connor, on their TV series in 1976, as a medley with *Caravan* and *I Don't Get Around Much Anymore*.

TEENAGE SYMPHONY

Previously unreleased Motown recording by the Jackson 5 featured on Michael's solo album, *LOOKING BACK TO YESTERDAY*, issued in February 1986 in the States and May 1986 in the UK.

Alternate version featured on the Jackson 5's 1986 compilation, *ANTHOLOGY*.

TELL ME I'M NOT DREAMIN' (TOO GOOD TO BE TRUE)

Song recorded by Jermaine Jackson, as a duet with brother Michael, for his self-titled album, issued in May 1984 – the album was titled *DYNAMITE* in the UK and many other countries.

'I co-wrote it with Michael Omartian and Jake Ruska,' said Bruce Sudano. 'We were working on Jermaine's record. Michael Omartian was producing the album for Jermaine. Michael and I became friends when he produced Donna (Summer)'s album, *SHE WORKS HARD FOR THE MONEY*, and we had co-written a couple of songs for that album. Michael had a track that Jermaine liked, and if I wanted to write something, it would probably get on the record.'

'Jermaine took the song and played it for his brother, Michael Jackson, who also liked it and it became a duet. Jermaine released it as his first single, radio went nuts about the song, and then Jermaine's record company got a call from Michael Jackson's record company, with a "Sist and Desist" from playing the song. Michael's *BAD* album was coming out and the company thought it would hinder Michael's new release.'

308

Jermaine concurred: 'A lack of communication between Clive Davis and CBS meant Arista were forbidden to issue the track as a single,' explained Jermaine. 'Basically, CBS were saying, why should we help you sell one of your albums?' As it happened, Michael's album *BAD* wasn't actually released until 1987.

White label promo copies released in the UK, backed with Jermaine's *Come To Me* and *Oh Mother*. Promo with picture sleeve issued in Japan.

B-side of Jermaine's *Do What You Do* in the UK – instrumental version also released on some formats, including the 12" of Jermaine's single, *Dynamite*.

Grammy nomination: Best R&B Performance by a Duo or Group with Vocal.

Featured in a 1984 episode of the TV series *Fame*, titled 'The Heart Of Rock 'N' Roll' – an episode Michael's sister Janet appeared in, as herself.

Cover version recorded by Robert Palmer, for his 1988 album, *HEAVY NOVA*.

THANK HEAVEN

Song written by Michael in 1998, and registered with the United States Copyright Office in April of the same year – remains unreleased.

THANK U (FALETTINME BE MICE ELF AGIN)

Sly & The Family Stone classic the Jackson 5 often performed in concert during their early years at Motown.

Performance included on a promotional film sent to concert promoters in 1970, to let them know who the Jackson 5 were – filmed at the group's first Motown concert in Philadelphia. The promo also featured a performance of *ABC* from the same concert. Snippets later included in the *Goin' Back To Indiana* TV special.

Original version sampled by Michael & Janet on their *Scream Louder* remix of their duet, *Scream* (and by Janet on *Rhythm Nation*).

No.1 for Sly & The Family Stone on both American charts in 1970 – not a hit in the UK.

THANK YOU FOR LIFE

Song written by Michael circa 1976, but failed to make his album, *OFF THE WALL*.

Registered with the United States Copyright Office in November 1984. Also cited by Michael in his court disposition in 1984, and again in his court disposition in November 1993 – remains unreleased.

THAT

Song written by Michael, and registered with the United States Copyright Office in November 1998 – remains unreleased.

THAT GIRL

Song written by Michael with brothers Jackie, Marlon, Randy and Tito. Recorded circa 1978-80 by the Jacksons, but failed to make the albums, *DESTINY* or *TRIUMPH* – remains unreleased.

THAT KIND OF LOVER

Song written circa 2001 by Michael with Ray Ruffin, for consideration for Michael's album, *INVINCIBLE* – remains unreleased.

Ruffin was asked to submit songs for Michael to consider, and he in turn invited boyband A1 – with whom he had collaborated previously – to work with him. Members of A1, interviewed on the *Big Breakfast* TV show in the UK in February 2001, stated they had written three songs for Michael, and said they felt it was a great honour for them to do so.

If ever recorded by Michael, all three songs remain unreleased.

310

THAT'S HOW LOVE GOES

Song Jermaine recorded on 6th January 1972, with the Jackson 5 on backing vocals, for his solo debut album, titled simply, *JERMAINE*.

Jermaine's debut single, issued in August 1972 in the States and December 1972 in the UK – charted at no.23 on the R&B singles chart and no.46 on the Hot 100 in the States, but wasn't a hit in the UK.

Performed by Jermaine, backed by his brothers, on *Soul Train* and *The Flip Wilson Show* in the States in 1972.

Alternate version by the Jackson 5, with Jermaine and Michael sharing lead vocals, remains unreleased.

Live version featured on the Michael/Jackson 5's *LIVE!* album, issued in September 1988 in the UK (no USA release). All songs on the album were recorded at a concert on 30th April 1973, at the Osaka Koseinenkin Hall in Japan. Also included on the limited edition CD, *IN JAPAN!*, released by Hip-Select in 2004 – only 5,000 copies pressed.

THAT'S HOW LOVE IS

Song Michael and his brothers recorded for Motown – remains unreleased.

THAT'S THE WAY (I LIKE IT)

Song the Jacksons performed on their TV series in 1976, with special guest, Dom Deluise.

No.1 on both American charts, and no.4 in the UK, for KC & The Sunshine Band in 1975. A remixed version charted at no.59 in the UK in 1991.

THAT'S WHAT CHRISTMAS MEANS TO ME

Song the Jackson 5 recorded for their *CHRISTMAS ALBUM* circa 1970, but which failed to make the final track listing – remains unreleased.

Originally recorded by Stevie Wonder.

THAT'S WHAT LOVE IS MADE OF

Song recorded for Motown between 1970-73, but unreleased until it was included on Michael's album, *LOOKING BACK TO YESTERDAY*, issued in February 1986 in the States and May 1986 in the UK.

The Miracles took the song to no.35 on the Hot 100 in the States in 1964.

THAT'S WHAT YOU GET (FOR BEING POLITE)

Written by Michael with brother Randy, and recorded by the Jacksons for their album, *DESTINY*, issued in December 1978.

'*That's What You Get (For Being Polite)* was my way of letting on that I knew I wasn't living in an ivory tower,' said Michael, 'and that I had insecurities and doubts, just as all other teenagers do. I was worried that the world and all it had to offer could be passing me by, even as I tried to get on top of my field.'

B-side of *Destiny* in the UK.

B-side of *Shake Your Body (Down To The Ground)* in the USA.

Official Versions:
Album Version.
Single Edit.
12" Version.

Mentioned by Michael at the beginning of his deposition hearing in Mexico in 1993 – he mentioned 'Jack Still', part of the song's lyric, separately, leading some fans to believe another song with this title existed.

THERE MUST BE MORE TO LIFE THAN THIS

One of three songs Michael worked on with Queen's Freddie Mercury, and recorded a demo duet version of with Freddie in the summer of 1983 – Michael composed some of his own lyrics as the 5-6 hour session progressed.

Song first considered for release on Queen's 1982 album, *HOT SPACE* – it failed to make the group's 1984 album, *THE WORKS*, as well. Solo version by Freddie featured on his album, *MR BAD GUY*, issued in 1985.

Recording of Michael and Freddie working on the song in 1983 surfaced on the internet in 2002 – this version featured Freddie talking about the song, and Michael singing solo, to piano accompaniment. A second, longer version has vocals by Michael and Freddie – both versions remains unreleased.

See also: *State Of Shock, Victory*.

THERE WAS A TIME

Song the Jackson 5 performed during their first national TV appearance, *The Hollywood Palace Special*, aired in the States on 18th October 1969.

Omitted from the accompanying soundtrack album, *MOTOWN AT THE HOLLYWOOD PALACE*, issued in March 1970 (no UK release).

Performed by the Jackson 5 on *American Bandstand* in February 1970, as part of a medley, with *Zip-A-Dee Doo-Dah*.

James Brown took the song to no.3 on the R&B singles chart and no.36 on the Hot 100 in the States in 1968 – not a hit in the UK.

THEY CAN'T TAKE THAT AWAY FROM ME

Snippet of a song Michael performed as part of a three song medley – also including *Gotta Dance* and *Putting On The Ritz* – on *The Jacksons* TV series in 1976.

THEY DON'T CARE ABOUT US

Written by Michael, and recorded for his HIS*TORY* album, issued in June 1995.

Lyrics deemed 'anti-Semitic' by Jewish groups:

Jew me, sue me, everybody do me;
Kick me, kike me, don't you black or white me.

Michael, who insisted it was a public awareness song, responded by releasing a statement that read:

'The idea that these lyrics could be deemed objectionable is extremely hurtful to me, and misleading. The song in fact is about the pain of prejudice and hate, and is a way to draw attention to social and political problems. I very much regret and apologise from the bottom of my heart if I have hurt anyone's feelings in conveying my own.'

Michael further stated he would re-record the song, changing 'jew me' to 'do me' and 'kike me' to 'strike me', and that apology stickers would be affixed to all existing copies of HIS*TORY*.

New pressings of HIS*TORY* in 1996 saw 'jew me' changed to 'chew me', and 'kike me' changed to 'hike me'.

'I'm talking about myself as the victim,' Michael later explained. 'David Geffen, Jeffrey Katzenberg, Stephen Spielberg, Mike Milkin – these are my friends. They're all Jewish, so how does that make sense? I was raised in a Jewish community.'

Chosen for single release by Michael, ahead of Sony Music's preference, *Money*.

Charted at no.4 in the UK but, unsurprisingly given the controversy it had stirred up, struggled to no.10 on the R&B singles chart and no.30 on the Hot 100 in the States.

No.1 in the Czech Republic, Germany, Hungary and Italy.

Official Versions:

Album Version (original).	Radio Edit.
Album Version (revised/clean).	LP Edit.
A Cappella.	Single Edit.
Charles' Full Dirty Mix.	Track Masters Instrumental.
Charles' Full Joint Mix.	Track Masters Radio Edit.
Charles' Full Joint Mix – No Intro.	Track Masters Remix.
Charles' Full Joint Mix – No Rap.	Dallas Main Mix.

Love To Infinity's Anthem Of Love Dub.
Love To Infinity's Anthem Of Love Mix.
Love To Infinity's Anthem Of Love Radio Edit.
Love To Infinity's Classic Paradise Dub.
Love To Infinity's Classic Paradise Mix.
Love To Infinity's Classic Paradise Radio Mix.
Love To Infinity's Hacienda Mix.
Love To Infinity's Walk In The Park Mix.
Love To Infinity's Walk In The Park Radio Mix.

Two promo short films made, both directed by Spike Lee.

Shooting of the first short film delayed by 20 days, as the Governor of Rio was fearful filming the city's shanty town area of Doña Marta might adversely effect Brazil's chances of hosting the 2004 Olympic Games. Finished promo censored by MTV and VH1 as, although the offending words were muffled, Michael could still be seen mouthing 'jew me, sue me.' Premiered on 22nd March 1996.

Michael was reportedly unhappy with the first promo, and had Spike Lee put together a second, featuring prison footage shot in New York that wasn't used in the first version. This more accurately reflected the angry, defiant mood of the song, but was banned by MTV and several other TV stations, so was only rarely screened and still awaits an official release.

Live performances screened in Germany and New Zealand, as part of televised concerts.

Eighteenth of Michael's 20 *'Visionary – The Video Singles'* reissues, with the music on one side of a Dual Disc and the accompanying short film on the other side. Issued in June 2006 in the UK – charted at no.26.

THINGS I DO FOR YOU

Written by Michael with brothers Jackie, Marlon, Randy and Tito, and recorded by the Jacksons for their *DESTINY* album, issued in December 1978.

B-side of *Lovely One* in the UK.

B-side of *Heartbreak Hotel* in the USA.

Performed by the Jacksons on *American Bandstand*, *Soul Train* and their own *Midnight Special* TV show in 1979, and during a Destiny Tour concert screened on BBC2 in the UK.

Performed by Michael during his Bad World Tour – one such concert screened on Nippon TV in Japan.

Live version, recorded at a concert at Madison Square Garden in September 1981, featured on the Jacksons album, *LIVE*, issued in November 1981.

Live recording released as a single, some with a promo picture sleeve, in the UK (no USA release) – failed to chart. This version also issued as the B-side of Michael's *Thriller* in the UK.

THINK HAPPY

Song the Jacksons recorded for their self-titled debut album, issued in November 1976.

Performed by the Jacksons on *Soul Train* in 1976 and their own TV series in 1977 – the *Soul Train* performance was included on the home video, *Soul Searching*, in 1984, along with *Shake Your Body (Down To The Ground)* and Jermaine's *Let's Get Serious*.

THIS HAD TO BE

Song written by Michael with George and Louis Johnson. Recorded by the Brothers Johnson, with Michael on backing vocals, for their 1978 album, *LIGHT UP THE NIGHT*.

The Brother's Johnson's *Strawberry Letter 23* was one of Michael's favourite songs of 1977.

THIS IS IT

Song written by Michael in 1980, and registered with the United States Copyright Office in November 1984 – remains unreleased.

THIS IS OUR TIME

Written by Michael with David Foster and Lauren Hill in 1999, and originally scheduled for Michael's album, *INVINCIBLE* – remains unreleased.

Despite rumours to the contrary, Lauren Hill has denied she has ever recorded a duet with Michael, but has said to do so is her dream.

THIS 'OLE MAN – ABC

Medley the Jackson 5 performed on the *Carol Burnett Show* in the States in March 1974. Host Carol played a class teacher who loosens up when her class – the Jackson 5 plus dancers – perform the medley.

THIS PLACE HOTEL

Alternative title for the Jacksons hit, *Heartbreak Hotel*, re-titled to avoid any confusion with Elvis Presley's classic – Michael, incredibly, maintains he wasn't aware of this when he wrote the song.

Live version with this title, recorded at a concert at Madison Square Garden in September 1981, featured on the Jacksons album, *LIVE*, issued in November 1981.

See also: *Heartbreak Hotel*.

THIS TIME AROUND

Written by Michael with Dallas Austin, Bruce Swedien and Rene, and recorded for his HIS*TORY* album, issued in June 1995.

Guest rapper: Notorious B.I.G.

'I got off the airplane somewhere in Texas, and answered my pager,' the late Notorious B.I.G. recalled in an interview in 1995. 'They were like, Michael Jackson called – he wants to do a song with you! I laughed 'cos I thought they were just frontin'… he wasn't in the studio when I did the song but when I was about to leave, he came through, listened to the joint, said he loved it and I jetted.'

Several promo remixes released, with *Earth Song*, in the States in 1995 but no commercial single release.

Charted at no.23 on the R&B airplay chart in the States.

Official Versions:
Album Version.
Dallas Clean Album Remix.
Dallas Main Extended Mix.
Dallas Main Mix.
Dallas Main Mix W/out Rap.
Dallas Radio Remix.
Dallas Radio Remix W/out Rap.
David Mitson Clean Edit.
D.M. AM Mix.
Georgie's House'n'Around Mix.
Instrumental.
Maurice's Club Around Mix.
Maurice's Club Around Radio Mix.
Maurice's Hip Hop Around Mix.
Maurice's Hip Hop Around Mix
  W/Drop.
Maurice's Hip Hop Around Mix
  W/Biggie Drop W/out Rap.

D.M. Bang Da Drums Mix.
D.M. Mad Club Mix.
D.M. Mad Club Mix – different.
D.M. Mad Dub.
D.M. Radio Mix.
The Don's Control This Dub.
David Mitson Clean Album Mix.
Georgie's House'n'Around Edit.

Maurice's Hip Hop Around Mix
  W/Biggie Drop.
The TimeLand Dub.
UBQ's Opera Vibe Dub.
Uno Clio Dub.
Uno Clio 12" Master Mix.
The Neverland Dub (Aftermath).

Sampled on *You've Really Got A Hold On Me*, with the late Notorious B.I.G., a track put together by DJ Vlad & Dirty Harry, on a tape titled *Rap Phenomenon*.

THREATENED

Written by Michael with Rodney Jerkins, Fred Jerkins III and LaShawn Daniels, and recorded for his album, *INVINCIBLE*, issued in October 2001.

Dedicated to 'The Guru of Special Effects', Rick Baker.

THRILLER

Title track of the album that would go on to become the no.1 best selling record ever released, *THRILLER*, issued in December 1982.

Written by Rod Temperton; an inspiration was the Jacksons' hit, *Heartbreak Hotel*. Early titles include 'Starlight', 'Starlight Sun' and 'Give Me Some Starlight' – the title was changed after Michael told Temperton he wanted something that would appeal to kids.

Featured a rap by horror actor, Vincent Price – an unused, third verse of the rap was included on the expanded, special edition reissue of *THRILLER* in October 2001.

Debuted on the Hot 100 in the States at no.20 – the highest new entry for over 20 years (John Lennon's *Imagine* also debuted at no.20 in 1971). Rose to no.4, to give Michael his seventh Top 10 hit from *THRILLER* – a new record from one album.

Charted at no.3 on the R&B singles chart in the States, and achieved no.10 in the UK, where it logged 18 weeks on the Top 75.

No.1 in Belgium.

RIAA Platinum Record (USA million seller).

Official Versions:
Album Version.	Remixed Short Version.
Edit.	Instrumental.
Voice Over Session.	

14 minute short film, directed by John Landis, cost in excess of $1 million. Premiered on MTV in the States on 2nd December 1983, and carried the following disclaimer:

> *Due to my strong personal convictions, I wish to stress*
> *that this film in no way endorses a belief in the occult.*

UK premiere, on Channel 4's *The Tube*, at 1.00am on 3rd December 1983 – repeated late the following evening by public demand.

Cited by Michael as the 'most fun short film or video' he's ever made. 'I just loooooved becoming a monster, because it gave me a chance to pretty much become someone else,' he said. 'It was just fun, hiding behind this mask and just really letting this part of you, your body, or your feelings out... it was just thrilling for me to do that. And the dance, and all the morphing, and all the fun things we did – it's so memorable!'

Michael's sister Janet reportedly appeared in the *Thriller* short film as a zombie.

Grammy Awards: Best Pop Vocal performance, Male and Best Video Album (for the home video, *Making Michael Jackson's Thriller*).

MTV Video Awards: Best Overall Performance, Viewer's Choice Award and Best Choreography.

American Music Video Awards: Best Home Video and Best Long Form Video (for *Making Michael Jackson's Thriller*).

Rolling Stone magazine: Video of the Decade (1980s).

MTV & TV Guide: Best Music Video of the Millennium.

Inducted into the Music Video Producers Hall of Fame in 1991, and recognised by the 2006 edition of *Guinness World Records* as the 'Most Successful Music Video'.

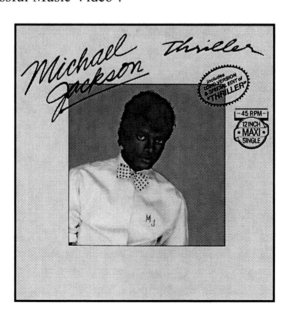

Live performances screened in Germany, Japan and New Zealand, as part of televised concerts.

Live performance by Michael, at his Dangerous Tour concert in Bucharest, Romania, on 1st October 1992, featured on the DVD released as part of his box-set, *THE ULTIMATE COLLECTION*, issued in November 2004.

Part of a lawsuit heard in Mexico in 1993, when Robert Smith (*aka* Robert Austin), Reynard Jones and Clifford Rubin claimed it infringed the song, *Run On Manchild* – the judgement was in Rod Temperton's favour.

Voted no.20 Best Song of all time in early 2000, in Channel 4 and music retailer HMV's 'Music of the Millennium' poll.

Short film invariably ranked no.1 in polls of the best music videos ever made, by such organisations as *Rolling Stone*, CNN, *Entertainment Weekly*, MTV and VH1.

Lead cover version on the 1984 album, *THE HAPPY CHIPMUNKS SING MICHAEL JACKSON'S GREATEST HITS*. The album also featured versions of: *Rockin' Robin, Say Say Say, Rock With You, Beat It, Don't Stop 'Til You Get Enough, Wanna Be Startin' Somethin', Human Nature* and *Billie Jean*. Due to complaints from David Saville, who created the Chipmunks, the album was withdrawn, and re-issued the following year as *THE HAPPY HAMSTERS SING MICHAEL JACKSON'S GREATEST HITS*.

Cover version by Ian Brown featured on his single, *Golden Gaze*, issued in the UK in 2000.

Sampled in 2001 by Allstars on *Things That Go Bump In The Night* – charted at no.12 in the UK.

Recreated sample featured on *The Way It Is*, a track from Prodigy's 2004 album, *ALWAYS OUTNUMBERED, NEVER OUTGUNNED*. Writer Rod Temperton, when approached by Prodigy's Liam Howlett, suggested they recreate the original music. 'He gave me permission to use the publishing side of the sample, then we could actually recreate *Thriller*,' said Howlett. 'We spent over a week in the studio and it was very hard to recreate, but we recreated the actual sample ourselves. He certainly wouldn't let us use the original recording.'

Sampled on numerous other tracks, including:
Muddfoot by Biz Markie.
No Guest List by Def Squad.
Rhythm Trax – House Party Style by DJ Jazzy Jeff & The Fresh Prince.
Mad Scientist by Large Professor.
100 Miles And Runnin' by N.W.A.
911 Is A Joke by Public Enemy.
Make Love (a parody) by Chef (from *South Park*).

First of Michael's 20 *'Visionary – The Video Singles'* reissues, with the music on one side of a Dual Disc and the accompanying short film on the other side. Issued in February 2006 in most countries – hit no.1 in Spain, but ineligible to enter the UK as it came with a free *Visionary* box to house all 20 Dual Discs, and UK chart rules prohibit freebies of any kind. Box-set with all 20 discs released in the States in November 2006, where the discs were not issued individually.

THRILLER MEDLEY

Medley registered with the United States Copyright Office in June 1984, featured: *P.Y.T. (Pretty Young Thing)*, *Billie Jean*, *Human Nature* and *Beat It*.

THROUGH THICK AND THIN

Song the Jackson 5 originally recorded for their 1975 album, *MOVING VIOLATION*, but failed to make the final cut.

Featured on the first 'new' Jackson 5 album released by Motown after Michael and his brothers signed for CBS/Epic, *JOYFUL JUKEBOX MUSIC*, issued in October 1976 in the States and December 1976 in the UK.

THROWIN' YOUR LIFE AWAY

Song written by Michael in 1988, and registered with the United States Copyright Office in September of that year – remains unreleased.

TIME EXPLOSION

Song featured on the Jackson 5 album, *MOVING VIOLATION*, issued in May 1975 in the States and July 1975 in the UK.

TIME OUT FOR THE BURGLAR

Co-written by Jackie and Randy Jackson with six other writers, and recorded by the Jacksons as the theme song for the Whoopi Goldberg movie, *Burglar*.

Originally titled simply 'Time Out' – changed to tie-in with the movie.

First Jackson 5/Jacksons recording that didn't involve Michael (or Marlon, who had left the Jacksons to pursue a solo career).

Charted at no.88 on the R&B singles chart in the States, but failed to make the Hot 100, and wasn't a hit in the UK.

TIME WAITS FOR NO ONE

Written by Jackie and Randy Jackson, and recorded by the Jacksons for their album, *TRIUMPH*, issued in October 1980.

Fifth single released from the album in the UK (no USA release) – listed as a chart 'breaker' for one week, but didn't sell well enough to enter the Top 50.

TO KNOW

Song the Jackson 5 recorded for their album, *LOOKIN' THROUGH THE WINDOWS*, issued in May 1972 in the States and October 1972 in the UK.

B-side of *Corner Of The Sky* in the USA.

B-side of *Hallelujah Day* in the UK.

TO MAKE MY FATHER PROUD

Song recorded by Michael on 11th April 1973, and first released – with added overdubs – on his *FAREWELL MY SUMMER LOVE* album, issued in May 1984 in the States and June 1984 in the UK.

Original recording featured on *THE BEST OF...*, part of Motown's Anthology series, issued in the States in March 1995 (no UK release).

TO SATISFY YOU

Song Michael wrote with Bryan Loren during the *DANGEROUS* sessions, but Michael didn't much like it, and let Loren record it for his 1992 album, *MUSIC FROM THE NEW WORLD* – Michael contributed backing vocals.

Also recorded – as *Satisfy You* – by Damion 'Crazy Legs' Hall, for his 1994 album, *STRAIGHT TO THE POINT*. The backing vocals, as done by Michael on Loren's version, were this time sung by Chanté Moore.

Solo version by Michael remains unreleased.

TO SIR WITH LOVE

Song Michael and his brothers recorded for Motown – remains unreleased.

Title song from the movie of the same name, starring Sidney Poitier – a no.1 on the Hot 100 in the States for Lulu in 1967.

TOBACCO ROAD

One of the songs the Jackson 5 performed at their Motown audition in 1968, and regularly sang in concert in the pre-Motown days.

Heard in *The Jacksons: An American Dream* TV series, but not performed by the Jackson 5.

TODO MI AMOR ERES TU

Spanish language version of Michael's *I Just Can't Stop Loving You*, recorded by Michael as a duet with Siedah Garrett.

Released as a single in some countries, including America (12" only), Spain and Columbia (7" blue vinyl); it was also added to *BAD* as a bonus track in some European and Latin American countries. Issued as a 7" single in Mexico – given away free with Michael's album, *BAD*.

Included on the compilation, *SIGNATURE SERIES*, released in the States in 1992, and the expanded, special edition of *BAD* in 2001, as a bonus track.

See also: *I Just Can't Stop Loving You*.

TODO PARA TI

Spanish language version of Michael's *What More Can I Give*, featuring contributions from Mariah Carey, Celine Dion, Gloria Estefan, Julio Iglasias, Ricky Martin and Jon Secada.

Recorded as a charity single, to aid the victims and their families of the 9/11 terrorist attack on the States, but Michael's record company refused to release it.

Made available as a download single in October 2003, but no commercial physical release.

See also: *What More Can I Give*.

TOMBOY

Song written by Michael in 1985, and registered with the United States Copyright Office in October that year. Considered by Michael for his album, *BAD*, but didn't make the final track listing.

Cited by Michael in his court disposition in November 1993 – remains unreleased.

Mistakenly believed by some fans to have been written by Quincy Jones.

TOO MUCH MONKEY BUSINESS

Original title of *Monkey Business*.

See also: *Monkey Business*.

TOO YOUNG

Song featured on Michael's album, *MUSIC & ME*, issued in April 1973 in the States and July 1973 in the UK.

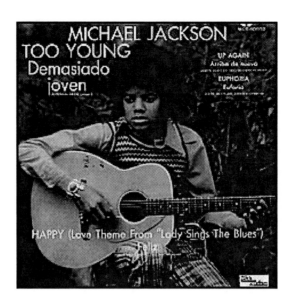

Released as a single in a limited number of countries, including Italy and Mexico. Italian sleeve, incorrectly, translated the title as *I Wasn't Born Yet*.

Hit versions:
Nat 'King' Cole – no.3 on the R&B singles chart in the States in 1951.
Bill Forbes – no.29 in the UK in 1960.
Donny Osmond – no.5 in the UK, and no.13 on the Hot 100 in the States, in 1972.

TORTURE

Written by Jackie Jackson with Kathy Wakefield, and originally planned as a duet between Jackie and Michael – Jermaine took on Jackie's vocals, as he wasn't sure he would be involved with the *VICTORY* album until the last minute, when he agreed to go on tour with his brothers.

Demo versions probably include one with Jackie and Michael singing lead, and maybe a solo version by Jackie.

Recorded by the Jacksons – with lead vocals credited to Michael and Jermaine – for the album, *VICTORY*, issued in July 1984.

Second single lifted from the album – charted at no.12 on the R&B singles chart and no.17 on the Hot 100 in the States, and no.26 in the UK.

Official Versions:
Album Version.   Extended 12" Dance Mix.
New Mix.   Instrumental.
7" Single Edit.

Promo short film directed by Jeff Stein. Michael and Jermaine refused to be involved with the promo, so their four brothers went ahead, and shot it without them.

TOUCH

Song featured on the Jackson 5's *SKYWRITER* album, issued in March 1973 in the States and July 1973 in the UK.

B-side of *Get It Together*.

Originally recorded by the Supremes, for their 1971 album of the same title – single achieved no.71 on the Hot 100 in the States.

TOUCH THE ONE YOU LOVE

Song recorded on 14th June 1973, and included in an up-dated mix on Michael's *FAREWELL MY SUMMER LOVE* album, issued in May

1984 in the States and June 1984 in the UK – demo version also known to exist.

Second and last single lifted from the album in the States, but failed to chart (no UK release).

B-side of *Girl You're So Together* in the UK.

Original recording remains unreleased.

TOY, THE

Song Michael wrote for a Richard Prior movie in 1981, and registered with the United States Copyright Office in November 1984. Also cited by Michael in his court disposition in December 1984 – remains unreleased.

TRACKS OF MY TEARS

Smokey Robinson song the Jackson 5 recorded in the pre-Motown days, first released in 1989 on the album, *BEGINNING YEARS 1967-1968*.

Song the Jackson 5 are believed to have performed at their Motown audition. It's always been thought the group only performed three songs at the audition, but new footage that has recently come to light suggests otherwise.

Title given to a pre-Motown compilation released in Holland in 2000.

The Miracles took the song to no.2 on the R&B singles chart and no.16 on the Hot 100 in the States in 1965, and to no.9 in the UK in 1969.

TRAGEDY OF A CHEER-LEADER

Song Michael cited he had written in his court disposition in November 1993 – remains unreleased.

TRUE LOVE CAN BE BEAUTIFUL

Song written by Jermaine Jackson with Bobby Taylor, and recorded by the Jackson 5 for their *ABC* album, issued in May 1970 in the States and August 1970 in the UK.

TRY A LITTLE TENDERNESS

Song the Jacksons performed on their TV series in 1976, with their special guest star, Sonny Bono (of Sonny & Cher), as part of a medley with *More Than I Know*, *Am I Blue* and *For Once In My Life*.

Hit versions:
Aretha Franklin – no.100 on the Hot 100 in the States in 1962.
Otis Redding – no.4 on the R&B singles chart and no.25 on the Hot 100 in the States, and no.46 in the UK, in 1967.
Three Dog Night – no.29 on the Hot 100 in 1969.
Ohio Players – no.40 on the R&B singles chart in 1981.
Commitments – no.67 on the Hot 100 in 1991.

TUBEWAY

Song written by Michael circa 1999, considered for but failed to make his album, *INVINCIBLE* – remains unreleased.

TURNING ME OFF

Song Michael cited he had written in his court disposition in November 1993 – remains unreleased.

TWENTY-FIVE MILES

Song Michael recorded in the early-to-mid 1970s for Motown, but remained unreleased until an overdubbed version appeared on his album, *THE ORIGINAL SOUL OF MICHAEL JACKSON*, issued in October 1987 in the States and February 1988 in the UK – demo version also known to exist.

Released as single, with the same picture sleeve as the album, in the States in October 1987 but failed to chart (no UK release).

Edwin Starr took his original version to no.6 on both American charts, and to no.36 in the UK, in 1969.

TWINKLE, TWINKLE LITTLE ME

Song the Jackson 5 recorded for their *CHRISTMAS ALBUM* circa 1970, but which failed to make the final track listing – remains unreleased.

The Supremes took the song to no.5 on the Christmas Singles chart in the States in 1965.

TWIST & SHOUT

Song heard in the TV mini-series, *The Jacksons: An American Dream* – it's possible the Jackson 5 performed the song in concert in the early days, but it's unlikely they recorded a version of it.

Hit versions:
Isley Brothers – no.2 on the R&B chart, and no.17 on the Hot 100, in the States in 1962, and no.42 in the UK in 1963.
Beatles – no.2 on the Hot 100 in 1964, and no.23 on the Hot 100 in 1986.
Salt-N-Pepa – no.4 in the UK in 1988, and no.45 on the R&B chart in 1989.
Chaka Demus & Pliers – no.1 in the UK in 1993.

U DON'T HAVE TO CALL

One of two songs written for Michael by Pharrell Williams, but recorded by Usher for his 2001 album, *8701*.

See also: *I Don't Know.*

UNBREAKABLE

Written by Michael with Rodney Jerkins, Fred Jerkins III, LaShawn Daniels, Nora Payne and Robert Smith, and recorded for his album, *INVINCIBLE*, issued in October 2001.

Backing vocals by Brandy, and featured a rap by the Notorious B.I.G.. 'I was actually with Biggie when he did that rhyme,' said producer Rodney Jerkins. 'He was working with Shaq (Shaquille O'Neal) on an album track called *You Can't Stop The Reign.*'

Cited by Michael, during his on-line chat with fans on 26th October 2001, as one of his three personal favourite tracks on the album. The same year, he explained the message behind the song: 'That I'm invincible, that I've been through it all. You can't hurt me. Knock me down – I get back up.'

Track Michael wanted to release as the first of seven planned singles from *INVINCIBLE*, accompanied by a 20 minute short film, set to co-star Mel Gibson and Chris Tucker. A shorter production schedule for the promo led to Sony insisting on issuing *You Rock My World* as the lead single instead.

Listed in *Music Week*, the UK's trade music magazine, as a forthcoming new release in early 2002, before Sony Music made it known in March they had officially discontinued promoting *INVINCIBLE*, just six months after it appeared – thus the international release as singles of *Unbreakable*, *Butterflies*, *Cry*, *Break Of Dawn*, *Speechless* and *Whatever Happens* were all shelved.

Test pressings and promos only released in the UK, included an instrumental version.

UNDER THE BOARD WALK

Song the Jackson 5 often performed and recorded in the pre-Motown days, not released until 1989, when an overdubbed version appeared on the album, *BEGINNING YEARS 1967-1968*.

Original, untouched recording made available as one of the bonus tracks on the albums, *BIG BOY*, issued in Japan in 1993, and *THE JACKSON FIVE FEATURING MICHAEL JACKSON*, released later the same year in the UK (no USA release).

Hit versions:
Drifters – no.4 hit on the Hot 100 in the States, and no.45 in the UK, in 1964.
Billy Joe Royal – no.82 on the Hot 100 in 1978.
Tom Tom Club – no.22 in the UK in 1982.
Bruce Willis – no.2 in the UK, and no.59 on the Hot 100 and no.72 on the R&B singles chart in the States, in 1987.

UNDER YOUR SKIN

Song written by Michael in 1979, and registered with the United States Copyright Office in November 1984 – remains unreleased.

UNKNOWN

Song written by Michael and registered with the BMI; it's unclear whether the song is titled 'Unknown' or the song title is unknown – remains unreleased.

UNTITLED

Untitled song – one of five hand-written by Michael circa 1979, to which the lyrics were included in a personal notebook, with young actor Mark Lester on the cover. Formed part of a 10,000+ piece collection of Jackson memorabilia purchased by Universal Express and some of its entertainment partners, in November 2006.

UNTITLED JACKSON 5 DITTY

Short, untitled ditty about themselves the Jackson 5 performed as part of a 'Salute to the Vocal Groups' medley with *Opus One, Yakety Yak, Bei Mir Bist Du Schon, Stop! In The Name Of Love* and *Dancing Machine*, on *The Carol Burnett Show* in the States in January 1975 – clip included on the Vol.31 DVD of the show.

UNTITLED JERMAINE JACKSON SONG

Untitled song Jermaine confirmed he was working on with Michael in 1973.

'I'm doing some producing on Michael now,' said Jermaine at the time. 'We have a studio at home now, my father did it for us. Sid Fein, who is a big arranger for television shows and movies, is doing an arrangement of one of my songs for Michael – it's about a bird.'

UP AGAIN

Song featured on Michael's album, *MUSIC & ME*, issued in April 1973 in the States and July 1973 in the UK.

Scheduled to appear on the B-side of *Doggin' Around* in the States in February 1974 – release cancelled, although test pressings exist.

UP ON THE HOUSE TOP

Song the Jackson 5 recorded for their *CHRISTMAS ALBUM*, issued in October 1970 in the States and December 1970 in the UK – featured a line specially written for each member of the group.

One of four tracks from the album included on the *Merry Christmas From Michael Jackson With The Jackson 5 EP*, issued in the UK in 1987 (no USA release) – charted at no.91.

Also issued as a white label promo in October 1987, complete with picture sleeve, credited to Michael Jackson With The Jackson 5. Promo single also released in the States.

UP THE LAZY RIVER

Song the Jackson 5 performed, along with *Opus One*, with the Mills Brothers, on the *One More Time* TV special in the States in January 1974.

UPPERMOST

Song featured on the Jackson 5's album, *SKYWRITER*, issued in March 1973 in the States and July 1973 in the UK.

UPSIDE DOWN

Diana Ross hit she performed at the Los Angeles Forum in 1981, when she called Michael up on stage, to sing the final chorus with her – later the same year featured in the *diana!* TV special, where Michael was Diana's special guest.

Diana took the song to no.1 on both American charts, and to no.2 in the UK, in 1980.

UPTIGHT (EVERYTHING'S ALRIGHT)

Stevie Wonder classic the Jackson 5 recorded a version of – remains unreleased.

Hit versions:
Stevie Wonder – no.1 on the R&B singles chart and no.3 on the Hot 100 in the States, and no.14 in the UK, in 1966.
Ramsey Lewis – no.30 on the R&B singles chart and no.49 on the Hot 100 in 1966.
Nancy Wilson – no.84 on the Hot 100 in 1966.
Jazz Crusaders – no.95 on the Hot 100 in 1966.

VIBRATONIST

Song written by Michael with Teddy Riley circa 1999, but failed to make his album, *INVINCIBLE* – remains unreleased.

VICTORY

One of three songs Michael worked on with Queen's front-man, Freddie Mercury, when Michael invited him to Hayvenhurst in the summer of 1983 (the other two were *State Of Shock* and *There Must Be More To Life Than This*). Only Michael, Freddie and Freddie's personal assistant, Peter Freestone, were present during the 5-6 hour session – so, with no drummer and Michael not keen on using a drum machine, Freestone slammed a bedroom door in time with the rhythm.

Song began life as a Queen track, possibly intended for the group's *HOT SPACE* album. Michael and Freddie's version wasn't completed, so wasn't included on the Jacksons album of the same title, issued in July 1984.

Queen's Brian May told *Q* magazine in 1998 that he tried to finish the three Freddie/Michael songs, but didn't know how.

May and Roger Taylor are reported to have recorded backing vocals for the Freddie/Michael demo in 2002, for inclusion on a Queen box-set – however, copyright difficulties meant the track couldn't be released.

May's mother gave two Michael Jackson fans a cassette with *Victory* (and the two other Jackson/Mercury songs) on it, after they contacted her – no official release.

WABASH CANNONBALL

Song Michael and his siblings used to sing with their mother in Gary, Indiana, as confirmed in Katherine's autobiography, *My Family, The Jacksons*.

WAIT

Written by Jackie Jackson with David Paich, and recorded by the Jacksons for their album, *VICTORY*, issued in July 1984.

Fourth and last single taken from the album in the UK – failed to chart.

WALK ON – THE LOVE YOU SAVE

Live medley recorded at the Jackson 5's homecoming concert in Gary, Indiana, on 29th May 1971, included on their album, *GOIN' BACK TO INDIANA*, issued in September 1971 in the States (no UK release). Footage screened on the group's *Goin' Back To Indiana* TV special, aired in the States on 19th September 1971.

WALK RIGHT NOW

Written by Michael with brothers Jackie and Randy, and recorded by the Jacksons for their *TRIUMPH* album, issued in October 1980.

Charted at no.7 in the UK, and no.50 on the R&B singles chart and no.73 on the Hot 100 in the States.

Limited edition picture disc released in the UK.

Official Versions:
Album Version.   7" Edit.
Special Extended Remix.   Instrumental.

WALL, THE

Song the Jackson 5 recorded for their album, *MAYBE TOMORROW*, issued in April 1971 in the States and October 1971 in the UK.

Featured on 'The Tiny Five' episode of the Jackson 5 cartoon series in 1971.

WANNA BE STARTIN' SOMETHIN'

Written by Michael, and recorded for his *THRILLER* album, issued in December 1982. Believed by some fans to be a hidden criticism of the media pressure Michael faced at this time, and would continue to face long into the future.

First song written by Michael for *THRILLER*: '(It's a song) which I had written when we were doing *OFF THE WALL*,' he said, 'but had never given to Quincy for that album.'

Cited by Michael as a song that disappointed him: 'Song-writing is a very frustrating art form,' he said. 'You have to get on tape exactly what's playing in your head. When I hear it up here (his head), it's wonderful – I have to transcribe that on to tape.'

Fourth single released from the album – peaked at no.5 on both American charts and no.8 in the UK.

Official Versions:
Album Version.   Single Version.
Brothers In Rhythm Mix.   Tommy D's Main Mix.
Instrumental.   12" Extended Mix.

Song chosen to open the Jacksons' Victory Tour and Michael's Bad World Tour concerts.

Live performance by Michael, at his Dangerous Tour concert in Bucharest, Romania, on 1st October 1992, featured on the DVD released as part of his box-set, *THE ULTIMATE COLLECTION*, issued in November 2004.

Live performances screened in Germany, Japan and New Zealand, as part of televised concerts.

Featured in 1990, along with *The Way You Make Me Feel*, in commercials for L.A. Gear – Michael was paid $10 million for his sponsorship of the brand.

Cover version by Jennifer Batten, while Whitney Houston performed a version live in concert, in Japan.

Sampled by:
Lord Tariq & Peter Gunz on *Startin' Somethin'*, from the 1998 album, *MAKE IT REIGN*.
Jamiroquai on the *Dinner With Greedo Mix* of *Love Foolosophy*, a track that featured on the 2001 album, *A FUNK ODYSSEY*.

Performed by Usher, Mya and Whitney Houston during the *Michael Jackson: 30th Anniversary Celebration, The Solo Years* concerts, staged at New York's Madison Square Garden on 7th and 10th September 2001.

Featured in the 2002 video game, *Grand Auto Theft: Vice City*, and its accompanying soundtrack.

WAY YOU LOVE ME, THE

Song written and recorded by Michael between 2000 and 2004, included on his box-set, *THE ULTIMATE COLLECTION*, issued in November 2004.

WAY YOU MAKE ME FEEL, THE

Written by Michael, in response to his mother's request for a song with 'a shuffling kind of rhythm' – recorded for his album, *BAD*, issued in September 1987.

Originally titled *Hot Fever*.

Third single from the album, and third single to top both American charts, a first for Michael.

No.1 in Ireland, and charted at no.3 in the UK.

Official Versions:

Album Version.	Dub.
Album Version incl. Vocal Fade.	A Cappella.
Dance Extended Mix.	Instrumental.
7" Mix.	Dance Remix Radio Edit.

Remix with more prominent vocals and harmonies replaced the original version on later pressings of *BAD*.

Promoted with a nine minutes short film directed by Joe Pytka. Co-starred Tatiana Thumbtzen, and featured a cameo appearance by Michael's sister, La Toya. Premiered on 31st October 1987. Extended 25 minute version also made – exclusively screened by Michael at his Neverland home.

Performed, along with *Man In The Mirror*, by Michael at the Grammy Awards in March 1988 at Radio City Music Hall, New York – despite four nominations, Michael failed to win a single award.

Featured in 1990, along with *Wanna Be Start' Somethin'*, in commercials for L.A. Gear – Michael was paid $10 million for his sponsorship of the brand.

Performed by Michael – solo and as a duet with Britney Spears – during the *Michael Jackson: 30th Anniversary Celebration, The Solo Years* concerts, staged at New York's Madison Square Garden on 7th and 10th September 2001.

Cover version recorded by Paul Anka.

Seventh of Michael's 20 *'Visionary – The Video Singles'* reissues, with the music on one side of a Dual Disc and the accompanying short film on the other side. Issued in March 2006 in the UK – charted at no.17.

WE ARE HERE TO CHANGE THE WORLD

Written by Michael with John Barnes, and originally recorded in 1986 by Michael for *Captain EO*, the 3D-movie he filmed exclusively for Disney – premiered at the Epcot Centre on 12th September 1986.

Footage of Michael rehearsing the song in the studio has appeared on the internet – no official release.

Released for the first time on Michael's box-set, *THE ULTIMATE COLLECTION*, issued in November 2004.

Cover version recorded by Deniece Williams, for her 1989 album, *AS GOOD AS IT GETS*.

WE ARE THE ONES

Song Michael wrote in 1978, and registered with the United States Copyright Office in November 1984 – remains unreleased.

WE ARE THE WORLD

Written by Michael with Lionel Richie, as America's answer to Band Aid's *Do They Know It's Christmas*, and recorded by USA For Africa to aid famine relief in Ethiopia – issued in March 1985.

USA For Africa: United Support of Artists For Africa.

Song completed on 21st January 1985, and recorded the following evening, immediately after the American Music Awards ceremony in Hollywood.

Sir Bob Geldof, in his autobiography, spoke of Michael practising the song in various keys. 'Each one was perfect,' he wrote, 'and for anyone else would have been a take, rather than a practise.'

Soloists, in order of appearance on the record: Lionel Richie, Stevie Wonder, Paul Simon, Kenny Rogers, James Ingram, Tina Turner, Billy Joel, Michael Jackson, Diana Ross, Dionne Warwick, Willie Nelson, Al Jarreau, Bruce Springsteen, Kenny Loggins, Steve Perry, Daryl Hall, Huey Lewis, Cyndi Lauper, Kim Carnes, Bob Dylan and Ray Charles.

Chorus included La Toya, Randy, Marlon, Tito and Jackie Jackson (but not Jermaine or Janet – the latter was particularly upset at not getting an invite).

No.1 on both American charts, and in Australia, Belgium, Holland, Italy, New Zealand, Norway, South Africa, Sweden and the UK.

RIAA Platinum Record (x4).

No.1 best selling single of 1985, and no.5 best selling single of all time, in the States.

Estimated global sales: 7 million (about the same as Band Aid's *Do They Know It's Christmas*).

Grammy Awards: Record of the Year, Song of the Year, Best Pop Vocal Performance by a Duo or Group, Best Music Video – Short Form.

American Music Award: Song of the Year.

People's Choice Award: Favourite New Song.

Official Versions:
Album Version.
Single Version.
Demo – Solo Version.

Second version by Children Of The World (a group of children including Drew Barrymore, Kim Fields and Alfonso Ribeiro) – Michael is on record as saying he prefers this version. 'Since first writing it, I had thought that song should be sung by children,' he said. 'When I finally heard children singing it on producer George Duke's version, I almost cried – it's the best version I've heard.'

USA Foundation for Africa, by the end of 1985, had raised around $40 million to aid famine relief in Africa.

Part of a lawsuit heard in Mexico in 1993, when Robert Smith (*aka* Robert Austin), Reynard Jones and Clifford Rubin claimed it infringed the songs, *What Becomes Of The Children* and *If There Be You* – the judgement was in Michael and Lionel Richie's favour.

Performed at the Pavarotti & Friends concert in 1999, by Pavarotti with Boyzone, Mariah Carey and Lionel Richie – Michael was scheduled to appear, but cancelled as his son Prince was unwell.

Performed by Michael and his guests as the finale of the *Michael Jackson: 30th Anniversary Celebration, The Solo Years* concerts, staged at New York's Madison Square Garden on 7th and 10th September 2001 – omitted from the televised edit.

Performed by Michael and his guests at his 'Celebration Of Love' 45th birthday party, staged in Los Angeles on 30th August 2003.

Demo version by Michael included on his box-set, *THE ULTIMATE COLLECTION*, issued in November 2004.

WE BE BALLIN'

Song originally co-written and produced by Rick 'Dutch' Cousin in 1997, and recorded by Ice Cube as *We Be Clubbin'*, for the movie *The Player's Club* (which Ice Cube also directed).

Remixed later the same year by Cousin, with added vocals by Michael (who sang the chorus) and Shaquille O'Neal, and re-titled *We Be Ballin'*.

'I produced and co-wrote the title track from *The Player's Club*, entitled *We Be Clubbin'*, in 1997,' confirmed Cousin. 'The song was an instant hit and the following year, we thought it to be a good idea to do a remix version of the song, entitled *We Be Ballin'*, featuring Michael Jackson and Shaquille O'Neal. The song was to be released on an NBA compilation album, set to be released that year, and was going to be featured in the infamous NBA 'I Love This Game' themed commercials. The NBA season was cut in half that year, due to the player initiated strike against the league, and the entire project seemed to just disappear… the only folks I know to have copies of the record are Michael Jackson, Ice Cube and myself, and maybe less than a handful of other people.'

Promo CD featured two mixes: Street Mix and Master Mix.

Two bootleg recordings known to exist, one without Ice Cube and Shaquille O'Neal – no official release.

Cover version by Ricky Romance, dating from 2003, featured Michael's original 1997 vocals.

WE CAN CHANGE THE WORLD

Written by Tito Jackson with Wayne Arnold, and recorded by the Jacksons for their album, *VICTORY*, issued in July 1984.

WE CAN HAVE FUN

One of 19 'Rare & Unreleased' tracks on the fourth CD of the Michael/ Jackson 5 box-set, *SOULSATION!*, issued in June 1995 in the States and July 1995 in the UK.

Recorded on 8th January and 11th February 1970.

WE CAN PUT IT BACK TOGETHER

Song Jermaine Jackson recorded for his 1980 album, *LET'S GET SERIOUS*, about getting back together with his brothers.

'*We Can Put It Back Together* is a very important song, very special to me,' said Jermaine. 'The song makes me cry sometimes, because it's about my brothers – I put in one word to tie-in a double meaning about a marriage that didn't make it, but basically, it's about my brothers.'

WE DON'T HAVE TO BE OVER 21 (TO FALL IN LOVE)

Jackson 5's second single, probably issued by Steel-Town Records in early-to-mid 1968 in the States (no UK release).

Reissued in March 1971, re-titled, *You Don't Have To Be Over Twenty One To Fall In Love*. Around the same time, an album titled *GETTING TOGETHER WITH THE JACKSON 5* appeared in the States (no UK release), but it only featured two songs by the group. The album sleeve featured amateur photographs taken at the Jackson 5's concert in Gary, Indiana, on 31st January 1971.

WE THANK YOU

Short song performed by the Jackson 5 at the close of their concerts.

Performed live during the group's tour of Europe in 1972, at the Royal Command Performance in the UK, attended by HM The Queen Mother.

Snippet included at the end of Michael's *The Legend Continues...* home video.

WE WISH YOU A MERRY CHRISTMAS

Snippet by the Jackson 5, which they sang at the end of *Have Yourself A Merry Little Christmas*, on their 1970 album, *CHRISTMAS ALBUM*.

Appeared on its own on the Japanese compilation, *FREE SOUL*, released in 1999.

WE'RE ALMOST THERE

Song Michael recorded for the album, *FOREVER, MICHAEL*, issued in January 1975 in the States and March 1975 in the UK.

Achieved no.7 on the R&B singles chart and no.54 on the Hot 100 in the States in 1975 (no UK release).

Performed by Michael on *American Bandstand* in January 1975.

Released as a single in the UK in 1981, as the follow-up to the chart topping *One Day In Your Life* – peaked at no.46.

B-side of *Happy (Love Theme From 'Lady Sings The Blues')* in the UK in 1983.

DJ Spinna Remix, as included on the Japanese compilation, *SOUL SOURCE – JACKSON 5 REMIXES 2*, issued in 2001, featured alternate vocals.

WE'RE COMING BACK

Song performed by the Jackson 5 on their second TV special on 5th November 1972, to the tune of *I Want You Back*, as they closed part one of their show for a commercial break.

WE'RE GONNA CHANGE OUR STYLE

Song featured on the Jackson 5 album, *JOYFUL JUKEBOX MUSIC*, issued in October 1976 in the States and December 1976 in the UK.

WE'RE GONNA HAVE A GOOD TIME

Song recorded at a Jackson 5 concert at Osaka Koseinenkin Hall in Japan on 30th April 1973, featured on the Michael/Jackson 5 album, *LIVE!*, issued in the UK in September 1988 (no USA release).

Included on the limited edition CD, *IN JAPAN!*, released by Hip-Select in 2004 – only 5,000 copies pressed.

Originally recorded by Rare Earth, for their 1972 album, *WILLIE REMEMBERS* – single charted at no.93 on the Hot 100 in the States.

WE'RE HERE TO ENTERTAIN YOU

Song included on the Jackson 5's album, *JOYFUL JUKEBOX MUSIC*, issued in October 1976 in the States and December 1976 in the UK.

Issued as a single in the Philippines b/w *We're Gonna Change Our Style*.

Snippet featured on Michael's home video, *The Legend Continues...*, released in 1988 (1989 in the States).

WE'VE GOT A GOOD THING GOING

Song Michael recorded for his album, *BEN*, issued in August 1972 in the States and December 1972 in the UK.

B-side of *We're Almost There* in the UK in 1981.

DJ Bobi James remix featured on the album, *SOUL SOURCE –
JACKSON 5 REMIXES 2*, released in Japan in 2001.

Hit covers versions (all titled *Good Thing Going*):
Sugar Minott – no.4 in the UK in 1981.
Yazz – no.53 in the UK in 1996.
Sid Owen – no.14 in the UK in 2000.

(WE'VE GOT) BLUE SKIES

Song featured on the Jackson 5's album, *MAYBE TOMORROW*, issued
in April 1971 in the States and October 1971 in the UK.

Featured in the 'Ray And Charles Superstars' episode of the Jackson 5
cartoon series in 1971.

WE'VE GOT FOREVER

Song Michael recorded for his album, *FOREVER, MICHAEL*, issued in
January 1975 in the States and March 1975 in the UK.

Performed by Michael in the States on *Soul Train* in 1975.

WE'VE HAD ENOUGH

Written by Michael with Rodney Jerkins, LaShawn Daniels and Carole
Bayer Sager, and featuring on his box-set, *THE ULTIMATE
COLLECTION*, issued in November 2004.

Originally rumoured to be a duet by Michael with sister Janet, about the
way the media mistreated Michael and his family.

WHAT A LONELY WAY TO GO

Song written by Michael circa 1975, and cited by him in his court
disposition in November 1993 – remains unreleased.

Jazz recording of the song surfaced on the internet in 2005 – reputedly
a duet by Michael and brother Jermaine, however, this proved to be a
fake.

WHAT ABOUT US

Song written by Michael, originally for his *DANGEROUS* album, demos of which evolved eventually into *Earth Song*. Demos, titled What About Us, leaked on the internet in 2003 – no official release.

WHAT BECOMES OF THE BROKENHEARTED

Jimmy Ruffin hit the Jackson 5 recorded a version of – remains unreleased.

Hit versions:
Jimmy Ruffin – no.6 on the R&B singles chart and no.7 on the Hot 100 in the States, and no.8 in the UK, in 1966.
Jimmy Ruffin (reissue) – no.4 in the UK in 1974.
Dave Stewart & Colin Blunstone – no.13 in the UK in 1981.
Paul Young – no.22 on the Hot 100 in 1992.
Robson & Jerome – no.1 in the UK in 1996.

WHAT DOES IT TAKE (TO WIN YOUR LOVE)

Song recorded by the Jackson 5 – remains unreleased.

Originally recorded by Jr. Walker & The All Stars, who took the song to no.1 on the R&B singles chart and no.4 on the Hot 100 in the States, and to no.13 in the UK, in 1969.

WHAT GOES AROUND COMES AROUND

Song included on Michael's album, *BEN*, issued in August 1972 in the States and December 1972 in the UK.

WHAT MORE CAN I GIVE

Written by Michael, and originally inspired by Nelson Mandela, a song he had planned to premiere at his 'Michael & Friends – What More Can I Give' concerts in June 1999, staged in the South Korean capital, Seoul, and in Munich, Germany.

'In an earlier conversation I had this year with President Mandela,' said Michael in 1999, 'we discussed the concept of giving, and the words 'what more can I give' kept coming into my mind... we all have to do what we can, to help end the needless suffering in the world.'

Re-written by Michael, following the '9/11' terrorists attacks in America on 11th September 2001 – recorded as a charity single with a host of stars, including Beyoncé, Mariah Carey, Celine Dion, Luis Miguel, Tom Petty, Carlos Santana, Usher and Luther Vandross.

Completed on 19th October 2001, premiered two days later at the 'United We Stand – What More Can I Give' concert at Washington DC's RFK Stadium, in front of 46,000 people. Concert edited and aired on ABC TV on 1st November.

'I'm not one to sit back and say, "Oh, I feel bad for what happened to them",' said Michael. 'I want the whole world to sing (*What More Can You Give*), to bring us together as a world, because a song is a mantra, something you repeat over and over. And we need peace, we need giving, we need love, we need unity.'

Promo short film premiered at the Radio music Awards in 2003.

Spanish language version, titled *Todo Para Ti*, also recorded – featured contributions from Michael, Mariah Carey, Celine Dion, Gloria Estefan, Julio Iglasias, Ricky Martin and Jon Secada.

Serious disagreements between Michael and Sony Music meant both charity singles went unreleased – however, 200 promo copies were distributed to the artists involved and music industry representatives involved with the project.

Made available as a download single in October 2003 – no other official release.

WHAT YOU DO TO ME

Song originally written by Michael in 1985, and registered with the United States Copyright Office in October the same year. Failed to make Michael's *BAD* album – remains unreleased.

Registered again in December 1998, possibly after being re-written, and considered for Michael's album, *INVINCIBLE* – remains unreleased.

WHAT YOU DON'T KNOW

Song featured on the Jackson 5's album, *DANCING MACHINE*, issued in September 1974 in the States and November 1974 in the UK.

Michael, in an interview with Don Cornelius in 1974, stated this song was originally recorded for one of his solo albums.

Performed solo by Michael on *Soul Train* in 1974, and by the Jacksons on their TV series in 1977.

Released as a single in France.

WHATEVER HAPPENS

Song written by Michael with Teddy Riley, Gilbert Cang, J. Quay and Geoffrey Williams, and recorded for his *INVINCIBLE* album, issued in October 2001.

Guest guitarist: Carlos Santana – his contribution was recorded in San Francisco in February 2001 (Michael couldn't attend due to other engagements).

'I was very honoured that he called on me to work with him and I love the song,' said Santana. 'He was really happy with it.'

WHATEVER YOU GOT, I WANT

Song featured on the Jackson 5 album, *DANCING MACHINE*, issued in September 1974 in the States and November 1974 in the UK.

Michael, in an interview with Don Cornelius in 1974, stated this song was originally recorded for one of his solo albums.

Lead single from the album in the States (no UK release) – peaked at no.3 on the R&B singles chart and no.38 on the Hot 100.

B-side of *The Life Of The Party* in the UK.

Performed solo by Michael on *Soul Train* in 1974.

Sampled by K-Ci & JoJo on *Baby Come Back*, a song they recorded for their debut album, *LOVE ALWAYS*, released in 1997.

WHAT'S A GUY GOTTA DO

Song written by Pharrell Williams in 2000, for Michael's album, *INVINCIBLE*, but failed to make the final selection – remains unreleased.

'Meeting Michael Jackson has been the best moment of all this,' said Williams. 'He said that song I made for him, *What's A Guy Gotta Do*, was alright. He said he liked it, but in the end it wasn't right for him.'

WHAT'S IT GONNA BE

Song written by Michael, and registered with the BMI – remains unreleased.

Not the same song Michael's sister Janet recorded with Busta Rhymes.

WHAT'S YOUR GAME

Song written by the Jackson 5, and recorded by four sisters managed by their father, M-D-L-T Willis – issued in November 1974 in the States (no UK released).

Charted at no.89 on the R&B singles chart.

WHAT'S YOUR LIFE

Song Michael cited he had written with brother Jermaine at his court disposition in November 1993 – remains unreleased.

WHATZUPWITU

Song recorded by Eddie Murphy, with Michael on backing vocals, for his 1993 album, *LOVE'S ALRIGHT* (no UK release) – recorded following Eddie's guest appearance in Michael's short film, *Remember The Time*.

Charted at no.74 on the R&B singles chart and listed at no.121 on the 'bubbling under' section of the Hot 100 in the States (no UK release).

Promo video, directed by Wayne Isham, featured Eddie and Michael dancing and singing on fluffy white clouds. No commercial release, except in Japan, where it was included on the DVD, *Music Video Clip! Dance 4*.

Official Versions:
Album Version.	Klub Mix Dub.
Hip Hop Remix.	Klub Mix Edit.
Hip Hop Remix Edit.	Klub Mix Full.
Eclipse Mix.	Instrumental.

WHEN BABIES SMILE

Poem written by Michael – included in his book of poems and reflections, *Dancing The Dream*, published in 1992.

WHEN I COME OF AGE

Song written specially for Michael by Hal Davis, Don Fletcher and Weldon Dean Parkes, about a boy's wishes and what he would like to become when he grows up.

Recorded by Michael in the early-to-mid 1970s, released for the first time on his album, *LOOKING BACK TO YESTERDAY*, issued in February 1986 in the States and May 1986 in the UK.

Demo version, with alternate ending – different lyrics – known to exist.

WHEN I LOOK AT YOU

Song recorded by the Jacksons, and featured as a previously unreleased track on their single, *2300 Jackson Street*, issued in July 1989 in the States and August 1989 in the UK.

Michael wasn't one of the Jacksons who recorded this song.

WHEN WE GROW UP (WE DON'T HAVE TO CHANGE AT ALL)

Song Michael performed as a duet with Roberta Flack, on a TV show titled *Free To Be...You And Me,* which aired on ABC TV on 11th March 1974 – the show went on to win an Emmy, for Best Children's Special. Michael and Roberta lip-synched their performance, therefore a recording of the song must exist – remains unreleased.

Accompanying soundtrack album featured a version of the song by Diana Ross.

TV show released on home video in the States in 2001 (no UK release).

WHEN YOU WISH UPON A STAR

Song Michael performed as part of a medley, with *Ease On Down The Road* and *Follow The Yellow Brick Road,* on the *Kraft Salutes Disneyland's 25th Anniversary Show* in 1980, accompanied by Mickey & Minnie Mouse, Donald Duck and Goofy – remains unreleased.

Snippet featured on Michael's home video, *The Legend Continues...,* as the credits rolled.

WHERE DID OUR LOVE GO

Supremes hit the Jackson 5 recorded a version of – remains unreleased.

Hit versions:
Supremes – no.1 on the Hot 100 and R&B singles charts, and no.3 in the UK, in 1964.
Donny Elbert – no.6 on the R&B singles chart and no.15 on the Hot 100 in 1971, and no.8 in the UK in 1972.
J. Geils Band – no.68 on the Hot 100 in 1976.

356

Manhatten Transfer – no.40 in the UK in 1978.
Tricia Penrose – no.71 in the UK in 1996.

WHERE DO I STAND

Written by Marlon Jackson for the Jacksons 1984 album, *VICTORY*, but failed to make the final track listing.

Recorded by Marlon for his debut solo album, *BABY TONIGHT*, issued in the States in 1987 (no UK release).

WHITE CHRISTMAS

Most successful Christmas song ever, which the Jackson 5 recorded a version of for their *CHRISTMAS ALBUM* circa 1970, but which failed to make the final track listing – remains unreleased.

Written by Irving Berlin for the film, *Holiday Inn*, and recorded by Bing Crosby in Los Angeles on 29th May 1942 – hit no.1 in the States and went on to become to the best selling single of all time.

Other hit versions:
Ravens – no.9 on the R&B singles chart in the States in 1948.
Mantovani – no.6 in the UK in 1952.
Drifters – no.2 on the R&B singles chart in 1954 (with several re-
    entries in later years).
Pat Boone – no.29 in the UK in 1957.
Andy Williams – no.1 on the Christmas Singles chart in the States in
    1963.
Otis Redding – no.12 on the Christmas Singles chart in 1968.
Freddie Starr – no.41 in the UK in 1975.
Darts – no.48 in the UK in 1980.
Jim Davidson – no.52 in the UK in 1980.
Keith Harris & Orville – no.40 in the UK in 1985.
Max Bygraves – no.71 in the UK in 1989.

WHO DO YOU KNOW

Song Michael wrote circa 1981, but failed to make his album, *THRILLER*. Cited by Michael in his court disposition in November 1993 – remains unreleased.

WHO IS IT

Song written by Michael, and recorded for his album, *DANGEROUS*, issued in November 1991 – early versions were allegedly titled *Lying To Myself* and *It Doesn't Seem To Matter*. The latter was mentioned in *Revolution* magazine, in a list of supposed songs for the album.

Extended demo version featured different harmonies, some of which have been released on various remixes.

Charted at no.6 on the R&B singles chart and no.14 on the Hot 100 in the States, and no.10 in the UK – hit no.1 in Zimbabwe.

Released instead of *Give In To Me* in the States, following Michael's brief *a cappella* rendition during his televised interview with Oprah Winfrey.

Official Versions:
Album Version.	Most Patient Mix.
A Cappella.	Oprah Winfrey Special Intro.
Brotherly Dub.	P-Man Dub.
Brothers Cool Dub.	Patience Edit.
Patience Mix.	Patient Beats.
House 7".	Tribal Version.
IHS Mix.	7" Edit.
Lakeside Dub.	7" Edit With Intro.
Moby's Raw Mercy Dub.	Brothers In Rhythm House Mix.

World premiere of promo short film, directed by David Fincher, on BBC2's *Def II* show in the UK on 13th July 1992. The following day, unhappy with the promo and its premature release, Michael withdrew it (though it was included on his home video, *Dangerous – The Short Films*).

Promoted in the States with a montage of Michael's previous short films and in concert footage.

Remix included on the first acetate version of the expanded, special edition of Michael's *DANGEROUS* album in 2001 – bonus disc cancelled.

WHO IS THE GIRL WITH HER HAIR DOWN

Song Michael cited he had written in his court disposition in November 1993 – remains unreleased.

WHO'S BAD

Alternative title, possibly related to the ad-libs at the end of the short film, for Michael's hit, *Bad*, as registered with the United States Copyright Office on a number of occasions in the late 1980s.

See also: *Bad*.

WHO'S LOOKIN' FOR A LOVER

Song recorded for Motown, and included on Michael's album, *LOOKING BACK TO YESTERDAY*, issued in February 1986 in the States and May 1986 in the UK.

WHO'S LOVIN' YOU

Smokey Robinson song the Jackson 5 regularly performed live in the pre-Motown days, and one of the songs they performed at their Motown audition in 1968.

Recorded for their debut album, *DIANA ROSS PRESENTS THE JACKSON 5*, issued in December 1969 in the States and March 1970 in the UK.

Recorded on 19th, 20th and 24th July 1969.

B-side of the Jackson 5's debut single for Motown, *I Want You Back* – listed alongside the A-side on the Hot 100 in the States, hitting no.1.

One of three songs the Jackson 5 performed on their first appearance on the *Ed Sullivan Show* on 14th December 1969 in the States – this was a shortened version of the song.

Live version, recorded in Indianapolis, Indiana on 29th May 1971, discovered in a North Hollywood vault by director Karen Arthur, just four days before the shooting of the TV mini-series *The Jacksons: An*

American Dream finished shooting in 1992 – the script was hastily re-written so the song could be included.

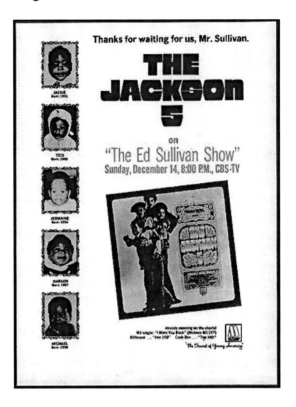

Remixed live version included on the soundtrack album, *THE JACKSONS: AN AMERICAN DREAM*, issued in October 1992 in the States and July 1993 in the UK.

Cassette single and promo CD single issued in the States (no UK release), promoted by a 'new' video directed by Steve Barron, featuring the group's *Ed Sullivan Show* performance – charted at no.48 on the R&B singles chart but failed to make the Hot 100.

Original live recording added as a bonus track to the 'Two Classic Albums on One CD' reissue of *GOIN' BACK TO INDIANA & LOOKIN' THROUGH THE WINDOWS*, issued in the States in August 2001 (no UK release).

Single version with extended vocals, taken from the mono version and 'folded' into the stereo version, included on Michael's solo compilation, *LOVE SONGS*, issued in the UK in 2002 (no USA release).

Originally recorded by the Miracles, and featured on their 1961 album, *HI, WE'RE THE MIRACLES*.

WHO'S RIGHT, WHO'S WRONG

Song recorded by Kenny Loggins, with Michael and Richard Page on backing vocals, for his 1985 album, *KEEP THE FIRE*.

WHY

Song written by Kenneth 'Babyface' Edmonds, and originally scheduled to appear on Michael's album, HIS*TORY* – until his three nephews, 3T (Tito's sons Taj, Taryll and TJ) claimed it.

'The song was supposed to be on Michael's HIS*TORY* album, but we loved it so much that we kinda ended up stealing it from him,' confirmed TJ in early 1996. 'I mean, once he played it for us and saw our faces he was like, "You guys want this song?" – and that's exactly what happened, and working in the studio with him was such an experience.'

Recorded by 3T, as a duet with Michael, for their debut album, *BROTHERHOOD*, released in 1996. Michael didn't actually record the song with his nephews, but allowed them to use his original version of the song, and turn it into a collaboration by adding their own vocals.

Hit no.2 in the UK, but struggled to no.71 on the R&B singles chart in the States, and only managed no.112 on the 'bubbling under' section of the Hot 100.

Promo short film featured Michael and his nephews – Michael, with Ralph Ziman, also directed.

Official Versions:
Album Version.
D.W. Bonus Mix.
Radio Edit.

Solo version by Michael remains unreleased.

WHY CAN'T I BE

Song written by Michael in 1980, and registered with the United States Copyright Office in November 1984. Also cited by Michael in his court disposition in December 1984 – remains unreleased.

WHY SHY

Song Michael cited he had written in his court disposition in November 1993 – remains unreleased.

WHY YOU WANNA TRIP ON ME

Song Michael recorded for his album, *DANGEROUS*, issued in November 1991.

Inspired by the things people say about Michael. 'We knew people were after him, people all talking about him,' said co-writer Teddy Riley. 'But we didn't get too direct, we didn't say anybody's name, 'cause when you're too direct it gets boring.'

Played over the closing credits on Michael's home video, *Dangerous – The Short Films*.

WILL YOU BE THERE

Written by Michael, and recorded for his album, *DANGEROUS*, issued in November 1991.

Lyrics included in Michael's book of poems and reflections, *Dancing The Dream*, published in 1992.

Featured the Andrae Crouch Singers on backing vocals, and opened with 67 seconds of Beethoven's *9th Symphony*, played by the Cleveland Orchestra – uncredited. $7 million copyright infringement lawsuit filed – settled in December 1992, and one outcome was all future copies of *DANGEROUS* must credit Ludwig Van Beethoven and the Cleveland Orchestra on *Will You Be There*.

Theme to the movie, *Free Willy*, and included on the soundtrack album.

Subject of a lawsuit filed by Albano Carrisi, who claimed the melody of the song was stolen from his composition, *I Cigni Di Balaka*.

Achieved no.7 on the Hot 100 and no.53 on the R&B singles chart in the States, and no.9 in the UK – hit no.1 in Zimbabwe.

Two versions of the short film, directed by Vincent Paterson, released – with and without footage of the movie, *Free Willy*. The short films used footage of Michael performing the song at MTV's 10th anniversary show in 1991, and from his own Dangerous World Tour.

RIAA Gold Record (500,000 copies in USA).

MTV Movie Award: Best Song in a Movie.

Official Versions:
Album Version.	Instrumental.
Edit.	Radio Edit.

Performed by Michael as MTV's 10th anniversary celebration, *MTV 10*, in 1991; two years later, at the NAACP Image Awards, he joined Patti LaBelle and The Voices Of Faith Choir, to perform a version of the song.

Live performance by Michael, at his Dangerous Tour concert in Bucharest, Romania, on 1st October 1992, featured on the DVD released as part of his box-set, *THE ULTIMATE COLLECTION*, issued in November 2004.

WINDOW SHOPPING

Song featured on the Jackson 5's album, *JOYFUL JUKEBOX MUSIC*, issued in October 1976 in the States and December 1976 in the UK.

Recorded on 15th December 1973 – a week before Jermaine married Berry Gordy's daughter, Hazel,.

Lead song on a four track Brazilian picture sleeve EP – also featured *You're My Best Friend, My Love, We're Here To Entertain You* and *Through Thick And Thin*.

Instrumental version appeared on the 1975 Motown album, *THE MAGIC DISCO MACHINE*, which featured unfinished/unreleased Motown tracks.

WINGS OF MY LOVE

Song Michael recorded for his debut solo album, *GOT TO BE THERE*, issued in January 1972 in the States and May 1972 in the UK.

Featured in the 'Who's Hoozis' episode of the new Jackson 5 cartoon series in 1971.

WITH A CHILD'S HEART

Stevie Wonder cover Michael recorded for his album, *MUSIC & ME*, issued in April 1973 in the States and July 1973 in the UK.

Peaked at no.14 on the R&B singles chart and no.50 on the Hot 100 in the States (no UK release).

Performed by Michael on *Soul Train* in the States in 1973.

B-side of *One Day In Your Life* in the UK in 1975.

Stevie Wonder's original, the flip-side of *Nothing's Too Good For My Baby*, was listed at no.8 on the R&B singles chart and no.131 on the 'bubbling under' section of the Hot 100 in 1966. Featured on Stevie's album, *UP-TIGHT EVERYTHING'S ALRIGHT*.

WONDERING WHO

Written by Jackie and Randy Jackson, and recorded by the Jacksons for their album, *TRIUMPH*, issued in October 1980.

B-side of *Can You Feel It*.

WORD TO THE BADD!!

Controversial song Jermaine recorded for his 1991 album, *YOU SAID, YOU SAID*, as a swipe at brother Michael, for not returning his calls.

Jermaine didn't originally plan to release the song, before it was leaked to American radio stations, around the time Michael's *Black Or White* made its debut.

Two versions: one, with lyrics directed at Michael; two, the album version with different lyrics not aimed at Michael. Promo 12" single released in the States featured a Jackson 5 introduction.

Media interest in the States helped the song to no.78 on the Hot 100 and no.88 on the R&B singles chart – not a hit in the UK.

WORDS WITHOUT MEANING

Song Michael co-produced with his nephews, 3T, for their debut album, *BROTHERHOOD*, released in 1995.

WORK THAT BODY

Song written by Michael with Bryan Loren.

Included on the first acetate version of the expanded, special edition of Michael's *DANGEROUS* album in 2001 – bonus disc cancelled.

A minute long snippet, along with *She Got It*, leaked on the internet in 2005 – no official release. Lyrics from the Jackson 5's *ABC*, as performed by an adult Michael, can be heard on this demo: 'Sit down, girl! I think I love you! No! Get up, girl! Show me what you can do!'

WORKIN' DAY AND NIGHT

Written by Michael, and recorded for his album, *OFF THE WALL*, issued in August 1979 – said by Michael to be very autobiographical in some ways, however, he wrote the song from a married man's viewpoint.

Michael's original demo recording featured as a bonus track on the expanded, special edition of *OFF THE WALL*, released in 2001.

B-side of *Rock With You* in the USA.

B-side of *Off The Wall* in the UK.

Live version, recorded at a concert at Madison Square Garden in September 1981, featured on the Jacksons album, *LIVE*, issued in November 1981.

Live performance by Michael, at his Dangerous Tour concert in Bucharest, Romania, on 1st October 1992, featured on the DVD released as part of his box-set, *THE ULTIMATE COLLECTION*, issued in November 2004.

Different live performance screened on Nippon TV in Japan.

Sampled by:
Will Smith on *Can You Feel Me*, a track he recorded for his 1991 album, *WILLENNIUM*.
Richie Rich on *Salsa House*, which appeared on at least two various artist compilations, namely *HOUSE SOUNDS OF LONDON* (1990) and *CLUB CLASSICS* (2003).

WORLD IS A MESS, THE

Song performed by the Jackson 5, as part of a sketch, on Cher's TV show in the States on 11th March 1975 – the song introduced a segment in which Cher and two other guests portrayed the confused, first inhabitants in the Garden of Eden. The Jackson 5 also performed *I Am Love*.

Remains unreleased.

WORLD OF SUNSHINE

Song featured on the Jackson 5's album, *SKYWRITER*, issued in March 1973 in the States and July 1973 in the UK.

Performed by the Jacksons, accompanied by film footage of them on skates, on their TV series in 1976.

WOULD YA? WOULD YA?

Song recorded by the Jackson 5 for Motown, and registered with the United States Copyright Office in January 1973 – remains unreleased. Written by Freddie Perren and Christine Yarian.

Also known to fans by the title, *Wouldja*.

XSCAPE

Song Michael recorded during the *INVINCIBLE* sessions.

Surfaced on the internet in 2002; Michael's attorneys immediately threatened legal action, if sites didn't remove access to download the track – no official release.

YAKETY YAK

Coasters hit the Jackson 5 performed as part of a 'Salute to the Vocal Groups' medley with *Opus One, Bei Mir Bist Du Schon, Stop! In The Name Of Love*, an untitled Jackson 5 ditty and *Dancing Machine*, on *The Carol Burnett Show* in the States in January 1975 – clip included on the Vol.31 DVD of the show.

The Coasters took the song to no.1 on both American charts, and to no.12 in the UK, in 1958.

YEAH

Song Eddie Murphy recorded, backed by an all star choir, for his 1993 album, *LOVE'S ALRIGHT*.

All star choir: Michael and his sister Janet, with Paul McCartney, Luther Vandross, Julio Iglasias, Elton John, Garth Brooks and Jon Bon Jovi

YESTERDAY

Beatles classic the Jackson 5 often performed in the early days, and during their Motown concerts in 1971, but never recorded.

Most covered song of all-time, according to *Guinness World Records*, with 2,500+ recorded versions by the year 2000.

Hit versions:
Beatles – no.1 on the Hot 100 in the States in 1965, no.8 in the UK in 1976.

Matt Monro – no.8 in the UK in 1965.

Marianne Faithful – no.36 in the UK in 1965.

Ray Charles – no.9 on the R&B singles chart and no.25 on the Hot 100 in the States, and no.44 in the UK, in 1967.

Wet Wet Wet – no.4 in the UK in 1997.

YESTER-ME, YESTER-YOU, YESTERDAY

Stevie Wonder song the Jackson 5 recorded a version of – remains unreleased.

Stevie took the song to no.2 in the UK, and no.5 on the R&B singles chart and no.7 on the Hot 100 in the States, in 1969.

YOU AIN'T GIVING ME WHAT I WANT (SO I'M TAKING IT ALL BACK)

One of 19 'Rare & Unreleased' tracks on the fourth CD of the Michael/Jackson 5 box-set, *SOULSATION!*, issued in June 1995 in the States and July 1995 in the UK.

Recorded on 8th January 1970 – originally titled, *You're A, B, C's And D's*.

YOU AIN'T GONNA CHANGE NOTHIN'

Song written by Michael in 1975, and registered with the United States Copyright Office in November 1984. Also cited by Michael in his court disposition in November 1993 – remains unreleased.

YOU ARE A LIAR

Song Michael cited he had written in his court disposition in November 1993, and one of the many songs he considered recording for his album, *INVINCIBLE* – remains unreleased.

Also known by the title, *You're A Liar*.

YOU ARE MY LIFE

Written by Michael with Babyface, Carole Bayer Sager and John McClain, and recorded for his album, *INVINCIBLE*, issued in October 2001.

Included on the album at the expense of *Shout*.

YOU ARE MY SUNSHINE

One of numerous songs the Jackson family used to sing in Gary, Indiana, while they were growing up, as confirmed by mother Katherine in her autobiography, *My Family, The Jacksons*.

YOU ARE NOT ALONE

Written by R. Kelly, and recorded by Michael for his album, HIS*TORY*, issued in June 1995.

'I was amazed when Michael called me because, for years, I just didn't expect to go to that level,' admitted R. Kelly. 'I was so nervous, I was afraid I wouldn't be able to finish the project. When I first got to the studio something weird came over me. Michael was on a different level, and it was a hell of a level to go to. But passion took me over, and it put a shield around me, and allowed me to be just a normal guy who felt like he worked with Michael all the time.'

Michael, after listening to the tape R. Kelly sent him, liked what he heard but felt the song needed a more prominent climax – which he wrote, with R. Kelly's approval.

Second single from the album – became the first single in the chart's 37 year history to enter Billboard's Hot 100 at no.1 in the States. Commemorated with a special award at the 6th annual Billboard Awards ceremony – Tina Turner collected the award on Michael's behalf, as he was in hospital, after he collapsed rehearsing for his planned HBO TV special, *Michael Jackson: One Night Only*. Feat recognised by *Guinness World Records* – Michael listed as the 'First Vocalist to enter the US Singles chart at Number One'.

Also hit no.1 on the R&B singles chart in the States, and in France, Ireland, New Zealand, Switzerland and the UK.

RIAA Platinum Record (USA million seller).

No.8 best selling single of 1995 in the UK.

25 years, seven months and one week between *I Want You Back* and *You Are Not Alone* hitting no.1 on the Hot 100 was a new record span between chart toppers (Cher beat this record in 1999, when her single *Believe* rose to no.1).

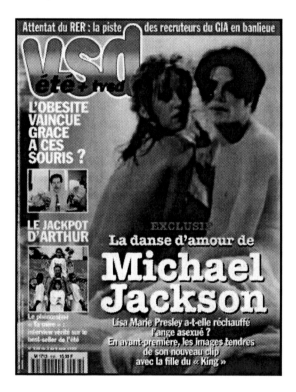

Short film, directed by Wayne Isham, co-starred Michael's then wife, Lisa Marie Presley – both, controversially, were seen almost naked on the edge of a swimming pool. Pool sequences shot at Raleigh Stages, theatre sequences filmed at Pantages Theater in Hollywood. Version released on the home video, *History On Film Volume II*, digitally altered to give Michael an 'angelic' look.

Grammy nomination: Song of the Year.

Official Versions:

Album Version.	Album Edit.
Album Version – different fade.	Jon B. Padappella.
Classic Club Edit.	Jon B. Remix Edit.
Radio Edit.	Knuckluv Dub Version.
Frankie Knuckles – Classic Club Mix.	R. Kelly Remix.
Frankie Knuckles – Franctified Club Mix.	R. Kelly Remix Edit.
Jon B. Main Mix.	

Performed by Michael at a number of events, including:

- MTV Music Video Awards, staged in New York's Radio City Music Hall on 7th September 1995.

- 15th Anniversary celebrations of Black Entertainment Television, in Washington DC on 22nd September 1995 (aired 6th December) – Michael became the first inductee in BET's newly founded Walk of Fame.

- The two Michael & Friends concerts, staged in Seoul, South Korea, on 25th June 1999, and in the Germany city of Munich two days later.

During Michael's *His*tory World Tour, a lucky girl was allowed on stage at each concert, to dance with Michael as he sang the song. Live performances from the tour screened in Germany and New Zealand.

Cover version recorded by Diana Ross, for her 1996 album, *VOICES OF LOVE*, as a prod – to see how Michael reacted to her version of the song. Interviewed on the UK's BBC Radio 1 in December 1996, Diana said, 'Just talking about him now makes my heart feel sad.'

Performed by Liza Minnelli during the *Michael Jackson: 30th Anniversary Celebration, The Solo Years* concerts, staged at New York's Madison Square Garden on 7th and 10th September 2001.

Sixteenth of Michael's 20 *'Visionary – The Video Singles'* reissues, with the music on one side of a Dual Disc and the accompanying short film on the other side. Issued in May 2006 in the UK – charted at no.30.

Law suit against R. Kelly filed in Belgium by brothers Eddy and Danny van Passel, who claimed the song sounded eerily similar to their song, *If We Can Start All Over.* 'It's identical,' said Danny, 'and I can't say more than that, except it's a protected copyright and you should ask permission first before you use it, and R. Kelly didn't ask for permission.'

YOU ARE SO BEAUTIFUL

Song Michael began writing during his court trial in 2005, inspired by and as a thank you to his fans for their ongoing support – remains unreleased.

YOU ARE THE ONES (INTERLUDE)

Song recorded by Michael's nephews, 3T, as a tribute to the Jackson 5 – included on the Jacksons TV soundtrack album, *THE JACKSONS: AN AMERICAN DREAM*, issued in October 1992 in the States and July 1993 in the UK.

YOU ARE THERE

Song featured on Michael's album, *FOREVER, MICHAEL*, issued in January 1975 in the States and March 1975 in the UK.

YOU CAN CRY ON MY SHOULDER

Song Michael recorded for his album, *BEN*, issued in August 1972 in the States and December 19772 in the UK.

B-side of *Ben*.

YOU CAN'T HURRY LOVE

Supremes cover recorded by the Jackson 5 – remains unreleased.

Hit versions:
Supremes – no.1 on both American charts, and no.3 in the UK, in 1966.
Phil Collins – no.1 in the UK in 1982, and no.10 on the Hot 100 in the
   States in 1983.

YOU CAN'T WIN

Song originally performed by Michael in the movie, *The Wiz* – premiered in Los Angeles in October 1978. Featured on the accompanying soundtrack double album, issued in September 1978 in the States and October 1978 in the UK.

Not featured in the Broadway musical on which the film was based – written especially for Michael's part as the Scarecrow.

First solo single by Michael released on CBS/Epic.

Charted at no.42 on the R&B singles chart and no.81 on the Hot 100 in the States – wasn't a hit in the UK.

Official Versions:
Album Version.   7" Part 1.
12" Extended Mix.   7" Part 2.

Snippet heard, on the radio when the children are in a car, in Michael's favourite film, *E.T. THE EXTRA-TERRESTRIAL.*

Included on the first acetate version of the expanded, special edition of Michael's *OFF THE WALL* album in 2001 – later withdrawn.

374

Performed by Jill Scott during the *Michael Jackson: 30th Anniversary Celebration, The Solo Years* concerts, staged at New York's Madison Square Garden on 7th and 10th September 2001.

YOU DON'T KNOW LIKE I KNOW

Sam & Dave song the Jackson 5 regularly performed live on the Chitli' Circuit circa 1965-67, and suggested by Shirley Cartman (Tito's music teacher) as a possible for the group's Motown audition in 1968 – rejected, as Sam & Dave were on a rival record label, Stax.

Hit for Sam & Dave in the States in 1966 – no.1 on the R&B singles chart and no.90 on the Hot 100 in the States (didn't chart in the UK).

YOU HAVEN'T DONE NOTHIN'

Musical assault on President Richard Nixon, written and recorded by Stevie Wonder for his Grammy Award winning 1974 album, *FULFILLINGNESS' FIRST FINALE*.

Credits 'Doo Doo Wopsssss by The Jackson 5', and Stevie could be heard singing, 'Jackson 5, sing along with me!'

Hit no.1 on both American charts and in Canada, and achieved no.30 in the UK.

YOU MADE ME WHAT I AM

Song included on the Jackson 5's album, *SKYWRITER*, issued in March 1973 in the States and July 1973 in the UK.

YOU NEED LOVE LIKE I DO (DON'T YOU?)

Song featured on the Jackson 5's album, *GET IT TOGETHER*, issued in September 1973 in the States and November 1973 in the UK.

Released as a single in France.

Originally recorded by Gladys Knight & The Pips – their version achieved no.3 on the R&B singles chart and no.25 on the Hot 100 in the States in 1970.

YOU ROCK MY WORLD

Written by Michael with Rodney Jerkins, Fred Jerkins III, LaShawn Daniels and Nora Payne, and recorded for his album, *INVINCIBLE*, issued in October 2001.

Originally titled *Rock My World*.

'My association with Michael came about after I was introduced to Carole Bayer Sager by Atlantic VP, Craig Kaman,' said Jerkins. 'She asked me if I would like to come to her house, and write with her and Michael – so I said, Cool! I flew to Los Angeles, and sure enough was there at her house... every time I see him, I tell him over and over – it's just incredible just to be here working with you, knowing how crazy I was about you when I was a kid.'

'We knew that it (*You Rock My World*) was going to be a corner-stone of the album, and it set the mood and the feel for the rest of the music,' said engineer Bruce Swedien. 'A lot of times, a real good piece of music will never get on the album, only because it just doesn't fit. You know Michael loves drama – if the music doesn't have drama, if it's just a derivative of a piece of music without drama, Michael's not going to go for it.'

Spoken intro by Michael and Chris Tucker – Tucker came into the studio to do a voice party for *INVINCIBLE*, but it wasn't until Rodney Jerkins heard it and thought it fitted the mood of the song, that it was agreed to use it for *You Rock My World*.

Lead single from the album – however, its release to radio stations had to be brought forward, after two New York stations broke the embargo Sony Music had placed on it.

Officially premiered on Michael's web-site on 24th August 2001.

Hit no.2 in the UK, and achieved no.10 on the Hot 100 and no.13 on the R&B singles chart in the States – on the strength of airplay alone, as no commercial single was released.

Fred Bronson, Billboard magazine's chart expert, felt it was 'a huge mistake' not to release the song as a single in the States: 'Certainly, if a commercial single had been available, it would have peaked higher – perhaps even at no.1.'

No.1 in France, Portugal and Spain.

Official Versions:

Album Version.	Instrumental.
A Cappella #1.	Radio Edit.
A Cappella #2.	Track Masters Remix (with Jay-Z).

Jay-Z chosen by Michael to remix the song because: 'he's hip, the new thing, and he's with the kids today. They like his work. He's tapped into the nerve of popular culture. It just made good business sense.'

Short film, directed by Paul Hunter, co-starred Chris Tucker, Michael Madson and Marlon Brando – three versions released, the longest almost 14 minutes long. Premiered on 21st September 2001 – based on a short story written by Michael with Paul Hunter.

NACCP Image Awards: Best Music Video.

Grammy nomination: Best Pop Vocal Performance, Male.

Performed by Michael and Usher during the *Michael Jackson: 30th Anniversary Celebration, The Solo Years* concerts, staged at New York's Madison Square Garden on 7th and 10th September 2001.

Originally scheduled to be the final release in Michael's *Visionary – The Video Singles* project, and was illustrated on a scrapped version of the *Visionary* box. Replaced by *Heal The World*, allegedly because Sony didn't want to afford Michael's *INVINCIBLE* album any publicity at all.

YOU TOLD ME YOUR LOVIN'

Song written by Michael in 1979, and registered with the United States Copyright Office in November 1984.

A second version, with words and music by Michael's brother, Randy, also exists – both versions remain unreleased.

(YOU WERE MADE) ESPECIALLY FOR ME

Song featured on the Jackson 5 album, *MOVING VIOLATION*, released in May 1975 in the States and July 1975 in the UK.

Performed by the Jacksons on their TV series in 1976.

Live performance by the Jacksons, at a concert in Mexico in 1976, included on the home video, *The Jacksons In Concert*, released in 1981 in the UK (no USA release).

YOU WERE THERE

Written by Michael, with Alan 'Buz' Kohan, at the Shrine Auditorium – venue for Sammy Davis, Jr.'s 60th Anniversary Show, on 13th November 1989. Performed by Michael – for the one and only time – at the show, after which he was heard saying he would never sing the song again, as it was 'Sammy's song.'

Registered with the United States Copyright Office in December 1989.

YOUNG FOLKS, THE

Song the Jackson 5 recorded for their second album, *ABC*, issued in May 1970 in the States and August 1970 in the UK.

B-side of *ABC* – featured a slightly different mix to the album version.

Featured in the 'Pinestock USA' episode of the Jackson 5 cartoon series in 1971.

Originally recorded by the Supremes, and included on their 1969 album, *CREAM OF THE CROP*. B-side of *No Matter What Sign You Are* – listed separately on the Hot 100, where it peaked at no.69.

YOUR LOVE IN MY LIFE

Song Michael produced for Colby O'Donis & Friends, for the album, *PARTY TIME*, released in 2004.

YOUR WAYS

Written by Jackie Jackson, and recorded by the Jacksons for their album, *TRIUMPH*, issued in October 1980.

B-side of *Walk Right Now* and *State Of Shock*.

YOU'RE A, B, C'S AND D'S

Original title of *You Ain't Giving Me What I Want (So I'm Taking It All Back)*, included on the Michael/Jackson 5 box-set, *SOULSATION!* in 1995.

YOU'RE GOOD FOR ME

Song recorded by the Jackson 5 circa 1973, but unreleased until it appeared on Michael's solo album, *LOOKING BACK TO YESTERDAY*, issued in February 1986 in the States and May 1986 in the UK.

YOU'RE IN GOOD HANDS

Song Jermaine Jackson recorded, with the Jackson 5 on backing vocals, for his 1973 album, *COME INTO MY LIFE*.

Achieved no.35 on the R&B singles chart and no.79 on the Hot 100 in the States, but wasn't a hit in the UK.

Performed by Jermaine on *Soul Train* in 1973.

YOU'RE MY BEST FRIEND, MY LOVE

Song featured on the Jackson 5 album, *JOYFUL JUKEBOX MUSIC*, issued in October 1976 in the States and December 1976 in the UK.

YOU'RE MY EVERYTHING

Temptations hit the Jackson 5 recorded a version of – remains unreleased.

The Temptations took the song to no.3 on the R&B singles chart and no.6 on the Hot 100 in the States, and no.26 in the UK, in 1967.

YOU'RE SUPPOSED TO KEEP YOUR LOVE FOR ME

Written by Stevie Wonder, and originally recorded in 1975 by Jermaine Jackson, with Stevie, Michael and Jackie Jackson on backing vocals.

'There's a song called *You're Supposed To Keep Your Love For Me*, which was recorded five years before it came out. Michael, Stevie, Jackie and myself sing backgrounds on it,' confirmed Jermaine. 'I'd been trying to get Stevie to put that song on one of my albums. He said, "I have to record this track 'cause it's kind of old now.". Just before, I had recorded four songs and so I said to Stevie, "Why don't you get this song ready for this album?" So he went into the studio to re-cut it, and he cut another two songs.'

Re-cut version, recorded solo by Jermaine, featured on his album, *LET'S GET SERIOUS*, issued in 1980.

Original recording, featuring Michael, remains unreleased.

YOU'RE THE ONE

Written by Michael with Alan 'Buz' Kohan.

Recorded by Jennifer Holiday, with Michael producing, for her 1985 album, *SAY YOU LOVE ME*.

YOU'RE THE ONLY ONE

One of 19 'Rare & Unreleased' tracks listed as appearing on the Michael/Jackson 5 box-set, *SOULSATION!* in 1995 – however, the track that actually appeared on the fourth CD was *Ooh, I'd Love To Be With You* (from the Jackson 5's *SKYWRITER*).

Written by Deke Richards, Freddie Perren & Fonce Mizell – registered in December 1972.

Recorded by Jackie for his debut solo album – it's unlikely this is the same version supposed to feature on *SOULSATION!*

Titled *Are You The One* in pre-release notes.

YOU'VE CHANGED

Song the Jackson 5 originally recorded for Steel-Town Records, for the B-side of their debut single, *Big Boy*, issued in the States in January 1968 (no UK release).

Re-recorded on 19th and 29th July 1969 by the Jackson 5 for their debut album, *DIANA ROSS PRESENTS THE JACKSON 5*, issued in December 1969 in the States and March 1970 in the UK.

Mistakenly titled 'You've Changed Me' on early American pressings of the album sleeve, as Motown confused the song with another in their extensive back catalogue.

YOU'VE GOT A FRIEND

Song Michael recorded for his debut album, *GOT TO BE THERE*, issued in January 1972 in the States and May 1972 in the UK.

Lead song on a 4-track picture sleeve EP released in Mexico.

Originally recorded by Carole King, for her Grammy winning album, *TAPESTRY*, released in 1971.

Hit versions:
James Taylor – no.1 on the Hot 100 in the States, and no.4 in the UK, in 1971.
Roberta Flack & Donny Hathaway – no.8 on the R&B singles chart and no.29 on the Hot 100 in the States in 1971.
Brand New Heavies – no.9 in the UK in 1997.

YOU'VE REALLY GOT A HOLD ON ME

Song recorded by Michael on 13th June 1973, and included in an updated mix on his album, *FAREWELL MY SUMMER LOVE*, issued in May 1984 in the States and June 1984 in the UK – demo version also known to exist.

Alternate version featured on the 1998 album, *MOTOWN SINGS MOTOWN TREASURES – THE ULTIMATE RARITIES COLLECTION*.

Originally recorded by the Miracles, for their 1963 album, *THE FABULOUS MIRACLES*.

Hit versions:

Miracles – no.1 on the R&B singles chart and no.8 on the Hot 100 in the States in 1963.

Gayle McCormick – no.98 on the Hot 100 in 1972.

Eddie Rabbit – no.72 on the Hot 100 in 1979.

ZIP-A-DEE DOO-DAH

Song the Jackson 5 recorded for their debut album, *DIANA ROSS PRESENTS THE JACKSON 5*, issued in December 1969 in the States and March 1970 in the UK.

Performed live by the Jackson 5 at the *Daisy* club on 11th August 1969, for 300 specially invited guests – attended by Berry Gordy. The group's recorded version featured a snippet of Sly & The Family Stone's hit, *Sing A Simple Song*.

Rehearsal footage by the Jackson 5 featured on a promotional film, sent to concert promoters in 1970, to help to make them aware of the group.

Title given to a budget Jackson 5 compilation, released by Music for Pleasure in the UK in January 1979 (no USA issue).

Song originally featured in Disney's 1947 movie, *Song Of The South* – Grammy Award for Song of the Year.

Hit version:

Bob B. Soxx & The Blue Jeans – no.7 on the R&B singles chart and no.8 on the Hot 100 in 1962-63, and no.45 in the UK in 1963.

ZIP-A-DEE DOO-DAH – THERE WAS A TIME

Medley – known as the 'Soul Medley' – the Jackson 5 performed on *American Bandstand* in the States in February 1970, with Michael strutting his stuff like James Brown – Michael and his brothers were also presented with Gold Discs.

RUMOUR HAS IT…

These songs may exist – but may not.

If they do exist, they may involve Michael – but they may not.

Some of the entries included in this section are BG (background) cues – not, as some fans believe, unreleased songs by Michael. BG cues are songs used as background music in a TV programme, and the title of the BG cue relates to the TV programme, not the song featured in the TV programme.

4 TRIBES

Remix version of *Wanna Be Startin' Somethin'* by Organ Donors, from the 2003 compilation, *BIG ROOM TUNES VOL.3* – mistakenly believed by many Jackson fans to be a new song.

1990

Song Michael is rumoured to have recorded for the shelved greatest hits package, *DECADE 1980-1990* – remains unconfirmed.

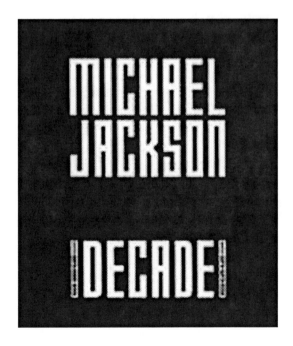

A SONG FOR YOU

ALL OF MY CHILDREN

BG cue.

ALWAYS

AN ANGEL CAME TO ME

ASK HER IT

BENJAMIN

Song about a boy who aspires to join the circus, recorded by the Dan Priddy – Michael is known to like the song, but reports on some fan sites he is on the song are incorrect.

BREAKING

One of four songs recorded by Michael, reportedly leaked to CFM radio in the States – the station claimed the songs were recorded and mixed at Capital Studios in Hollywood. All four songs remain unconfirmed.

See also: *Dead Or Alive*, *Healing My Feelings*, *What About Me*.

BUBBLE

CAN'T STOP ME NOW

Instrumental demo version exists as a bootleg, but is believed to be a fake.

CRUSH

Song Michael is rumoured to have planned to record as a duet with Lenny Kravitz, with a release date of early 2001 originally talked about – rumour may have arisen as Kravitz was working on the film *Blue Crush* around this time.

Instrumental demo surfaced on the internet in 2005.

DAWN OF A BRAND NEW DAY

Song rumoured to have been recorded by Michael and his brothers for Motown circa 1973 – remains unconfirmed.

DEAD OR ALIVE

One of four songs recorded by Michael, reportedly leaked to CFM radio in the States – the station claimed the songs were recorded and mixed at Capital Studios in Hollywood. All four songs remain unconfirmed.

See also: *Breaking*, *Healing My Feelings*, *What About Me*.

DEEP IN THE NIGHT

One of three titles – along with *Fever* and *Superfly Sister* – scribbled on a note, in a recording studio where Michael was working. May be a song title in its own right, or part of a song's lyrics, or just an idea.

DIRTY MINDS

Song Michael is rumoured to have recorded in 2003 – remains unconfirmed.

DO YOU EVEN CARE

Song Michael is rumoured to have recorded in 2003 – remains unconfirmed.

DON'T LEAVE ME IN THE DARK

Song Michael is rumoured to have recorded in 2003 – remains unconfirmed.

DRAGON FLY

BG cue.

DUST IN THE WIND

Re-make of a Kansas song (which featured on their 1977 album, *POINT OF KNOW RETURN*), allegedly recorded by Michael with Mariah Carey. Slated to appear on a six or seven track EP by Mariah titled *Don't Hesitate*, circa December 1996 – remains unconfirmed.

According to reports, the EP wasn't released, largely as a result of behind the scenes problems between Mariah and her husband, Tommy Mottola – president of her (and Michael's) record company, Sony Music Entertainment.

Kansas took the song to no.6 on the Hot 100 in the States.

EASY

BG cue.

ENTERTAINMENT TONIGHT

BG cue.

EVERYTHING ELSE IS A LIE

Song the Jacksons – minus Michael – are rumoured to have worked on circa 1996, for their shelved Humanity project.

FAINT

Song Michael is rumoured to have worked on circa 2003, claimed to feature Ashanti and Ja Rule on vocals – remains unconfirmed.

FAMILY AFFAIR

Touted as a song Michael planned to record for the film, *Addams Family Values* – unconfirmed.

FEVER

One of three titles – along with *Deep In The Night* and *Superfly Sister* – scribbled on a note, in a recording studio where Michael was working. May or may not be a song title.

Also rumoured to be the title of a song that failed to make the final track listing of Michael's album, *DANGEROUS* – however, it may have been confused with *Hot Fever*.

FORCE

Song Michael is rumoured to have written circa 2003, with Irv Gotti, Ashanti and Ja Rule, and recorded with Ashanti and Ja Rule.

FOREVER

Song Michael is rumoured to have worked on circa 2003 – remains unconfirmed.

GET IN TO THE GROOVE

Rumoured title of Michael's original demo versions of his hit, *Black Or White* – unconfirmed.

GET OUT OF MY MIND

Song written by the French composer, Nicolas Piedra, and recorded by the French artist, Ayhnik.

Recorded by Ashanti & Ja Rule – first surfaced on the internet in March 2003, with reported backing vocals from Michael. Ashanti's record management strongly denied Michael had been involved with the track, despite the vocals sounding suspiciously like his.

GET YOUR WEIGHT OFF ME

Instrumental demo rumoured to be from Michael's *INVINCIBLE* sessions. Surfaced on the internet in 2004 – no official release.

GIRL OF ANOTHER LOVE

Song Michael is rumoured to have considered for his album, *DANGEROUS* – remains unreleased.

Also known by the title, *Girl Of Another*.

GOT IT BACK LIKE THAT

Track Nas was rumoured to have recorded, featuring Michael, for his new album due September 2006 – not released.

HEALING MY FEELINGS

One of four songs recorded by Michael, reportedly leaked to CFM radio in the States – the station claimed the songs were recorded and mixed at Capital Studios in Hollywood. All four songs remain unconfirmed.

See also: *Breaking, Dead Or Alive, What About Me*.

HEARTLIGHT

Song Michael is rumoured to have recorded, before *Someone In The Dark*, for the storybook album, *E.T. THE EXTRA-TERRESTRIAL*.

Recorded by Neil Diamond, for his album of the same title, in 1982.

HEAVEN IS HERE

HOT LITTLE BITCH

Rumoured collaboration by Michael with Prince – possibly confused with *Hot Thing*, from Prince's album, *SIGN O' THE TIMES*.

HOUSE OF STYLE

BG cue.

HUMANITY

Song the Jacksons – minus Michael – are rumoured to have worked on circa 1996, for the shelved project of the same title.

I GOT HUSTLE

Song that gives Michael a co-writing credit – however, it's likely one of Michael's compositions is sampled, rather than it being a new track. Song sampled may be *Centipede* – unconfirmed.

I WANT TO EAT YOU UP

Allegedly the original title for Michael's hit, *Rock With You* – title supposedly changed, to better fit Michael's image.

I'LL GIVE YOU MY LIFE

Song Michael is rumoured to have recorded in 2003 – remains unconfirmed.

I'LL TRY ANYTHING ONCE

One of two songs Michael allegedly wrote for Kylie Minogue – slated to appear on her *FEVER* album in 2001, but remains unconfirmed.

See also: *Time Bomb*.

I'M NOT ALONE

A Cappella snippet – the opening lyrics of Michael's *P.Y.T. (Pretty Young Thing)*, heard on an unfinished demo by Michael. Michael also sang a few bars of the 'song' at the end of *The Way You Make Me Feel*, as seen on a bootleg DVD of the Dangerous Tour rehearsals.

Surfaced on the internet in 2003 – however, although some fans think differently, it's unlikely this is actually a new song.

INEVITABLE

Song Michael is rumoured to have recorded in 2003 – remains unconfirmed.

IT'S GONNA BE A BEAUTIFUL NIGHT

Rumoured collaboration between Michael and Prince – remains unconfirmed.

LIAR, LIAR

Song Michael is rumoured to have recorded in 2003 – remains unconfirmed.

LORE OF AGES

LOVE IN THE WRONG WAY

Song the Jacksons – minus Michael – are rumoured to have worked on circa 1996, for their shelved Humanity project.

MAYBE TOMORROW

Different to the well known Jackson 5 recording.

MESSAGE IN OUR MUSIC

Song rumoured to have been recorded by the Jacksons – later appeared on the O'Jays album, *IN THE MUSIC*, released in 1976.

MONSTER

MY TENDER HEART

Song Michael is rumoured to have worked on in 2003 – remains unconfirmed.

NEVER STOP ME

Song Michael is rumoured to have worked on in 2003 – remains unconfirmed.

NO EXCUSE

Song Michael is rumoured to have worked on in 2003 – remains unconfirmed.

NOBODY ELSE

Song Michael is rumoured to have recorded in 2003 – remains unconfirmed.

NOW THAT I FOUND LOVE

Song reported in April 2006, claimed to be the first single from a new, as yet untitled Michael Jackson album, set for release in 'late 2007' – reportedly a collaboration between Michael, 50 Cent and Lucy Diamonds.

'It was kinda weird because I didn't even hear about it until after it hit *Rolling Stone*,' said writer Lucy Diamonds. 'It's not true, and I just wanted to say *Now That I Found Love* is my song. Not Michael

Jackson's and not 50 Cent's, so if anybody on G-Unit is trying to do it, they can't.'

OPEN MIND

Song Michael reportedly worked on in 2003 – remains unconfirmed.

PAPERBACK WRITER

Beatles hit a Dutch magazine alleged Michael had recorded in 1997, for a forthcoming album – remains unconfirmed.

PRAYER FOR PEACE

Song Michael reportedly worked on with Barry Gibb of the Bees Gees in 2003 – however, in October 2005, Barry confirmed the song's actual title was *All In Your Name*.

See also: *All In Your Name*.

PRESSURE I FEEL, THE

Song Michael is rumoured to have worked on in 2003 – remains unconfirmed.

RESPECT

Song Michael is rumoured to have worked on in 2003 – remains unconfirmed.

RESURRECTION

Rumoured title of a project shelved in late 2003, as a result of Michael's arrest and child molestation charges – it remains unconfirmed if there is a song with this title.

REVOLUTION

Song Michael is rumoured to have written circa 2001.

RUMORS

Song mistakenly believed by some fans to have been written by Michael, for Lindsay Lohan's album, *SPEAK*.

Actually written by Michael's nephews Taryll and TJ, with Corey Rooney – may have been written about Michael.

SATURDAY

SECRET PASSAGE

BG cue.

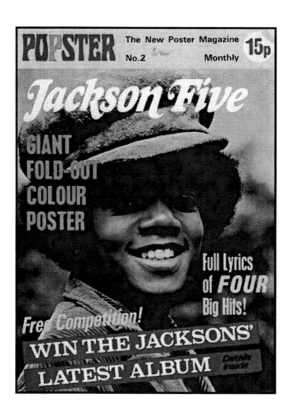

SEPTEMBER DAY

Song Michael is rumoured to have recorded in 2003 – remains unconfirmed.

SOMETHING SPECIAL

Track Quincy Jones recorded for his 1981 album, *THE DUDE*, believed by many fans to feature a contribution by Michael – remains unconfirmed.

STAND OUT

Track that surfaced on the internet and rumoured to be by Michael – actually by Tevin Campbell, and originally released on Disney's *A GOOFY SOUNDTRACK* album in 1995.

STILL GOT IT

Song Michael is rumoured to have written circa 2003.

STRONG

Song Michael is rumoured to have worked on in 2003 – remains unconfirmed.

STUDIO 54 DISCO MIX

Disco mix that supposedly included a sample of Michael's voice – considered by most fans to be a fake. Michael did regularly visit the legendary Studio 54 club in the mid-1970s.

SUN IN THE NIGHT

Song Michael is rumoured to have worked on in 2003 – remains unconfirmed.

SUNFLOWER

TAKE MY HAND

Song Michael is rumoured to have worked on in 2003 – remains unconfirmed.

TELL THEM WHY

Song about Michael, rumoured to have been recorded by Janet with Houston & Chingy, for her 2006 album, *20 Y.O.* – didn't appear on the album and remains unconfirmed.

THANK YOU

Song Michael is rumoured to have recorded in 2003 – remains unconfirmed.

THIS'LL MAKE YOU CRY

'TIL DEATH DO US PART

Song the Jacksons – minus Michael – are rumoured to have worked on circa 1996, for their shelved Humanity project.

TIMB BOMB

One of two songs allegedly written by Michael for Kylie Minogue in 2001, for the American release of her album, *FEVER* – remains unconfirmed.

See also: *I'll Try Anything Once.*

TINGLE

In April 1984, *Breakaway* magazine's Richard Hack reported 'Tingle' would be the title of Michael's new album – he stated there would be three short films and a film. However, Hack quickly back-tracked, admitting he had been fooled by a spoof written about Michael's new album.

TO THE WORLD

Song Michael reportedly co-wrote with Carole Bayer Sager circa 2000 – remains unconfirmed.

TRASH

Song Michael is rumoured to have co-written with Irv Gotti, and worked on circa 2003 – remains unconfirmed.

TRIAL OF THE CENTURY

'New' song, reportedly by Michael with 50 Cent, Lucy Diamonds and DJ Whoo Kid, slated to hit the streets in May 2006 – quickly confirmed to be a hoax.

TRIPLE THREAT CABLE

BG cue.

TRUE LIFE

BG cue.

TRUST ABOUT YOUTH

Song Michael allegedly wrote circa 1991 and considered for his album, *DANGEROUS* – remains unconfirmed.

TRUST IN MY HEART

Song Michael is rumoured to have recorded in 2003, for an album he was working on at the time – unconfirmed.

TURN ON THE ACTION

Track Quincy Jones recorded for his 1981 album, *THE DUDE*, believed by many fans to feature a contribution by Michael – remains unconfirmed.

ULTRASOUND

BG cue.

VERDICT

VISIONS

Song Michael is rumoured to have recorded in 2003 – remains unconfirmed.

WAY IT IS, THE

Song Michael is rumoured to have worked on in 2003 – remains unconfirmed.

WE WILL ALWAYS BE TOGETHER

Song the Jacksons – minus Michael – are rumoured to have worked on circa 1996, for their shelved Humanity project – remains unconfirmed.

WHAT ABOUT ME

One of four songs recorded by Michael, reportedly leaked to CFM radio in the States – the station claimed the songs were recorded and mixed at Capital Studios in Hollywood. All four songs remain unconfirmed.

See also: *Breaking, Dead Or Alive, Healing My Feelings*.

WHAT IS

WHO DO YOU KNOW

WOOP-T-WOO

Song that credits Michael as a co-writer, along with Khadejia Bass, Lamar Mitchell and Rufus Moore. Michael is also rumoured to sing backing vocals, but his involvement remains unconfirmed.

Recorded by Olivia for her eponymous debut album in 2001.

WORLD'S TOGETHER

Listed as a Michael Jackson song on at least one lyrics internet site – remains unconfirmed.

WOULDN'T U LOVE 2 LOVE ME

Song rumoured as a possible collaboration by Michael with Prince, supposedly passed on and *I Just Can't Stop Loving You* chosen instead – remains unconfirmed.

YOU CAN DO ANYTHING

Song reported to have been penned by Babyface, Carole Bayer Sager and Carole King, for Michael's *INVINCIBLE* album – remains unconfirmed.

Recorded by Carole King for her 2001 album, *LOVE MAKES THE WORLD*.

YOU CRY

Track slated to be a new song, and made available over the internet – proved to be *Be Not Always*, from the 1984 Jacksons album, *VICTORY*.

YOU-N-YOURS

Song that gives Michael a co-writing credit – however, it's likely one of Michael's compositions is sampled, rather than it being a new track. Song sampled may be *Centipede* – unconfirmed.

By the same authors:

ISBN: 07552 00640 *Michael Jackson – The Early Years*
ISNB: 07552 00918 *Michael Jackson – The Solo Years*

The aim of these two volumes is to tell Michael's incredible story as accurately, honestly and comprehensively as possible, by focussing on his music.

The Early Years includes a complete, chronological listing of every album (with track listings), one-off single and collaboration Michael has released in the USA and/or UK in the pre-Motown era, for Motown (solo and with the Jackson 5), and with the Jacksons. The book includes a Chartography (USA/UK), Discography (USA & UK), and a fascinating listing of rarities from around the world.

The Solo Years follows a similar format, but focuses on Michael's solo career. The book includes a Chartography (USA/UK), Top Singles & Albums, Discographies (USA & UK), Awards, Movies & Videography, and a list of Jackson rarities from around the world.

RRP: *The Early Years* – £10.95 / $14.95.
The Solo Years – £12.95 / $17.95.

ISBN: 07552 00985 *Jacksons Number Ones*
ISBN: 07552 01760 *ABBA Gold Hits*

Jacksons Number Ones details the 50 no.1 hits the Jackson family have achieved in the USA (Pop/R&B) and UK, plus a further seven chart toppers with a Jackson connection. The book includes a comprehensive Fact File section, including: Top 100 Jackson Singles, Chartography (USA & UK), plus the Jacksons in the USA, UK and Around the World.

ABBA Gold Hits follows a similar format, but details Top 10 hits – the 'Gold Hits', as we have called them – by Björn, Benny, Agnetha & Frida, on six continents, in no less than 22 countries. The book details pre-ABBA and post-ABBA successes – including 25 pages on Sweden alone.

RRP: *Jackson Number Ones* – £10.95 / $14.95.
      ABBA Gold Hits – £10.95 / $14.95.

All our books are available direct from our publisher, as either books or eBooks, or from a number of online stockists, for example amazon.com and amazon.co.uk.

LaVergne, TN USA
20 August 2009

155448LV00004B/194/A